THE PERILOUS QUEST

RICHARD B. GRANT

THE PERILOUS QUEST

IMAGE, MYTH, AND PROPHECY
IN THE NARRATIVES OF
VICTOR HUGO

DUKE UNIVERSITY PRESS
DURHAM, N.C.   1968

PRINTED IN THE UNITED STATES OF AMERICA
BY KINGSPORT PRESS, INC., KINGSPORT, TENN.

ACKNOWLEDGMENTS

I would like to take this opportunity to express my appreciation to the Duke University Council on Research, whose generous grant has made possible the publication of this study.

In a more personal vein, I wish to thank my father, Professor Elliott M. Grant, who not only made valuable suggestions and criticisms, but also read proof with great care. But especially do I wish to thank my wife Elizabeth, who worked hard with me during all stages of preparation of this study, and to whom it is gratefully dedicated.

RICHARD B. GRANT

TABLE OF CONTENTS

INTRODUCTION

The full history of scholarship and criticism on Victor Hugo is a vast subject, too vast for this brief introduction. Yet it is perhaps worthwhile to give a brief *état présent* of Hugo studies in order to put this essay into some perspective. Any reader of the critical commentaries that flourished during the poet's lifetime is immediately aware that the judgments rendered were largely inspired by extra-literary considerations. In the early part of Hugo's career, his efforts were judged by the canons of neoclassical taste; later, when Hugo became a champion of republicanism and an enemy of the Second Empire and the Roman Catholic church, political or religious criteria usually determined the critic's attitude. Among those who remained faithful to literary criteria, certain ones revealed shrewd insight, but there was little really serious criticism of any kind, except perhaps for Baudelaire's. With the poet's death in 1885, journalism was liberated from his presence and could turn its full attention to other matters. By this date, there had appeared the handsome "Ne varietur" edition of Hetzel and Quantin (1884), but as it had no critical apparatus and did not include much that Hugo wrote, something better was clearly needed. With the turn of the century, the Librairie Ollendorff, thanks to the efforts of Paul Meurice, Gustave Simon, and Cécile Daubray, from 1904 to 1952 put together the impressive Edition de l'Imprimerie Nationale (E.I.N.), still valuable despite errors and lacunae.[1] More recently still, Gallimard, in the Pléiade series, has published first *Les Misérables,* then *La Légende des siècles, La Fin de Satan, Dieu,* and very recently two volumes of theater and a volume of lyric poetry. Simultaneously, conscious that the texts themselves were faulty, René Journet and Guy Robert embarked upon a reexamination of the manuscripts and are publishing their findings at a steady rate. But despite the fact that the E.I.N. is no longer accepted as definitive, it is still the best general compilation of Hugo's vast work, and it contains as well a manuscript *Reliquat,* the editor's *Historique* of the genesis of the work, and a sample of critical reaction. Therefore, except

1. For all specific information on editions, books, and articles beyond what is given in this introduction, see the Bibliography.

for parts of Chapter V of this study, and unless otherwise noted, all quotations from Hugo are from this edition.

Interest in Hugo has of course not been limited to the publication of editions and the examination of manuscripts. There has been for many years great interest in both his life and the ideas that he held and propounded. Normally, the two have been combined by writers and what has emerged has been biography written from a politico-religious point of view. For instance, Edmond Biré's late nineteenth-century biography is systematically hostile, whereas Raymond Escholier's boasts the eulogistic title of *La Vie glorieuse de Victor Hugo* (1928). With such a tradition of partisanship, one can only admire the skill and objectivity of André Maurois' fine biography, *Olympio, ou La Vie de Victor Hugo* (1954), the best recent study of its kind.

As far as ideas are concerned, there has been some sharp disagreement as to whether Hugo had any coherent philosophical vision at all. Gustave Lanson at the turn of the century reminded us that "c'est un poète, non pas un philosophe" and insisted that "V. Hugo ne pense que par images." Lanson added: "Il crée des mythes" and deduced that "le mythe est la forme essentielle de son intelligence."[2] But at about the same time Charles Renouvier gave to Hugo the title of "Philosophe" and tried to incorporate the oscillations of his thought into some kind of larger synthesis. André Bellesort would later call Hugo a "songeur incohérent et romanesque,"[3] but more recently, Jacques Roos in *Les Idées philosophiques de Victor Hugo* has reverted to the idea that Hugo's thought is coherent if irrational.[4] Regarding the general problem of his thought, there has been considerable speculation about Hugo's debt to various occult doctrines, a curiosity legitimized by the poet's own dabbling in Spiritism. Certainly scholars like A. Viatte and D. Saurat are convinced of Hugo's Illuminism and more generally of his gnostic or Manichean view of man. But Journet and Robert are less sure of the poet's exact debt to occult religions.[5] It is probable that the debate will never be completely resolved. As for the political side of his thought, there is unanimous agreement that he drifted steadily from conservatism to liberalism, and various detailed studies, like

2. *Histoire de la littérature française* (7th ed., Paris, 1902), pp. 1037–38.
3. *Victor Hugo, sa vie, son œuvre* (Paris, 1930), pp. 233, 235.
4. (Paris, 1958), p. 142.
5. *Notes sur Les Contemplations* (Paris, 1958), p. 13.

Savey-Casard's *Le crime et la peine dans l'œuvre de Victor Hugo,* have recently provided extra depth of detail.

There has been some attempt to unite biography and art by showing Hugo's works as projections of the author's psychic patterns. The most famous of these efforts is no doubt Charles Baudouin's *Psychanalyse de Victor Hugo* (1943). For some time after its publication, it met with considerable academic coolness, but today such a distinguished scholar as Pierry Albouy does not hesitate to accept its basic thesis: that the relationships between mother and son and between Victor and his brothers are projected into the imagery of his works. But Baudouin's Freudian interpretation, valid as we are convinced it is for Hugo the man, has little to say of importance concerning the works themselves as independent artistic creations. His analysis of *Ruy Blas,* for example, can only be called absurd. Another such study, J.-P. Weber's *Genèse de l'œuvre poétique* (1960), has the same strengths and limitations. It too falters badly in the realm of criticism, as when it claims that Gwynplaine of *L'Homme qui rit* is a woman. A more sober psycho-literary effort is Paul Zumthor's *Victor Hugo, poète de Satan* (1946), to which many critics today owe a great debt.

But whatever one may believe about Hugo the man or the thinker, it should be remembered that he is above all a literary creator. Recognizing this fact, the literary historians have done and are still doing a valuable job in ferreting out sources and in general preparing the way for the critics. The monumental edition of *La Légende des siècles,* edited by Paul Berret, was a fine example of this kind of work. Other important attributions of source can be found in any complete bibliography. As to literary criticism proper (as distinct from intellectual history, biography, or vague critical impressionism), there was little written that is today considered important until the early twentieth century, when Paul and Victor Glachant did a study of Hugo's theater that can still be read with profit. In 1904 and 1905 Edmond Huguet's two studies on Hugo's metaphors and sense of color, light, and shadow added something. But little else was done during a period dedicated to literary history. It is true that Charles Renouvier's *Victor Hugo le poète* was an effort in this direction and was popular enough to have many editions, but when we read his judgment that the poets of the Pléiade of the sixteenth century "n'ont rien écrit qui soit encore bon à citer aujourd'hui que dans le joli et le frivole,"[6] our confidence in his judgment is seriously shaken. It was not until the late 1930's that a real change took place. Léon Emery's profound *Vision et pensée chez Victor Hugo* (1939) heralded the present generation's interest in Hugo as a visionary. Herbert Hunt's *The Epic in Nineteenth Century France* (1941) was more traditional, but both works pointed to the importance of "vision" and myth.

Since World War II, and particularly in the last decade, there has been a veritable explosion of scholarly and critical work on Hugo. J.-B. Barrère destroyed the old label of Hugo as a "garde national épique" with his provocative study, *La Fantaisie de Victor Hugo* (1949–1960). In 1962, the centennial year of *Les Misérables, Europe* devoted a special issue to the novel, and in that same year, a colloquium at Strasbourg led to the publication of one of the finest collections of articles ever assembled.[7] The approach of the distinguished contributors to this volume was reflected shortly afterward in two very important works, Albert Py's *Les Mythes grecs dans l'œuvre de Victor Hugo* and Pierre Albouy's *La Création mythologique chez Victor Hugo*. These three volumes and many brief articles published recently have revolutionized Hugo scholarship. As the editor of the Strasbourg *Hommage à Victor Hugo* put it, "il était permis de croire que Victor Hugo était un des écrivains les mieux étudiés, un de ceux sur lesquels il ne reste presque rien à trouver. Erreur profonde," and he goes on to remind us that although Hugo has often been studied in terms of his religious, political, social, and philosophical views, "on n'étudie guère l'*écrivain*." He urges critics to undertake studies of structure, style, and all literary aspects of Hugo's art and recommends that new discoveries in the field of depth psychology and mythology be used as tools.[8] Victor Hugo, this critic feels sure, would have had some sympathy for this more literary approach. As he had said in his own work of literary criticism, *William Shakespeare*, "Fouillez les étymologies, arrivez à la racine des vocables, *image* et *idée* sont le même mot."[9] Pierre Albouy echoes this sentiment when he writes: "Le symbole," which he defines as the key idea, "donne naissance au *mythe*, qui explique et illustre l'idée par

6. Cited from third edition (1900), p. 34.
7. *Centenaire des Misérables (1862–1962). Hommage à Victor Hugo* (Strasbourg, 1962).
8. *Ibid.*, p. 5.   9. E.I.N., p. 292.

un récit."[10] In fact, the historian of primitive religions, Mircea Eliade, has gone as far as to claim that the "roman du XIXᵉ siècle . . . en dépit de toutes les 'formules' scientifiques, réalistes, sociales, a été le grand réservoir des mythes dégradés."[11] It was perhaps with this in mind that Georges Piroué, a novelist himself, wrote in his stimulating (but chaotic and totally unscholarly) *Victor Hugo romancier: ou les dessous de l'inconnu*, "Il y a de quoi surprendre que . . . la critique ait encore si peu exploré ce terrain vierge et fertile qu'est le roman hugolien."[12] Albert Py, in his study of Hugo's poetry, has tried to show how two of these old myths which had lost their vigor have been given new life by Hugo. If one combines the legend of Orpheus and that of Prometheus, he argues, one arrives at the heart of Hugo's creation. These two myths are indeed of great importance to our understanding of Hugo's form, although Py's work sometimes seems to confuse them. As to the meaning of the myths, Py claims that until the period of exile, there was none. After the poem "Ecrit après la visite d'un bagne" (1853), political, social, and even metaphysical interpretations are given to the myths.[13] Py seems delighted that these forms took on intellectual meaning: "L'intérêt des poèmes prométhéens de Hugo réside . . . dans la façon dont les thèmes prométhéens se combinent avec les idées qui, réunies entre 1853 et 1855, constituent le message métaphysique et religieux du mage de Jersey."[14] Actually, both Albouy and Py, despite their interest in the literary side of Hugo, end up with consideration of ideas. Their approach is both valid and necessary if the center of interest is Hugo, for he certainly gave to his imagery meaning which the critic should set forth. But what has been lacking in Hugo criticism is a systematic literary analysis of the works of art as form rather than as idea. Although A. Glauser has done this for the "pure" poetry,[15] it also needs to be done for the fiction, or more precisely, for the narrative story line.[16] Nineteenth-century criticism never dealt with this problem and it is only in more recent times that this aspect of literature has attracted interest,

10. *La Création mythologique chez Victor Hugo* (Paris, 1963), p. 41.
11. *Images et symboles* (Paris, 1952), p. 12.   12. (Paris, 1964), p. 11.
13. *Les Mythes grecs dans la poésie de Victor Hugo* (Genève, 1963), p. 211.
14. *Ibid.*, p. 217.   15. *Victor Hugo et la poésie pure* (Genève, 1957).
16. Victor Brombert's seminal article "Victor Hugo, la prison et l'espace," *Revue des Sciences Humaines*, CXVII (Janvier-Mars, 1965), 59–79, is an effort in this direction, but in only twenty pages he could not, of course, treat each work in detail.

particularly with the growth of myth analysis. Northrop Frye has claimed that all literature is based on the quest myth, a view that we cannot accept, but we would agree that the vast majority of works of nineteenth-century French literature fall into this category. This is certainly true for Hugo's prose fiction and his epic poetry, and Hugo even tried to incorporate some mythic patterns into his theater.

If one starts with the concept of an heroic quest toward an ideal, then it is obvious that the hero must play a central role, and indeed, much of our essay will deal with the successive ways in which Hugo portrayed this central character. In one way or another, the path that the hero chooses, the obstacles that he faces, and the goal that he seeks will form the guiding thread of the narrative. To avoid over-rigid schematization of these separate parts (hero, path, obstacles, and goal), which tends to force a text to fit a preconceived mold, we will at times stress one aspect, at times another, in an attempt to respect the integrity of each work. Proceeding from the action, the critic encounters the fact that the aspects of the quest are expressed not only literally but in imagery as well. Therefore, this essay will analyze imagery in detail, but only those images that are essential to the elaboration of the heroic quest. For anyone interested in the totality of Hugo's imagery, Albouy and others are more useful. But for Victor Hugo, imagery was only part of the story. By his middle years he would put it to the service of myth, and in his declining years myth would in turn yield to prophecy, which, as Apocalypse, is a literary form as well as a set of ideas.

In studying this long evolution our purpose is twofold. First, it is to follow the development of the basic motifs of the quest to show what is central to Victor Hugo's imagination. In so doing, we shall inevitably repeat some conclusions of critics like Baudouin, Albouy, Py, Brombert, and others, but with a difference, in that we shall at the same time show this evolution within the framework of the artistic unity of each work rather than "in Hugo." This framework indicates our second purpose, something that is rarely attempted: to analyze as art each main work containing a narrative line.

The difficulty in writing a book of any kind on the works of Victor Hugo is that his universe is, to use one of his own images, a vast ocean under whose surface lies a dazzling array of forms, repeated over and over in almost, but not quite, identical manner. This abundance can overwhelm the diver-critic; he may be tempted to include every detail, but if he does, his criticism will have such bulk as to be almost unreadable. What is needed is simplification. To this end we have by the nature of our topic eliminated the lyric poetry (except for an occasional corroborative quotation and for one section of one chapter), because lyric poetry has no plot, even when, as in *Les Contemplations,* it can be argued that there is a "story line" of a *chasse spirituelle* and in *Les Châtiments* a progression from Nox to Lux. Also rejected is *Dieu,* with its semblance of a narrative, because it is primarily lyrical and ideological. Excluded as well are all of Hugo's formally rhetorical works, such as *William Shakespeare, Promontorium Somnii,* etc., because form, not ideas, is our concern. The play *Les Jumeaux* is omitted because it is incomplete, the *théâtre en liberté* because the plots are too sketchy and the play *Mille francs de récompense* because it seems somehow outside the main current of Hugo's literary career. *Torquemada,* too, has been omitted, perhaps arbitrarily, but it is a late anomaly despite its interest and scarcely merits a separate chapter. What remains is the long prose fiction, the main plays, *La Légende des siècles,* and *La Fin de Satan.*

In a further effort at streamlining, we have tried to keep to a reasonable number the examples that could be used in support of our analyses. Any reader familiar with Hugo will be able to think of others that we have omitted, but there seems little point in belaboring the obvious. In like fashion, we have of course used the best scholarly research and criticism, but only the essentials.[17] Completeness of acknowledgment would not reveal truth but obscure it by making the text too turgid to read.

17. For the reader interested in a more detailed bibliography, see the recent compilation by Elliott M. Grant, *Victor Hugo: A Select and Critical Bibliography* (Chapel Hill, N.C., 1967).

THE PERILOUS QUEST

THE EARLY ROMANCES

Han d'Islande

Victor Hugo's earliest published effort of full-length fiction was *Han d'Islande*, begun in 1820 when he was eighteen but not published until 1823. Its odd qualities have caused some problems in criticism, and even today one needs to ask again: What is *Han d'Islande?* Hugo called it "une espèce de roman en prose," a rather vague term. The Edition de l'Imprimerie Nationale (E.I.N.) quotes a few reviews of the day that tried to grapple with the text and give it some generic label. It was called "composition" and "ouvrage" and one even finds the admission that "il serait difficile peut-être de dire à quel genre appartient un tel ouvrage et quelle muse l'a inspiré."[1] Even Hugo's own word "roman" is obscure, for it does not distinguish between romance and novel. A novel, to make this distinction clear, deals with characters with their complex social masks, set in and a product of a given historical society. Romance, on the other hand, deals in archetypes. As Northrop Frye puts it: "The Romancer does not attempt to create 'real people' so much as stylized figures which expand into psychological archetypes."[2] The setting of romance is usually not defined in the time and space of history but takes place in something resembling a dream world. Frye points out that normally romance and novel do not remain totally separate but fuse in the actual practice of prose fiction, "just romantic enough for the reader to project his libido on the hero and his anima on the heroine, and just novel enough to keep these projections in a familiar world."[3]

This desire for both familiarity and dream is what lies behind the popularity of the genre that we know as the historical novel. In this phrase, "novel" actually means "romance" with enough history worked in to satisfy the reader's desires for something "realistic." This term, "historical novel," comes to mind when one considers *Han d'Islande*. On

1. "Revue de la critique," in *Œuvres complètes de Victor Hugo* (Paris, 1904–1952) (hereinafter cited E.I.N.), Roman—I, 350–51.
2. *Anatomy of Criticism* (Princeton, N.J., 1957), p. 304.
3. *Ibid.*, p. 305.

the historical side, Hugo reached back into the late seventeenth century and situated his narrative in Norway. To support this choice, Hugo did some research. Sister Mary O'Connor's study of the sources[4] proves that some of the characters do have an historical origin. Hugo obviously read Pierre-Henri Mallet's *Histoire de Dannemarc* for the details of the heroine's father, Jean Schumacker, Count Griffenfeld. His humble origins, his rise to power and subsequent fall due to the jealous machinations of his enemies, a rigged trial, years of prison and final release are all incorporated into Hugo's tale. Schumacker died in 1699 and was buried in Jutland. There are many other details Hugo found in Mallet that are genuinely historical and that appear openly in *Han*.

But despite Hugo's research, the total impression is hardly historical. André Maurois is convinced that Hugo made no serious study of his subject,[5] and Mlle Péès, a careful scholar, thinks that much of Hugo's researched local color is "un étalage d'érudition factice."[6] This reaction is due to the superficiality of Hugo's knowledge, but the more fundamental reason for this widespread reaction is that the author has transformed his sources and added so much unrealistic material that *Han* emerges a full-blown melodramatic romance.

If *Han* is a romance and if romances are projections of the psyche, should one not examine Hugo's life to "explain" the form that his romance takes? Hugo himself encouraged this approach when he stated that the work would be a means whereby he could express his love for Adèle Foucher, to whom he had declared himself in 1819:

> le besoin d'épancher certaines idées qui me pesaient . . . me fit entreprendre une espèce de roman en prose. J'avais une âme pleine d'amour, de douleur et de jeunesse . . . je n'osais en confier les secrets à aucune créature vivante. . . . Je voulais peindre une jeune fille qui réalisât l'idéal de toutes les imaginations fraîches et poé-

---

4. *A Study of the Sources of Han d'Islande and Their Significance in the Literary Development of Victor Hugo* (Washington, D.C., 1942), pp. 1–30. See also Servais Etienne, *Les Sources de Bug-Jargal avec en appendice quelques sources de "Han d'Islande"* (Bruxelles, 1923), and Mlle Simone Péès, "L'Origine de la couleur locale scandinave dans le *Han d'Islande* de Victor Hugo," *Revue de littérature comparée*, IX (1929), 261–85.

5. André Maurois, *Olympio, ou la vie de Victor Hugo* (Paris, 1954), p. 111.

6. Péès, p. 264.

tiques. . . . Je voulais placer près de cette jeune fille un jeune homme, non tel que je suis, mais tel que je voudrais être.[7]

In the preface to the second edition (1833), he reaffirmed the theme of the idyll based on his love for Adèle but judged his work with understandable severity, commenting: "Il n'y a dans *Han d'Islande* qu'une chose sentie, l'amour du jeune homme, qu'une chose observée, l'amour de la jeune fille."[8] There are some objections to this biographical approach. First, despite the fact that Baudouin has psychoanalyzed Hugo and many scholar-critics are now convinced that there is great truth in his findings, psychoanalysis applied to the text can tell us more about the author than the work, as we indicated in the Introduction. Second, since *Han* has numerous literary[9] and historical sources, the form of the narrative may well be influenced by these sources and therefore independent of the author's psyche. Curiously, an imitated form is usually considered a weakness, a "lack of originality." But as all literary forms are derived from others, this insistence on novelty can be easily exaggerated. A traditional form is a source of strength as much or more than an indication of sterility. At any rate, in *Han* the form is clearly visible as that of a romance, with overtones of myth.

The world of romance lies midway between the world of reality (novel) and that of true myth. In its pure form it is the setting for a very traditional tale. A hero of noble but hidden birth, having led an exemplary life, embarks upon a quest, usually for an ideal maiden held prisoner by a villain. The central theme of the quest generates a series of adventures whose settings are dark forests and enchanted castles. Inevitably, the hero faces various obstacles, but he overcomes them and triumphs to marry the girl and live happily ever after.

It should be said from the outset that in general Victor Hugo was a creator of romance characters. The common charge that his characterization is poor is accurate in that it reflects critical awareness that the personages who appear in his works lack the human complexity so necessary to the true novel. But as Hugo is a maker of archetypal figures,

7. *Victor Hugo, raconté par un témoin de sa vie* (chap. 37), cited in the "Historique" of *Han d'Islande*, E.I.N., p. 348.
8. Preface to *Han d'Islande*, E.I.N., p. 14.
9. O'Connor, pp. 40–97.

he should not be judged purely on a mimetic basis. His genius lies elsewhere.

The hero and general form of romance are particularly visible in *Han d'Islande*. The real identity of the hero Ordener is unknown to most of the characters at the beginning. He undertakes his quest to save the pure and lovely Ethel Schumacker and her old father, the ex-grand-chancellor who had some years previously been unjustly convicted of treason. In one scene, we see the old man in prison (a social form of the villain's castle) with his daughter at his feet: "son front chauve et ridé était appuyé sur ses mains et l'on ne voyait que sa barbe blanche qui pendait en désordre sur sa poitrine" (p. 166). On another occasion he laments: "je ne suis plus puissant" (p. 33). His daughter is the typical maiden in distress except for her dark hair, no doubt Hugo's tribute to Adèle Foucher. Otherwise, a captive herself, she weeps, prays, and loves the hero in her "tristesse et innocence" (p. 36). Into this classic situation comes Ordener Guldenlew (or Guldenloewe), who vows to get back a secret box containing the inevitable documents that prove old Schumacker's innocence.

Arrayed against the hero is an imposing set of evildoers. It is standard in romance tales to find, as on a chessboard, a dark or evil equivalent to each white piece.[10] Against the deposed Grand-Chancellor is positioned the wicked Count d'Ahlefeld, whose treachery caused Schumacker's downfall. His wife, the evil Countess, serves as a "black queen" and their putative son Frederic is the rival for Ethel's hand. The list of villains does not stop here. There is an evil advisor to d'Ahlefeld, one Musdœmon (actually Frederic's real father), whose name tells us that he has the soul of a rat. Above and apart from them all we find the titular figure, the monster Han himself. So perfectly does *Han* seem to fit romance patterns that Georges Piroué writes: "Parti à l'aventure en quête d'un monstre, d'une cassette et d'un cœur, il va par monts et par vaux, dans la brume et dans la tempête. . . . Hercule amoureux, chevalier légendaire d'une ballade allemande ou d'un conte russe."[11]

We remarked above that romance is halfway between the novel and myth, its forms repeating in secularized manner a more primitive religious ritual. It is difficult to define myth closely and yet flexibly, but one can say rather generally that it is the story of gods, and although these

10. Frye, p. 196.
11. *Victor Hugo romancier: ou les dessous de l'inconnu* (Paris, 1964), p. 24.

tales take various forms, one often finds a solar god, an old man who has lost his power, a pure maiden, and dragons that have laid waste a land. The god defeats the dragons of sterility, unites with the maiden (earth), restores the old man (the year) to his rightful throne (or in other versions replaces him as the next year), and Eden, or summer, is re-created. We mention this mythic plot because the aged old man who has lost his power is recreated as Schumacker. We see him at sunset (the decline of the year), he has a fertile daughter, and the hero's family name means Golden Lion, a suggestion of a solar god. As we continue our analysis of the text, we shall show other manifestations of hidden myth, for of course the myth must be disguised, or displaced, because the story is set in "real" time and place.

Ordener's adventures begin with a visit to the local morgue to check the body of a captain killed by Han. This officer was carrying the metal box containing the papers. Ordener's arrival at the morgue is announced by his knocking three times (a ritual number) before penetrating into the world of the physically dead. It will not be his last descent into the underworld. Here the hero meets Benignus Spiagudry, the morgue's caretaker whom the hero forces to accompany him on his quest of Han, in the supposition that this bandit now has the box.

Setting out for Han's lair, the pair traverse a part of Norway, a country chosen no doubt because of the popularity of the exotic "Romantic North," and also because its wild and supposedly infertile terrain offers a fine demonic antithesis to the ideal world of the pastoral genre:

> Ce n'était point une chose commode que de voyager dans ce pays. Tantôt il fallait suivre pour chemin le lit pierreux d'un torrent desséché. . . . A la triste monotonie de cette route se joignait l'incommodité d'une pluie fine et pénétrante qui avait envahi le ciel . . . et accroissait les difficultés du chemin. Nul oiseau n'osait se hasarder dans l'air. (pp. 197–98)

Their first stop along the way is at the demonic tower of Vygla where, in the best tradition of the *roman noir*, they are driven by a terrible storm. An old crone, whose "figure sèche et anguleuse avait quelque chose de cadavéreux" (p. 89), opens the door. By a trick of intentional ambiguity, Hugo makes the reader believe that the travelers are in the lair of the ogre Han, but it is merely the dwelling of the provincial executioner, Nichol

CHAPTER I

Orugix. Spiagudry prefers the storm outside, but like all heroes Ordener has no fear and so they enter. The place is furnished with gallows and instruments of torture visible in the red light of glowing fires. Three sleeping children are taken for cadavers by the frightened Spiagudry. This tower, which is appropriately called "le garde meuble de l'enfer" (p. 91), is straight out of the tradition of the *roman noir*.

Soon other refugees from the storm arrive; one is Han in disguise, the other a noble minister of the gospel named Athanase Munder, whose grave and serene appearance (p. 117) is but one of his virtues. At this moment he is on his way to seek a stay of execution for various convicted prisoners. Munder is a minor figure, but one of great importance. He is in total harmony with God[12] so that when he offers a safe-conduct pass to Ordener that will permit the hero to be accepted among the wild hill-country people, we recognize an old friend of romance: the agent of Providence who gives a talisman to the questing hero at the beginning of his adventures.[13] This offer and its acceptance indicate what we know from other characteristics of the hero: having God's favor, his quest should be successful. The pass does indeed later save Ordener's life. This scene at Vygla is the second entrance by the hero into the world of the dead, here represented in its social form, through the presence of the district executioner and the tools of his trade. The demonic inhumanity of society's killings is demonstrated by Orugix's worries concerning his job. His only concern is the payment that he receives for his butchery. Otherwise he drinks, eats, hangs, and sleeps in peace.

Leaving the tower unscathed, Ordener and his companion continue on their way. Their route takes them through more desolate country, past swamps, roads littered with stones (p. 114), bogs (p. 115), through "forêts druidiques" and sunsets described as the death of the sun (p. 138). On this journey, Spiagudry makes a reference to a work, "Descente de Saint Georges aux enfers," by one Melasius Iturham. The reference to this non-existent author and work[14] is not a pure coincidence. Like St.

12. He gives a benediction to the assemblage, stressing the bounty of God to those who live in Him (p. 94).
13. For an excellent statement of the basic pattern of myth and romance adventure, see Joseph Campbell, *The Hero with a Thousand Faces* (New York, 1949). Citations taken from Meridian Books edition (New York, 1956), pp. 69–77.
14. Maximilien Rudwin, *Satan et le Satanisme dans l'œuvre de Victor Hugo* (Paris, 1926), p. 49, errs in reading the text as Sturham and in assuming that this concocted title and author are real.

8

George, Ordener is in a demonic kingdom and is facing dragons. Arriving at Oëlmoe, they learn that Spiagudry has a price on his head, for he had permitted the mutilation of a body in the morgue. Appalled by the news, Spiagudry wishes to flee "ce maudit faubourg de l'enfer" (p. 141). Cowardice and fear are never well rewarded in the world of romance. As they continue, Spiagudry begins to see glowing eyes in the dark and has premonitions of disaster, but Ordener remains blissfully unaware of them. His only concern is to climb a peak from which he can see Ethel's prison far on the horizon. While Ordener is sighing with rapture far above the waiting Spiagudry, Han comes along and kills the morgue-keeper. Ordener had promised the victim that no harm would befall him as long as they were together (p. 153). As usual in romances, the prediction comes true, for they had momentarily become separated. Ironically, the box of documents was all the time in Spiagudry's possession, a fact that Ordener had not known. Han throws it and the body into a nearby lake and disappears.

Descending from his peak, the hero is very little disturbed by his companion's disappearance and soon goes on his way. As Spiagudry had said: "Quoi de plus . . . glorieux . . . que d'exposer noblement sa vie pour délivrer son pays d'un monstre" (pp. 142–43). Ordener ignores ominous presages (e.g., p. 207) as he approaches the grotto of Walderhog where he knows Han will be. Again it is the third experience, as in ritual, that is the important one, for here the hero faces not just physical or even social death as in the first two encounters but some form of ultimate evil. The motif of the descent into Avernus is made nearly explicit. Someone sees him, "une figure enveloppée d'un manteau ou d'un linceul, descendre le long des roches et disparaître sous la voûte formidable de la caverne" (p. 207). This cave is full of skeletons and at the end, "un monument de forme singulière, situé au milieu de la salle souterraine, appela son attention. Trois pierres longues et massives, posées debout sur le sol, en soutenaient une quatrième, large et carrée. . . . Sous cette espèce de trépied gigantesque s'élevait une sorte d'autel. . . . Ordener reconnut une de ces colossales constructions druidiques" (p. 208).[15] Han rises from beneath this altar, gives a ritual warning three times (p. 209), and attacks the hero with "un rire atroce"; but Ordener is fearless,

15. This altar is not an invention of Hugo's but a detail that he found in Mallet. See O'Connor, p. 16.

having entered the cave feeling "une joie céleste" (p. 207). To get the box of documents, says the hero, "J'en donnerais [des ordres] au démon de l'enfer" (p. 211). Engaging in battle, Ordener gains an advantage but by a noble gesture permits the other to recover. Soon Ordener is disarmed and about to be killed when the arrival of chance passers-by chases the villain away.

Who is this evil Han of Iceland? With his eyes like burning coals is he merely another of those innumerable imitations of Maturin's Melmoth?[16] Although it is true that devilish figures in caves were popular at this period of French literature, Hugo brings to his creation some novel attributes. Critics have pointed out that Han bears a striking resemblance to Spanish brigands that Hugo's father wrote about in his memoirs.[17] These outlaws, Fra Diavolo and Empecinado, fought against General Hugo and at that time, Victor, hostile to his father, tended to sympathize with the "proscrit espagnol," an attitude that the poet would keep even after his reconciliation with his father. In *Han* there are certain similarities with these Spaniards. Fra Diavolo was, like Han, "de petite stature," with eyes "vifs et pénétrants." Both had a price on their heads and both were elusive, again like Hugo's titular character. But a better explanation, if we must have one, is suggested by Charles Baudouin, who proposes that these grotesque figures are projections of Hugo's own feelings of inadequacy.[18] However this may be, Han inaugurates a series of grotesque figures which, as J.-B. Barrère has pointed out, start with the "frénétique" and move toward the "grotesque," starting with Han and moving through Quasimodo ultimately to Gwynplaine.[19]

Han's biography is fanciful indeed. His ancestor was Ingolphe the Exterminator, who had in earlier times fled to Iceland and sired a son. Ever since, each generation has also produced one son, down to Han. By transferring the name to Iceland, incidentally, Hugo manages to reinforce the sense of bleak sterility of the titular "hero." We first learn of him as a foundling discovered by peasants who wished to kill him. But a worthy

16. There are other literary sources as well. Amédée Guiard, *Virgile et Victor Hugo* (Paris, 1910), p. 51, rightly concludes that Han's origins are to be found in part in Virgil's cyclops and the monster Cacus, passages which Hugo had translated into French verse. See also J.-B. Barrère, *La Fantaisie de Victor Hugo*, I (Paris, 1949), 30–32.

17. *Victor Hugo raconté* (chap. V).

18. Charles Baudouin, *Psychanalyse de Victor Hugo* (Genève, 1943), pp. 13–14.

19. Barrère, *Fantaisie*, I, 51–79.

bishop, anticipating Claude Frollo's action in behalf of the grotesque Quasimodo, "s'y opposa et prit l'oursin sous sa protection, espérant faire un chrétien du diable" (p. 66). The experiment failed, as Han burned down the episcopal palace and ran away. Ever since, he has roamed the land killing with delight, laughing satanically, his long steel-like fingernails leaving claw marks on his victims. Although he possesses superhuman strength, he is small in size. His ethic is to return good with evil, for the simple pleasure of it, and he hates men "parce qu'ils m'ont fait du bien" (p. 317). He had some years earlier interrupted an idyllic love between two young people and, symbol of diabolic intervention, had raped the girl. Her offspring was one Gill Stadt, who has died when the story opens and whose body is in the morgue at Drontheim. Han sees his line dying out, as he is apparently unable to have more children. His only companion is a huge polar bear named "Friend" with whom he shares an underground cave near Walderhog. Here Han can indulge his cannibalism by crunching bones, drinking blood from skulls, etc. This is the creature whom Ordener fights, the ultimate dragon of evil, and the presence of a pagan altar in the cave provides a suggestion of a demonic cult,

It is with this episode that we realize that the narrative is taking an unusual direction, for Ordener fails now and later to slay the dragon. Han does indeed die at the end, but only by his own hand after voluntarily surrendering to the authorities. Further, although there is no doubt as to Han's demonic nature, for he even calls himself a devil (p. 127) and his glowing eyes are in the best tradition of the diabolic, he actually feels himself to be morally superior to some of the other villains, and one even has the impression that Hugo shares his attitude. Speaking to the evil Grand-Chancellor d'Ahlefeld, the one who had trumped up a false charge against Schumacker, Han judges him: "Si nos deux âmes s'envolaient de nos corps en ce moment, je crois que Satan hésiterait avant de décider laquelle des deux est celle du monstre" (p. 187). And when he gives himself up, he becomes transfigured: "Alors les pieds dans le sang, il promena son œil farouche et hardi sur le tribunal, les archers et la foule, et l'on eût dit que tous ces hommes palpitaient d'épouvante sous le regard de cet homme désarmé, seul et enchaîné" (p. 312). It is of importance, surely, that at this point and at this point only, Hugo refers to Han as a man, rather than as a devil or a beast or a monster. Addressing the court, the outcast cries out: "Ecoutez, juges, n'attendez pas de moi de longues paroles," although he does take time out to recount his past misdeeds. He repeats his statement that his nature is to "haïr les hommes, ma mission [est] de leur nuire," but he concludes melancholically: "Je suis las de la vie. . . . J'ai assez de sang; je n'ai plus soif. A présent, me voici, vous pouvez boire le mien" (p. 313). The total effect of all this language is to suggest that some René, some Romantic hero, lurks beneath Han's forbidding exterior. A solitary wanderer, he is not even a bandit in the traditional sense: "Ne l'appelez pas bandit, car il est toujours seul" (p. 60), we are told.

In short, Hugo's text is somewhat startling. We progress with the hero from physical death to manifestations of society's hell, arriving at the ultimate demon only to learn that the evil figure is not so wicked as one would have expected. Han has a suggestion of a redeeming side, manifested negatively in his judgment upon other villains and positively by the deep (if grotesque) love that he bore for his son.

Who, if anyone, is the ultimate adversary? Is it the rival for the maiden's hand, Frédéric d'Ahlefeld? Hardly. A *précieux*, whose main interests are the novels of Mlle de Scudéry and the lace on his clothes, he cannot be taken seriously and is soon eaten by Han d'Islande. Nor is it Ulrica d'Ahlefeld, the woman that the evildoers wish Ordener to marry for reasons of state. Such a figure can be the evil counterpart to the pure, virtuous heroine, but in this narrative she never even appears on the scene and remains but a name.

What of the "black king and queen," the d'Ahlefelds themselves? Here the chances seem good. The Grand-Chancellor is the "mortel ennemi" (p. 25) of Schumacker, and it was his betrayal that overthrew him. He is described as infernal (p. 112), but like Macbeth, he is a weaker character than his wife, who plays something of the role of the wicked witch of fairy tales. She does not quite have the evil beauty needed for the part, being fifty years old, but she does lie around on a "riche sopha" (p. 53) with a "sourire faux" and a "rayon de l'enfer" (p. 242) in her glance. She even gloats over the misfortunes of the innocent Ethel. But she has one redeeming feature, the same one that will later redeem Lucrèce Borgia: "Dans une femme dégradée, même quand l'épouse a disparu, il reste encore quelque chose de la mère" (p. 76). When in the final poetic justice all the evildoers receive their punishment, she learns of her son's death and goes mad, but one can see in her Hugo's idea that no mother is ever evil incarnate, for she is, like her creator Hugo, a creator of lives. Hugo's hostility will be reserved for the *impuissants*.

If there is an incarnation of ultimate evil in *Han d'Islande,* it can only be Musdœmon, the guiding spirit of evil in all the twists and turns of the plot, who betrays everyone until he is himself betrayed. In the final scene in which he is hanged in prison, we find the theme that will appear so frequently in Hugo, that of the "frères ennemis." To our surprise, we learn that Musdœmon is in reality the brother of Nichol Orugix, the executioner who comes to kill him. The victim pleads for mercy, but to no avail, for he had himself been responsible for his brother's exile to the provinces. With the usual cringing and whining, he is dropped through a trap door at the end of a noose. Unlike even Frédéric's mother, he has never loved anyone in any way except himself. This is total evil in any theological sense. Hugo will later represent this idea in the form of the eunuch Zaïm of *La Légende des siècles.*

Thus Ordener does not himself slay any of the villains and despite his heroic efforts, does not even find the *cassette* with the precious documents. These are brought to light by pure chance. The hero is curiously incapable of effective action, with the result that the story's action is inevitably transferred to the more evil figures. But because his heart and his love are pure, because he nobly sacrifices himself, Providence continues to smile upon him and provides him with a happy outcome from all his afflictions.

Ordener's relationship with Ethel also merits analysis. We remember that Hugo admitted that he had projected his love for Adèle Foucher into this tale and that the girl is the "idéal de toutes les imaginations." In spatial terms, this ideal is viewed as lofty or exalted, that is, upward. Ordener thinks of her as an "être qui serait enlevé au monde réel pour assister au monde idéal" (p. 39). The distinction between real and ideal world is made in these terms: "de temps en temps, une fondrière, une pierre, une branche d'arbre, heurtant ses pieds, le rappelaient brusquement de l'idéal au réel. Il . . . regrettait d'être tombé de son beau voyage céleste dans son pénible voyage terrestre" (p. 115). This upward vision is given spatial function in the narration itself when Ordener climbs to the top of the ruin from which he can see the light in the window of Ethel's prison shining far on the horizon. This event is then translated into abstract terms as Hugo comments: "Il faut que l'homme gravisse longtemps et péniblement pour voir un point de bonheur dans l'immense nuit" (p. 165). But this triumph is largely an illusion, as will be Satan's many years later in *La Fin de Satan,* as the fallen archangel flies in vain toward the distant star. Although the hero may see her prison far away, by going upward he does not really succeed in approaching her. To achieve real union, he must plunge down into Hell, which, as we know, he has done three times already, and which he will do again.

We left the hero after his indecisive encounter with Han in the grotto of Walderhog. Immediately afterward, stumbling around in the darkness outside, a darkness which seems somehow equated with his failure to understand the machinations of the villains, he sees a mysterious group of men who suddenly disappear into the earth. A flash of lightning reveals "une sorte de puits large et circulaire. . . . Il s'approcha du gouffre." He spots a ladder "et s'enfonça dans l'abîme sans savoir si elle le conduirait jusqu'au fond, sans songer qu'il ne reverrait peut-être plus le soleil" (p. 223). He finds himself in a lead mine amid a group of miners who have been tricked by Musdœmon into rebelling against the king in the name of Ethel's father. The scene is described with the imagery of demonology: "on eût dit . . . une de ces assemblées fabuleuses, dont parlent les vieilles chroniques, de sorciers et de démons qui . . . illuminaient la nuit les vieux bois et les châteaux écroulés" (p. 226). Here Ordener is saved by his safe-conduct pass and even agrees to accompany the rebels on their march. Why? Hugo intervenes to explain: "Ce fut . . . un généreux désir d'approfondir, à tout prix, cette ténébreuse aventure, mêlé à un dégoût amer de la vie, à un insouciant désespoir de l'avenir; peut-être je ne sais quel doute de la culpabilité de Schumacker, inspiré . . . par un instinct inconnu de la vérité, et surtout par son amour pour Ethel" (p. 229).

This underground experience soon leads to another hellish scene, although not underground in a strict sense. The miners are ambushed in a deep ravine, unable to escape. The battle between the insurgents and government troops is complicated by the fact that Han appears, killing people on both sides, rolling rocks down the hillside, and indulging in cannibalism. The miners are slaughtered and Ordener and the leaders are taken prisoner. Curiously, during the fight Ordener is hardly mentioned, the action shifting to the miners. This eclipse of the hero during combat is unusual in romance, where he is supposed to do deeds of great valor.

But at least his presence permits him, when the captured insurgents are later put on trial for treason, to arise in court and claim that he alone was responsible and that Schumacker is innocent of the charge of fomenting rebellion. Thus does he foil the villains' plot.

Convicted of treason, Ordener awaits execution in his cell. Suddenly Ethel arrives with the ultimate temptation. The d'Ahlefelds have charged her to tell him that if he will marry their daughter Ulrica, he can be freed. But the hero is not the type to listen to such a gross suggestion. Even on the verge of death, "il éprouvait la joie la plus céleste" (p. 310) at her presence, a phrase which repeats the same language used when he entered Han's cave. "Elle était belle comme un ange qui remonte de l'enfer au ciel" (p. 302). Ordener refuses the literal light of day, freedom, and life, in order to descend into death for his beloved. At this moment Athanase Munder, the good minister, appears and an altar is set up in the cell. Before this celestial counterpart to Han's demonic cave altar, the two are married "après s'être donné rendez-vous dans l'éternité" (p. 307). Soon the villains are exposed by the providential appearance of the documents, hero and heroine are freed, and the work ends on the happy note of romance: "Bientôt de belles et douces fêtes solennisèrent le sombre hymen au cachot. La vie commença à sourire aux deux jeunes époux qui avaient su sourire à la mort." And finally, "De cette alliance d'Ordener et d'Ethel naquit la famille de Danneskiold" (p. 344).

In this wild tale, how many of the patterns of action represent either the normal episodes of romance or sheer coincidence on the one hand, and how many represent a particular pattern of Hugo's creativity? Of course, the two can coincide. It is instructive in this connection to compare *Han d'Islande* with an early effort that the ten-year-old Victor called *Le Château du diable*.[20]

This youthful playlet has a plot remarkably similar to that of *Han*. A peasant tells a local lord, Raoul, that there is nearby an old abandoned castle, called "le Château du diable" because according to rumor, the Evil Spirit and his *lutins*, or imps, haunt the place, killing all unwary travelers who pass by during the night. Many knights have already died trying to overcome the demon, and in the best tradition of the chivalric novel, their

20. This play does not appear in the E.I.N. Our text is that published by J.-J. Thierry and Josette Mélèze in *Victor Hugo: Théâtre complet* (Paris, 1963), 2 vols., in the "Pléiade" series.

arms hang in the Great Hall. Raoul of course accepts the challenge, knowing well that "un brave chevalier doit punir l'oppression, défendre l'opprimé."[21] On the way, Raoul's servant is set upon by a devilish imp and beaten, but somehow the hero doesn't "see" this action and accuses his servant of talking nonsense when he complains. Then comes a change of décor, a *sombre caverne* with a tomb in it bearing the inscription: "Fuis ces lieux ou crains la mort" (p. 1292). Servant and master are magically separated and in Act III we find Raoul in a Promethean pose, chained to a rock in the cave, not by spirits, it turns out, but by brigands. Here he is offered the choice of marrying the Queen of the Brigands and becoming their leader or of being hurled from a cliff. Refusing to betray his beloved Adelaide, he jumps off, followed by his fiancée so that they may be united in death. But this tragedy is only an "illusion comique." The entire castle, robbers, etc., were a test of the fidelity of the lovers by Adelaide's father. Their leap was onto mattresses.

The several details which link this play to *Han* (in addition to a knightly hero and evil castle) are: (1) while on the road to adventure, he is unaware of danger and unable to protect his companion; (2) he is passive like Ordener and here actually chained to a rock; (3) he is faced with a choice between death and marrying an evil woman, and because of his self-sacrifice, he achieves happiness. These motifs repeated some years later in *Han* suggest that they may have a special function in Hugo's universe.

But a further question must be raised. Are we taking all this juvenilia too seriously? Is *Han d'Islande* worth considering at all, for not only is it atrociously written, but it is pretty clear that Hugo had his tongue deep in his cheek as he wrote most of it. Some of Han's blood-drinking speeches leave one helpless with laughter. Hugo throws in such ridiculous names as Oglypiglap and has the nerve to dub a professor of rhetoric "Syngramtax" (p. 315). It has even been suggested that the name of the minor character Spollyson means "C'Polisson," Victor Hugo.[22] Phrases like "tramer d'infâmes machinations" abound, parodies of other works are slipped in without much subtlety. Barrère has noted that "C'est Nichol Orugix, bourreau du Dromtheimhus" is a parodied classical alexandrine, and that the phrase "Oh! que j'aime bien mieux le cor au fond des bois!"

21. *Ibid.*, II, 1286.
22. Géraud Venzac, *Les Premiers Maîtres de Victor Hugo* (Paris, 1955), p. 36.

is an obvious *coup de chapeau* to his friend Alfred de Vigny."[23] The confrontation of Han and Ordener in the cave sounds like a parody of Corneille, and to restrict ourselves to but one more example, at a moment when the plot is at its most intricate, Hugo informs us with owlish solemnity: "Le lecteur n'a pas oublié les fâcheuses nouvelles qui tourmentaient le vieux gouverneur au chapitre XX de cette véridique histoire" (p. 170). Not only has the reader totally forgotten, he couldn't care less by now, and the last adjective must have been inserted for comic effect. The answer to our query must be that comic parody of romance uses the same forms as serious romance, and that therefore both can be of value for the critic.

The key to an understanding of Hugo is to be found most clearly in those parts of the book that show either a marked deviation from traditional romance patterns or, conversely, obsessively repeated patterns. A prime example of the former is the whole episode of the rebellious miners. Normally, romance supposes a stable feudal society, complete with kings and happy peasants. In *Han* we are told that the miners are genuinely suffering. They are underpaid and overtaxed, and their condition seems to reflect genuine economic inequities, not merely the machinations of passing evil grand-chancellors. This situation is troubling in a romance, even if it were handled with greater technical skill than Hugo had at his disposal in 1820. To have a noble marriage at the end requires that the revolt be crushed, as it is, and yet although the ringleaders among the miners are pardoned, justice has hardly triumphed. This whole episode suggests, as we of course know, that Hugo will increase the role given to "les misérables" in his later career. Another variant from traditional romance is the passivity of the hero and the transfer of normal heroic energy to Han, the titular figure, who becomes the vital center of the work, absurd though he be. This weakening of the virtuous hero will become increasingly marked with the passage of time.

The motif that recurs the most frequently is that of the descent into an underworld while seeking the Truth. Given the fact that romance is derived from myth, we should not be surprised at Ordener's multiple descents into Hell, but as they occur so frequently, we may provisionally conclude that they foreshadow Hugo's later creation of mythic literature.

Our conclusions, while answering some questions, also force us to ask

23. Barrère, *Fantaisie*, I, 55.

some others which are not clearly answered in the text. For instance, what will be the future of the pure but passive hero? How demonic is the demon? Another early work will explore these questions further.

Bug–Jargal

THERE ARE two versions to Victor Hugo's next effort at prose fiction, *Bug-Jargal*. The first was begun in 1818 and published in five instalments in *Le Conservateur littéraire*.[24] If we may believe the amusing anecdote cited in *Victor Hugo raconté . . .* , the inspiration came at a dinner where a friend proposed that each person write a tale, to be collected under one title. The narrative setting would be a soldier's tent on the eve of battle, and so the book would be called *Contes sous la tente*. Hugo boasted he could write his in two weeks and won a bet that he could. In actual fact, his was the only one written.[25]

The plot of this original and much shorter version shows the same preoccupation with the exotic that was visible in *Han d'Islande,* for the scene is laid in Santo-Domingo. There is, however, a considerable difference between the atmosphere of this narrative and that of *Han.* The action takes place in 1791 and the plot is built around a slave revolt that actually occurred in that year. Hugo has set his narrative much nearer to the present than in *Han,* and although distant in space, the area was well known to a French reader because it was a French colony. Consequently, the absurdities of some monster's drinking blood from skulls cannot be tolerated. The sense of verisimilitude is much greater, and we feel closer to Walter Scott than to the pseudo-supernatural *roman noir*. Here is a résumé of the plot:

Léopold d'Auverney visits his uncle in Santo-Domingo. A plantation owner of the cruel type, the uncle jails a Negro slave, Pierrot, who had offended his master by protecting a fellow slave from punishment. Léopold befriends Pierrot, who seems admirable in every way. These personal happenings are set against a background of social unrest and shortly a violent rebellion breaks out. During the carnage, Pierrot makes off with Léopold's uncle to save him from being butchered by less

24. Reproduced in the E.I.N., Roman—I, 537–61.
25. "Historique" of *Bug-Jargal, ibid.,* pp. 565–66.

responsible slaves. Léopold, assuming that his new friend has killed his uncle and betrayed their friendship, follows with an armed force only to be himself captured by Biassou, a brutal slave leader, and told that he will die. The hero is saved by Pierrot, who turns out to be Bug-Jargal, another of the rebellious leaders, but, as we can guess from his actions as Pierrot, a wholly admirable one, exercising clemency wherever possible. His participation in the struggle had been the result of the execution of his own wife and children by evil colonialists. But although Léopold is saved, the "conte" closes with something of a tragedy. Bug-Jargal had himself been captured and was given his liberty, leaving ten hostages behind, so that he could arrange Léopold's escape. Having succeeded in his mission, he returns to the French camp to free the hostages and is executed just before word arrives that he is to be spared. If there is any point to this tale other than sheer entertainment, it seems to be to evoke, if in rudimentary fashion, the local color of the tropics and its possibilities for violence and also to suggest that an outcast and "inferior" race may be superior to Europeans, an idea that was popular in eighteenth-century thought and fiction.[26]

One can sense the immense difference in tone between this work and *Han,* where the monster appears frequently under thin disguises, and although his interlocutors wonder vaguely where they have heard the voice before, they never recognize him. The disguise is merely that the slave has two names, one as slave, the other as leader. In a similar way, Léopold does not suggest as strongly the mythic character of the hero. He is not a Golden Lion but merely a French aristocrat. Even the evil characters, the wicked uncle who maltreats his slaves and the evil rebel Biassou, are historically credible and even real. Such impossible names as Musdœmon, Oglypiglap, Syngramtax, etc., are nowhere to be found.

But the second version of 1826 is so different from this first one that, despite a basic plot similarity, it is not the same work. Between these two dates Victor Hugo fell in love and married, and Eugène, the poet's brother, went insane from jealousy on their wedding day. Further, Victor had already completed *Han* and had these patterns fresh in his mind. The result of this revised effort would be the addition of many extra details and two major characters who do not appear in the first version. Their

26. Etienne, pp. 17–39.

presence transforms the primitive narrative into a more complex literary expression.

The first of these two new characters is the heroine, Marie. In the 1818 version, Léopold goes to Santo-Domingo to the plantation of his uncle "dont je devais épouser la fille" (p. 540). This mechanical device for explaining the hero's arrival in the tropics is dropped, having served its purpose, and there is no further mention of any heroine. By providing one in the 1826 version, Hugo moves closer to the normal patterns of romance. The other figure added is a monstrous creation, roughly equivalent to Han and Musdœmon rolled into one, an evil slave named Habibrah, a deformed, cringing being who murders his master and later tries to kill the hero.

The plot, though more complex than the original, is still rather rudimentary. The dead uncle can no longer be saved by Pierrot, and so Hugo imagines that the slave has fallen in love with Marie and rescues her at the moment of the insurrection, which happens to be Léopold's and Marie's wedding day. Again the hero imagines all kinds of villainy on Pierrot's part, but the noble savage reunites the hero and the heroine, and he then sacrifices himself as in the first version. The reasons for his saving Léopold's life are that the young European had saved his life early in the tale, had been kind to him, and above all, was the man that Marie had chosen to marry. At the end of *Bug-Jargal*, however, we do not find the traditional happy ending any more than in the original version. Pierrot is dead as before, and although Léopold and Marie are apparently alive and married, there is only one oblique reference to their future, no account of their marriage, and Marie must have died soon afterwards, because Léopold seems to be a widower at the time that he tells the tale. To cap the sad ending, the narrator is killed in battle the next day.

Despite the many differences between this story and *Han d'Islande*, many patterns visible in the latter story recur. One observes particularly that key scenes are constructed around some descent into a cave or a grotto. There are six of these in *Bug-Jargal*, four of which are demonic.

The first is the scene during which Léopold visits the noble slave Pierrot, in jail for having protected the fellow worker from the evil master. Like Han in his cave, he has a faithful animal with him, but now it is not a ferocious bear with the ironic name of Friend, but a friendly dog, Rask. The prison cell is demonic in that it suggests the injustice that our Western societies inflict upon the exploited classes and races.

The second episode repeats the ambush in the valley that we saw in *Han d'Islande.* Here it is the military column sent out to break the slave revolt that is attacked, but it manages to break out of the trap. During the fighting Léopold is taken prisoner by Biassou, and Pierrot as Bug-Jargal is taken by the French. An interesting detail of this scene is that the blacks, at Bug-Jargal's command, roll stones down the mountain slope against the soldiers exactly as Han had. Here are the two texts compared:

> Ces éclats de rocs se suivaient dans leur chute avec une horrible rapidité; on les entendait se briser à grand bruit les uns sur les autres, et rebondir parmi les soldats, qui, rompant leurs lignes, se hâtaient de descendre en désordre de la hauteur et fuyaient dans toutes les directions. (*Han d'Islande,* p. 261)

> Alors les noirs commencèrent à rouler sur nos colonnes d'énormes quartiers de rochers. . . . Nos soldats . . . expiraient en désespérés, écrasés par les rochers. . . . Une horrible confusion régnait dans l'armée. (p. 429)

The wording is not identical but the situation is.

The third, and one of the most important scenes, takes place in the enemy camp. "Nous parvînmes à l'entrée d'une grotte, taillée par la nature" (p. 442). Led inside, Léopold sees the egocentric Biassou, seated. The hero comments: "Je voyais briller ses yeux flamboyants, constamment attachés sur moi" (p. 443). Biassou announces that the hero will die and asks his *obi* (priest) to make an altar to say a Mass (pp. 444–46). The ceremony is a grotesque parody of the Christian Mass, with a stolen chalice and packing crates for an altar. The parallels with the scene in Han's cave are striking. The hero met Han in a cave *where there was an evil altar.* The flaming eyes and piercing glance are also common to both scenes. When Han jumped on the Druid altar, "de là son œil fixe plongeait sur le jeune homme." Surely, the motif of a demonic altar in a cave with some evil figure present must be more than a coincidence. If we should leap ahead to a late poem of *Les Quatre Vents de l'Esprit* entitled "Ils sont toujours là," we read:

21

> Baal se contemple
> Et s'adore, assis sur l'autel;
> Il triomphe; il a dans sa crypte
> La vieille Inde et la vieille Egypte. . . .
> Et la sombre terre endormie
> Rêve que ce monstre est son dieu.

The theme and even the words are about identical. But if we return to the earlier period in Hugo's life and recall that in *Notre-Dame de Paris* we will again find the setting of a cave, a cathedral, which has its altar (albeit in what seems to be an orthodox rather than a demonic context) and its living demonic figure, Quasimodo, we may begin to realize the importance of this image in Hugo's imaginative patterns.

The final demonic scene takes place in another cave over a rushing torrent. Léopold, about to be executed by Biassou, has been handed over to the masked *obi,* who turns out to be Habibrah and who is eager to execute the hero himself. The tables are turned after Pierrot intervenes to rescue Léopold, and Habibrah becomes the victim. The situation is reminiscent of the one in *Han* where Musdœmon expects life and meets death. His cell was described as a cave: all was "nocturne et secrète" and its form is that of a "cachot obscur" (p. 336).

> —Je laisserai ma vie dans ma dernière morsure; mais elle sera mortelle.
>
> En parlant ainsi, il étreignait en ennemi celui qu'il venait d'embrasser en frère. . . . avec la fureur rusée du démon. Mais les quatre hallebardiers . . . avaient prêté assistance au bourreau, et bientôt Musdœmon, qui n'avait d'autre force que sa rage, fut contraint de lâcher prise. . . .
> —Mourir! démons de l'enfer! (pp. 336–37)

A few moments later, his body is dropped into the water.

Habibrah finds himself hanging from a tree root over the torrent. Like Musdœmon, he begs his former victim for mercy. When Léopold reaches down to help him, Habibrah clutches his hand and tries to pull them both down into death. Like the halberdiers who come to Orugix's aid, Pierrot intervenes once again just in time. "Habibrah avait consumé toute sa force dans son dernier effort. Ses doigts . . . furent enfin contraints de me lâcher . . . . et en me jetant une malédiction que je n'entendis pas" (p.

523), he falls. The parallels are obvious; Hugo is reworking the same scene[27] and preparing for Claude Frollo's death in *Notre-Dame de Paris*.

He also repeats that moment when the evildoers suddenly turn and become judges of others. Speaking to Léopold when about to kill him, he cries out:

> Si j'entrais dans vos salons, mille rires dédaigneux m'accueillaient; ma taille, mes difformités, mes traits, mon costume dérisoire, jusqu'aux infirmités déplorables de ma nature, tout en moi prêtait aux railleries de ton exécrable oncle. . . . Réponds, crois-tu que de pareilles humiliations soient un titre à la reconnaissance d'une créature humaine? Crois-tu qu'elles ne vaillent pas les misères des autres esclaves, les travaux sans relâche, les ardeurs du soleil, les carcans de fer et le fouet des commandeurs? (p. 515)

His job as buffoon anticipates Triboulet as his description looks ahead to Quasimodo:

> Habibrah . . . était un de ces êtres dont la conformation physique est si étrange qu'ils paraîtraient des monstres, s'ils ne faisaient rire. Ce nain hideux était gros, court, ventru, et se mouvait avec une rapidité singulière sur deux jambes grêles et fluettes, qui, lorsqu'il s'asseyait, se repliaient sous lui comme les bras d'une araignée. Sa tête énorme, lourdement enfoncée entre ses épaules . . . était accompagnée de deux oreilles si larges, que ses camarades avaient coutume de dire qu'Habibrah s'en servait pour essuyer ses yeux quand il pleurait. Son visage était toujours une grimace. (p. 449)[28]

Biassou is another evil character, at times ridiculous in his lurid uniform, but not without a certain dignity as the following passage shows:

> Biassou fit un signe de la main; le tumulte cessa comme par un prodige; chaque nègre reprit son rang en silence. Cette discipline, à laquelle Biassou avait plié ses égaux par le simple ascendant de la pensée et de la volonté, me frappa . . . d'admiration. Tous les soldats de cette armée de rebelles paraissaient parler et se mouvoir

27. Baudouin, p. 230, makes this point emphatically.
28. Baudouin, p. 14, likens Habibrah to the infant Hugo. The poet had written that he was born nearly deformed. See *Victor Hugo raconté*.

sous la main du chef, comme les touches du clavecin sous les doigts du musicien. (p. 449)

And if there is a redeeming side to these evil characters, how much more is redemption visible in Pierrot, who is so transformed from dark to light that he becomes almost the hero of the tale. Physically attractive, humanly sensitive, highly intelligent, deeply humanitarian, he will even face death to be faithful to his word. But despite these virtues, he is an outcast. He combines, one year before the *Préface de Cromwell,* the sublime, not with the grotesque, but with the taboo. Being a Negro, he cannot hope to win Marie. Not only is she engaged to Léopold, but miscegenation is unthinkable within the context of the romance and one suspects also within Hugo's mind.

The reader's first encounter with Pierrot takes place early in the story, not at a demonic cave but at a miniature paradise:

> Mon oncle avait fait construire, sur les bords d'une jolie rivière . . .
> un petit pavillon de branchages, entouré d'un massif d'arbres épais,
> où Marie venait tous les jours. . . .
>
> J'avais soin d'orner moi-même tous les matins cette retraite des
> plus belles fleurs que je pouvais cueillir. (p. 389)

To this bower Pierrot comes each night to serenade the heroine, much to her alarm, for she cannot guess who it can be. On one occasion he drives the girl out in fear, overpowers Léopold in the darkness, and leaves the place in disorder (p. 389), a sign of his disruptive presence.[29] One is tempted to think of the serpent in the Garden of Eden, but this parallel is perhaps not the most rewarding way of viewing the text. When we remember that Pierrot will shortly sweep Marie up in his arms and carry her off into the jungle, the lair of diabolical slaves who burn, pillage, and murder, surely we may think of the classic myth of Proserpina. Into an ideal fertile world (the bower) comes dark-browed Pluto, ruler over a dark (Negro) world, for although a slave, all the others obey him in-

---

29. In his song to Marie, he warns her of the coming desolation of Paradise: "Il y a quelquefois au fond du désert un ouragan jaloux du bonheur de la fontaine aimée; il accourt, et l'air et le sable se mêlent sous le vol de ses lourdes ailes; il enveloppe l'arbre et la source d'un tourbillon de feu; et la fontaine se dessèche, et le palmier sent se crisper sous l'haleine de mort le cercle vert de ses feuilles" (p. 393).

stantly, for he is an African king.[30] He disappears with the girl and hides her in the grotto in the forest.

But here the myth must be replaced with another. The idea of rescuing one's wife from Hades can only be the myth of Orpheus and Eurydice. Léopold finds himself cast in the former role and at first he seems active enough in his search.[31] But soon he is taken prisoner and leaves the action to others. Who, then, can play the role of Orpheus? The curious answer is that it is none other than Pluto himself, Bug-Jargal. One of the characteristic traits of Orpheus was his singing, and we first encounter Pierrot singing sweetly in the night, accompanying himself not on a lyre of course, but on its tropical equivalent, the guitar. His voice is in harmony with the forces of nature as he sings of his love, so much so that Habibrah tries to make Léopold think that it *is* the voice of nature (p. 394), even though the language is clearly recognizable as Spanish.[32] It is he who succeeds in reaching Marie in the burning fort and rescuing her.

The last of the six grotto scenes takes place in the wilderness where Pierrot has hidden his fair captive, and to which he leads Léopold. Not the Hell of Pluto's realm, it is explicitly called an Eden (p. 508). "Nous débouchâmes sur une jolie savane verte, arrosée d'eau fraîche . . . de la forêt. Une caverne, dont une multitude de plantes grimpantes, la clématite, la liane, le jasmin, verdissait le front grisâtre, s'ouvrait sur la savane" (p. 497). The heroine faints with joy as Léopold appears, and Pierrot revives her by sprinkling a few drops of water on her face, a gesture that seems ridiculous until we realize its baptismal overtones: the death to her relationship with Pierrot and rebirth to that with Léopold. The moment is in fact so sacred that Hugo's own defense breaks down. Myth is replaced much too openly with his own psychological projections. Pierrot runs from the cave covering his eyes, begging that the lovers not kiss before him ("pas devant moi au moins! s'écria une voix déchirante," p. 497). One can easily sense that the theme of the "frères ennemis"

30. As Pluto represents winter or night, and Proserpina summer or day, Pierrot's language in song is suggestive: "Tu es blanche, et je suis noir; mais le jour a besoin de s'unir à la nuit pour enfanter l'aurore et le couchant, qui sont plus beaux que lui!" (p. 393).
31. Albert Py, *Les Mythes grecs*, stresses the "Orphic" motif in the singer and truth-finder. Even when he is looking for Eurydice, the woman is overshadowed by "la révélation qu'il était allé sans en avoir nettement conscience, quérir" (p. 205).
32. The language of exile in Hugo's vision. His theme song is: "Yo que soy contrabandista."

already announced in *Han d'Islande* explodes here shortly after Victor's marriage to Adèle Foucher, with Eugène's insane jealousy purified and ennobled. Significantly, this action is taking place immediately following the wedding of Léopold and Marie, and Pierrot and Léopold are sworn brothers, always calling each other "Frère."

The result of the double myth, however, is total confusion by the end of the narrative. The bacchantes who later tore Orpheus apart are present in the form of *griotes*, but it is Léopold whom they menace. Pluto becomes Orpheus; both Léopold and Pierrot die but not in ways that fit any pattern of traditional myth. Only Marie seems to fit the pattern, fading out of the picture as Eurydice faded back into Hades.

To outline the coincidence of a plot with that of Greek myths is not of great value in itself. All romance tales, if one look carefully enough, tend to project mythic plots. It is any variation in the pattern that is important. Here the variation is this very confusion of roles which in turn is caused by the weakening of the traditional hero. Despite his passivity, Ordener did make free choices and triumphed at the end. But in *Bug-Jargal* a clear, vital center is lacking. If Hugo had continued in this direction, he would merely have turned his original demons into virtuous heroes and come the full circle back to the traditional romance in the form of the *bon nègre* moralizing tale of the eighteenth century, or if he had concentrated on the demons and had kept them demonic, he would have fallen into the excesses of Sade's demonology. Hugo managed to avoid both pitfalls and maintained the uneasy balance between heroic and demonic that has given his work its force as well as its ambiguity.

The early romances show Hugo's basic creative nature: that of a mythmaker. With this observation there arises a question: What is the nature and role of imagery in this total vision? Imagery expressed in conventional similes and metaphors is infrequent in these early works, save for those clichés of the *roman noir* which indicate the angelic or demonic qualities of heroine or villain. But it was precisely at this time that Hugo, as leader of the new Romantic school in rebellion against the Greco-Roman imagery of Neoclassicism, turned away from the traditional imagery of literature with its overtones of classic mythology. Further, he was about to turn his energies to the theater, and the presence of flesh-and-blood actors and the limitations of the conventional stage would tend to reduce his world to a more human one. Therefore, from

26

1826 to 1841 approximately, Hugo found that his images were cut off from any traditional transcendent cosmic vision, with the result that he would have to create for himself not only their forms but their meaning (if any). This process finds its greatest expression in *Notre-Dame*, perhaps because its prose fiction form gives greater freedom in this direction, but it will also be visible in the plays, even in his earliest theatrical ventures, which we shall next examine.

CROMWELL AND ITS
PREFACE

DURING these formative years, the versatile Hugo was also trying his hand at writing plays. The juvenile *Le Château du diable* mentioned in the previous chapter was in theatrical form, and in the years following 1812, he wrote an imitation of a classical tragedy, *Irtamène* (1816), and a comedy, *A Quelque Chose hasard est bon* (1817–1818). But he soon centered his attention on historical drama with *Inez de Castro,* probably written in 1818,[1] which he followed with a theatrical version of Sir Walter Scott's *Kenilworth* under the title of *Amy Robsart,* written in 1822 and revised in 1827.[2] This imitation of Scott is important for an understanding of Hugo's development in general and of *Cromwell* in particular. Jean Gaudon has dismissed this kind of melodrama as merely a repetition of other efforts:

> Le poète le plus inventif de son époque reste fidèle à un cadre vieux d'un demi-siècle et reprend, de drame en drame, tous les accessoires d'une terreur qui avait été à la mode sous la Révolution. . . . Ce ne sont que souterrains, cachots et oubliettes, châteaux qui sont des mondes sans communication avec le monde, murs qui s'ouvrent pour le coupable et se referment sur l'innocent persécuté.[3]

When the play had its first and only performance in 1828, the critic for the *Journal des Débats* observed that the subject had already been treated "sur trois théâtres différents," and he dismissed the effort as a "vieille nouveauté."[4] We can only agree with the critics just cited, but if our hypothesis that these traditional forms can be seen to take on special meaning in certain cases has any validity, we should take a close look at *Amy Robsart.*

1. *Victor Hugo: Théâtre complet,* éd. J.-J. Thierry et Josette Mélèze (Paris, 1963), II, 1732.
2. For the text of the original version, see E.I.N., Théâtre—IV, 439–52.
3. *Victor Hugo, dramaturge* (Paris, 1955), pp. 48–49.
4. E.I.N., p. 455.

Before beginning any analysis, one may well ask how important is the theater in Hugo's work. Does it merit a central place? Charles Baudouin seems to think so, suggesting that the theater corresponds to the deepest psychological needs of Victor Hugo. Baudouin's idea is that Hugo's desire to create a *spectacle* is a projection of his own voyeurism (*voir = savoir*) in matters sexual, and all of this fits into Hugo's obsessive theme of *l'œil.*[5] Perhaps this is true, but surely more traditional reasons can explain Hugo's interest. The theater in France has always had immense prestige because of the reputation of the seventeenth-century giants. Therefore, we should not be surprised if the boy's imagination turned in this direction. On a more adult intellectual level, the theater in France has always been the way to succeed, the means of propagating ideas, an arena of intellectual struggle, whether to challenge neoclassical doctrine in 1830, or as with Sartre in the mid-twentieth century, to demolish bourgeois principles. Hugo himself recognized this function of the theater in his preface to *Lucrèce Borgia* (1832): "le théâtre, on ne saurait trop le répéter, a de nos jours une importance immense, et qui tend à s'accroître sans cesse avec la civilisation même. Le théâtre est une tribune. Le théâtre est une chaire" (p. 443). Finally, on the personal level, a cheering audience asking for the author at the final curtain is a sweet triumph indeed and, by the time of *Hernani*, Hugo would badly need the money that dramatic success can bring. So we agree with critics who consider his theater important but would hesitate to make it absolutely central. After all, the poet was writing as much lyric poetry in the 1830's as he was drama, and *Notre-Dame de Paris* shows his continuing interest in prose fiction.

Another question must accompany this importance of Hugo's theater. Does the change in literary genre from prose fiction to play require any new critical approach? In theory, yes. The origins of the theater in corporate religious ritual, whether Dionysiac or Christian, with its death and rebirth motifs are well known (even Hugo's *Le Château du diable* has a comic variant of it in its ending) and should lead the critic to search for these stylized patterns. Further, because an audience cannot reread a page, a dramatic author must repeat his situations often enough so that even if missed the first time, the audience can soon grasp the point. If the

5. Charles Baudouin, *Psychanalyse de Victor Hugo* (Genève, 1943), chap. III.

play is in verse, rhyming words can help the communication of key themes, and so forth. But in practice, Hugo's prose romances are, as we have already seen, so full of recurring mythic patterns that the differences are not likely to be significant. The distinctions are further blurred when we realize that *Amy Robsart* is an adaptation of an historical novel, and when we come to *Cromwell* itself, the fact that its length is nearly twice that of an ordinary play makes it seem even less an example of a distinct genre with its own rules and conventions.

Hugo himself showed in the famous preface to the play that despite his insistence on the distinction between lyric, epic, and dramatic, he really had no clear sense of genre. Isolating the various remarks in the *Préface*, we obtain the following yield: the third stage of world literature, after the lyric and epic periods, is *le drame,* whose "caractère" is "la vérité" (p. 20), hardly a clear distinguishing test. We read further that "le drame vit du réel," (p. 21), the latter word defined as a mixture of the sublime and the grotesque, and that "le drame peint la vie." Do not such phrases apply as well or better to the novel? Finally, drama wishes to "peindre ce qu'elle [la société] pense" (p. 21), which suggests the essay. To sum it up, not only does Hugo say that "Il y a tout dans tout" (p. 22), a phrase which blurs generic boundary lines to the point that he proposes Dante's *Inferno* and Milton's *Paradise Lost* as dramas, but he concludes: "le drame est la poésie complète" (p. 22). For Hugo, it would seem that "drama" is merely a word for serious contemporary literature, with its attributes in no way different from those of a dramatic romance, except that he desires a theater written in verse. Yet even this last distinction he abandons toward the end of the *Préface:* "Au reste, que le drame soit écrit en prose, ce n'est là qu'une question secondaire. . . . Dans des questions de ce genre, il n'y a qu'une solution. Il n'y a qu'un poids qui puisse faire pencher la balance de l'art, c'est le génie" (pp. 39–40). Hugo does require that a play have unity of action, but he warns against simplicity of action (p. 28), permitting the free development of subplots and thereby approaching the greater complexity of prose fiction. We may conclude, therefore, that the distinctions of genre are weak enough both in the author's statement and in his actual practice so that we may safely ignore them for the purposes of this study.

To return to *Amy Robsart:* the play tells the familiar story of Dudley, Duke of Leicester, secretly married to the lower-born Amy. The tension develops from the fact that he is Queen Elizabeth's favorite and that the Queen is in love with him and is even on the verge of declaring herself to him. The ambitious Leicester is aware of the Queen's feelings and senses that to reveal that he is not a bachelor after all, and therefore not a possible husband and king for Elizabeth, might easily precipitate disaster. Not only would he fall from favor, but the Queen is ruthless enough to be capable of destroying the innocent Amy. Into this delicate situation comes the villain, Richard Varney, low-born and even more ambitious than Leicester. As Leicester's confidant, he urges his master to repudiate Amy so that his master's, and therefore his own, rise to power will not be checked. Varney reminds Dudley of "la nécessité de toujours monter quand on a mis le pied sur l'échelle de l'ambition" (p. 343). For the Duke, his destiny must either be "le trône" or "l'abîme." Influenced by this Iago and vacillating between pure love and strong ambition, he realizes that to make public his marriage would be to uproot the great oak that protects Europe with its shade, to use the play's image, and reduce him to the rank of a simple country squire (p. 319). Arriving at his castle for a visit, the Queen senses his ambition and uses vertical imagery to describe the situation: "Il me semble qu'en ce moment même où vous baissez si humblement votre front, vous élevez votre pensée bien haut" (p. 297). Leicester does think briefly of giving up his political ambitions, but, and again we see the absence of heroic energy in the hero, he finally abdicates his responsibility and begs the villain to advise him and to lead him. But Varney has also been warned by the Queen: "Varney . . . sachez modérer vos désirs; car . . . l'ambitieux se marque son but, mais c'est toujours au delà qu'il tombe" (p. 314). Their attempt to rise leads to a fall for them all. The innocent Amy plunges to her death through a trap-door. Leicester's fall is an inward one. He awakens too late ("mon aveuglement a cessé," p. 375) to the fact that Amy was his angel and that Varney is the devil. The latter's end is also a fall, with the imagery of Hell suitably present. He is trapped in a burning tower which collapses in flames as the imp Flibbertigibbet, a semi-comic demonic *lutin*, watches in delight.

This play begins to make clear what the prose romances had only suggested. The imagery of rise and descent is directly associated with failure and success. To rise is to fall. Had Leicester humbled himself by marrying openly, his happy life would not have been threatened with destruction, and in humble love with Amy he could have risen to heights of virtue. He was not so wise as Ordener, who abandoned all for love and thus won. Another noticeable progression here is that the rise and descent imagery has a clear socio-political dimension. Although Hugo's story is not original, he provides his own meaning to it through patterns of imagery. What is rather sketchily developed in *Amy Robsart* is to be repeated and expanded in his next dramatic attempt.

After contemplating writing a play on Corneille in 1825, Hugo decided to do one on Oliver Cromwell, the Lord Protector of England. Because of the abnormal length of the text, it has rarely been produced, and, in addition, its famous preface has overshadowed it. But as our interest is in the fictional forms, the play must surely be more important than any theory by its author. Hugo himself warned against overlooking the drama: "Tandisque les critiques s'acharnent sur la préface et les érudits sur les notes, il peut arriver que l'ouvrage lui-même leur échappe" (p. 97). With our knowledge of subsequent academic scholarship, we recognize that Hugo was very wise.

The first act of the play takes place in a tavern in London, where both Cavaliers and Roundheads are meeting to plot Cromwell's assassination. Sworn enemies, they are nonetheless united for the moment because of Cromwell's desire to become king. The setting is called both an "antre" and a "caverne de Cacus" (p. 105). These words suggest the value of the proscenium box for an author obsessed with caves and grottoes. The cave, in this case the tavern, is the stage itself. We are already accustomed in Hugo's work to having a hero enter to do battle or in some other way to confront death at the hands of a monster, but here the pattern seems inapplicable. The traditional ogre has been replaced by the numerous conspirators, and one can hardly decide whether they are heroes or villains. The spectator's sympathies might lie with them against a regicide and usurper, but it soon becomes clear that Hugo is presenting them in a comic light, thus diminishing their heroic stature for either good or evil. One of the Cavaliers is a foppish poet, Lord Rochester, interested only in his pastoral quatrain, and others among this group show other signs of pettiness. Nor are the Puritans any better. The fanatic Roundhead Carr, seeing Rochester's rich habiliments, wildly equates the Cavaliers with Sodom, Satan, and Vishnu all at once. In this serio-comic atmosphere, they fulminate against the usurper. Even the Old Testament imprecations that the Puritans hurl at Cromwell are carefully chosen for their comic effect. For example, Barebone says:

> Il veut être, échauffé par l'impure Abisag,
> Roi comme fut David;—qu'il le soit comme Agag! (p. 96)

Hugo heightens the comedy by contriving to bring in Puritan names that would surely amuse a French Catholic audience, e.g., Vis-pour-ressusciter-Jéroboam-D'Emer (p. 91). Still, the Biblical imagery, even if largely comic in effect, does inevitably have its apocalyptic dimension. Carr, for example, adds to the references to the Old Testament his own statement of Hell. In the presence of the vile Cavaliers, he feels that "Mes pieds marchent ici sur des charbons d'enfer" (p. 82).

Into this odd demonic cave where the identity of the true demon is uncertain, if indeed there is any true demon at all, *someone* must enter; a hole is to be filled. It turns out that the "hero" who appears is another comic figure, none other than Cromwell's harmless, scatterbrained son Richard, who has come to carouse and drink. The conspirators are at first sure that they have been discovered, but after some carefully contrived ambiguous language, we learn that Richard is truly unaware of the reason for the meeting in the tavern and receives the accolade from Rochester: "Il a l'air d'un bon diable" (p. 102).

Where, then, is the true hero? And as a hero requires a heroine, where is the maiden in distress? Or have these figures disappeared? Act II provides an answer of sorts. The titular character makes his first appearance and completely dominates the action through Act IV. He has the intelligence and energy needed for a heroic role, but he cannot be a hero in the traditional style of romance. He has no lady fair to rescue and no arduous quest to undertake, for we learn that he has the Parliament under his thumb, and they will soon come crawling to his feet to offer him the crown. This protagonist seems a far cry from the typical hero of the Ordener type and much closer to Leicester of *Amy Robsart* in his desire for the crown and his hesitation whether to reach for it. He is even less a hero than Leicester, for he has no pure Amy to love, being already married to an ordinary bourgeois female, one Elizabeth Bourchier. Hugo had to be true to history in this respect. But we may make an even bolder parallel: To some extent Cromwell is a carefully disguised Han d'Islande.

First his size. In *Han*, we quote from a crowd scene:

—Quel homme est-ce donc que ce Han? demanda-t-on.

—C'est un géant, dit l'un.

—C'est un nain, dit l'autre.

—Personne ne l'a donc vu? reprit une voix. (p. 23)

This Hugolian dialogue recurs in less extreme but still recognizable form in CROMWELL, V, xii:

Voix dans la foule

Cromwell!—C'est là Cromwell?—Ce roi!—Ce régicide!

—Il est fort laid!—Qu'il est petit pour un héros!

—On l'aurait dit plus grand.—Je le croyais moins gros. (p. 401)

Another suggestion of similarity is in the eyes. In *Han,* Spiagudry sees "là derrière ce mur . . . ces deux yeux flamboyants comme des comètes, qui se sont fixés sur nous" (p. 158). In *Cromwell,* verisimilitude and the limitations of the stage require that this trait be reduced to popular rumor, but the language is similar:

PREMIÈRE FEMME

Dit-on pas qu'il a fait pacte avec le diable?

DEUXIÈME FEMME

On conte que la nuit ses yeux semblent ardents. (p. 386)

Also, at least in the popular imagination, the two have a Protean quality. In *Han,* the monster is thought to be able to change his shape at will and even to be able to fly (p. 261). In the play, Rochester cries out:

. . . il est protée! il est magicien.

On l'aborde; on croit voir un lion royal.—Bien;

Tâchez de l'endormir. Bst! un coup de baguette,

Le lion qui dormait est un chat qui vous guette;—

Le chat devient un tigre aux rugissements sourds.—

Puis, la griffe se change en patte de velours. (p. 420)

These Protean figures, evil or not, have at least the virtue of loving their sons. Han, we remember, mourned deeply the death of Gill Stadt, even if his grief took the odd form of stealing his skull from the morgue and drinking blood from it. Gill's death leaves Han's life meaningless:

"Maintenant, juges, mon fils est mort; je viens ici chercher la mort. L'âme d'Ingolphe me pèse, parce que je la porte seul et que je ne pourrai la transmettre à aucun héritier. Je suis las de la vie, puisqu'elle ne peut plus être l'exemple et la leçon d'un successeur" (p. 313). Cromwell feels the same way, *toutes proportions gardées*. The tone is of course less extravagant, for both Cromwell and Richard are actual historical personages.

CROMWELL

Richard—mon héritier—il faut présentement
Vous ouvrir la milice avec le parlement.
Je vous fais colonel, pair d'Angleterre et membre
Du conseil privé.

The idle youth replies in a manner that can only disappoint his father. He refuses, saying:

J'aime les bois, les prés, le loisir, le repos;
J'aime à chasser les daims et des cerfs par troupeaux." (p. 427)

The father then remarks "amèrement à part," "Que sert ce que je fais?" This theme of the conflict between generations continues *Han* and anticipates the relationship between Claude and Jehan Frollo in *Notre-Dame* and much later M. de Gillenormand and Marius of *Les Misérables,* not to mention the even more elaborate disappointment with the younger generations that one will find in *Les Burgraves.* All of these variations on the father-son theme probably reflect the early strained relations between Hugo and his own father, even though they were now on good terms.

Act II shows us this Han in his lair, the banquet hall at Whitehall, where Cromwell receives foreign ambassadors and manipulates them as he pleases. Here he also learns of the conspiracy to assassinate him just as Han had learned that a price had been put on his head. The Protector's assistant says, showing that Cromwell will continue to be the dramatic center and energy of the play:

. . . il faut les surveiller de près.
D'eux-mêmes ils viendront se jeter dans nos rets. (p. 191)

But the tension is maintained because Lord Rochester (now in disguise as Cromwell's chaplain) learns of the counterplan to seize the plotters and

35

hopes to foil it. So much for this over-long and often pointless act, but it does show that the Ordeners and Léopolds are gone and have been replaced by a semi-villain.

Act III introduces us to Les Fous, to use Hugo's own subtitle to the act. These are four court jesters who occasionally gambol around the stage like a kind of chorus. This is not their first appearance in Hugo. There were imps in his very early *Le Château du diable*, witches (the *griotes*) cavort around Biassou's camp, and in *Amy Robsart*, Hugo transformed Scott's Flibbertigibbet into a serio-comic imp from Hell. Here in *Cromwell*, there is more than a suggestion of demonology, but as in Act I it is in a comic vein. The jesters appear on stage singing:

> Oyez ceci, bonnes âmes!
> J'ai voyagé dans l'enfer.
> Moloch, Sadoch, Lucifer
> Allaient me jeter aux flammes
> Avec leurs fourches de fer. (p. 193)

Immediately after this song, they equate the Devil with Cromwell, an idea that recurs in later songs (e.g., p. 198), but the reader again has difficulty in deciding whether to take this demonology seriously.

Against this semi-comic background the serious aspect of the play unfolds. Cromwell, like Leicester, half wishes to be king. On the one hand, he contemptuously refuses the order of the Golden Fleece presented to him by the Spanish ambassador (p. 118) and, speaking more generally of the monarchy, soliloquizes:

> Qu'est-ce, un trône, d'ailleurs? un tréteau sous un dais,
> Quelques planches, où l'œil de la foule s'attache,
> Changeant de nom, selon l'étoffe qui les cache.
> Du velours, c'est le trône; un drap noir,—l'échafaud! (p. 169)

In this verse is visible one of the key image patterns of the play. The attempt to rise to the throne may turn out to be a trip to the executioner's block, an idea suggested in *Amy Robsart* but here made more explicit. Early in Act I, for instance, Lord Broghill declared to the other conspirators as if speaking to Cromwell: "Tu ne montais si haut que pour tomber si bas!" (p. 55). This language is repeated by Cromwell's wife in Act II, as she urges her husband to remain simple, as Amy had begged the same of Leicester (pp. 120–21). Cromwell's wife even reminds him that his own mother "quand vous montiez, mesurait votre chute" (p. 121). His daughter Francis [*sic*], a royalist, is horrified at the idea that anyone except Charles be King of England. Even the poet John Milton makes an occasional appearance to warn him of the danger of reaching upward: "Ce n'est pas que je veuille ici te rabaisser," he says (p. 224), but royalty is not the way to greatness or even to survival.

Act IV should give Cromwell some insight into this truth. Having learned that the Royalist conspirators have planned to drug him and then to sneak into the palace and kidnap him, he first drugs the drugger, Rochester, and then disguises himself as a sentinel at the palace gate. With the disguise, incidentally, he creates another link with Han, who appeared frequently incognito.

For this act Hugo sets a scene which, even if outdoors, gives the impression of being a closed-in lair where the unwary may be trapped. "A droite, des massifs d'arbres; au fond, des massifs d'arbres, au-dessus desquels se découpent en noir, sur le ciel sombre, les faîtes gothiques du palais. A gauche, la poterne du parc, petite porte en ogive très ornée de sculptures.—Il est nuit close" (p. 288). Here Cromwell waits for the kidnappers to appear. Before their arrival, the four jesters arrive to provide a comic suggestion of Hell, one commenting on the darkness:

> Il faudrait l'œil d'un clerc.
> Voir?—dans le four du diable il fait vraiment plus clair! (p. 290)

With the arrival of Lord Ormond and his party, Cromwell is in a position to overhear their conversation, from which he learns the truth of what they think of him. From his lowly position as sentinel he is also able to capture the whole group. It would seem that both knowledge and effective action are made possible by a lowly position.

Hugo closes his act with an amusing experiment. The Royalists emerge from the palace with a drugged "Cromwell," actually Lord Rochester, who had occupied the ruler's bed, and when the young man awakes in the park outside, he thinks that he is dead and in Hell:

> Suis-je déjà pendu? Serais-je dans l'enfer?
> Ce palais flamboyant, ces spectres, ces armées
> De démons secouant des torches enflammées;
> C'est l'enfer! Car Wilmot [i.e., Rochester] comptait peu sur le ciel.

Regardant le Protecteur

Oui, voilà bien Satan; il ressemble à Cromwell! (p. 337)

He continues in this vein for the rest of the scene, which one of the jesters calls a "scène de l'autre monde en celui-ci visible" (p. 344). Rochester's mistake can hardly form the basis for any sustained imagery without becoming tedious. Still, it shows Hugo's pattern of thinking in vertical imagery. He has Rochester say:

Je suis mort.—Ce Cromwell pourtant me déconcerte.
Ici . . . déjà!—Je l'ai laissé là-haut hier. (p. 342)

Cromwell too thinks in vertical terms. His desire to be king is expressed (traditionally enough) in words of ascent. Hearing that his rubber-stamp Parliament is offering him the crown, he exults:

Ah! je le tiens enfin, ce sceptre insaisissable!
Mes pieds ont donc atteint le haut du mont de sable! (p. 133)

He goes on to say:

Tu ne sais pas, ami, comme il est importun,
Quand on sort de la foule et qu'on touche le faîte,
De sentir quelque chose au-dessus de sa tête!
Ne serait-ce qu'un mot, ce mot [king] alors est tout.

Cromwell soon becomes aware, however, that the entire nation is restive and unhappy at his idea, and he in turn resents his limited power. Tied down by politics, he is not free like the traditional solitary hero:

Ah! si j'étais né roi
Je chasserais cela! [the crowd] Mais un chef populaire
Doit pour mener la foule, hélas, savoir lui plaire. (p. 214)

The lesson is clear: To avoid destruction, he must refuse the heights and concern himself with what is beneath him. This idea is forcefully expressed through the imagery of the setting for Act V.

The scene is the Great Hall of Westminster Abbey: "A droite, une charpente revêtue de planches figurait les degrés d'un trône" (p. 348). This temporary platform, erected for the coronation, is receiving its finishing touches as the curtain rises, at the hands of the same group of workmen who, in 1649, had built the platform on which Charles I was beheaded, a coincidence not overlooked by these workers. One remarks: "Ce trône de Stuart complète l'échafaud" (p. 350), thus associating rise and fall in one sentence. A Roundhead warns: "S'il veut s'élire roi, qu'il tombe" (p. 351), and another repeats the idea:

> Voilà son échafaud!
> Il y sera monté pour tomber de plus haut. (p. 356)

The Roundheads are planning to assassinate Cromwell as soon as he is crowned.

The danger of becoming king is expressed by the workers through the imagery of their own carpentry. One comments: "Ce trône est moins solide [than the one at Charles' coronation]; en y montant, il tremble" (p. 350). The symbolic meaning is made explicit by an earlier development of the image:

> Au moindre vent qui change, au moindre bruit qui vibre,
> L'édifice effrayant s'écroule, et, dans la nuit,
> Un trône, un peuple, un monde ainsi s'évanouit! (p. 295)

The conspirators put the matter squarely: "S'il fait ce dernier pas [up the ladder to the throne], [il] se jette au précipice" (p. 346).[6] The ominous predictions of John Milton and of Cromwell's wife and daughter seem to be coming true. Milton once more rushes forward with a final "Mané, Thécel, Pharès" (p. 406), but Cromwell shrugs his shoulders and climbs. A conspirator whispers delightedly: "Il monte! je respire," for now they can in good conscience assassinate him. But at the last moment, no doubt because of the exigencies of history, Hugo has Cromwell come to a realization of what he is about to do. He seems to awaken as from a trance and rejects the crown with the comment:

> M'édifier un trône! Eh! c'est creuser ma tombe.
> Cromwell, pour y monter, sait trop comme on en tombe. (p. 409)

6. This idea of climbing a ladder to death had already been elaborated in a comic context when Lord Rochester in his disguise as a Puritan preacher had to give his opinion whether to burn or to hang someone. He explains his choice of the gallows:

> Ah! . . . le gibet? C'est cela . . .
> On y monte au moyen d'une échelle . . . Voilà.
> Et . . . Dieu fit voir en rêve à son berger fidèle
> Qu'on monte au ciel de même au moyen d'une échelle. (p. 216)

Before leaving this scene of near-coronation, we might point out another dimension to it. The act takes place in Westminster, an abbey, in which workmen have put together a platform, onto which Oliver climbs, sits in a chair, while prayers and other rites of a politico-religious nature are performed. By wording the action in this way, we may observe an analogy with Han's grotto, with its Druid altar, its three rocks supporting a horizontal slab upon which the monster crouches. There is also a parallel to be made with the episode in Biassou's camp when Habibrah put together a rickety altar from packing crates in order to parody the Mass. Can we not see here in *Cromwell* Victor Hugo already recoiling from the monarchical principle, both because it belongs to the past, like the druidical cult, and because it has proved itself bloodthirsty and grotesque? At any rate, to go up directly is to fail, in politics as in love. Should one then go down to succeed, as in the case of Ordener or Orpheus? It would appear so. John Milton suggested this course of action, albeit indirectly, when he urged Oliver to refuse the crown:

> Démens tes vils flatteurs, montre-toi noble et grand.
> Juge, législateur, apôtre, conquérant,
> Sois plus que roi. Remonte à ta hauteur première. (p. 225)

Cromwell seems to accept this advice in his final rejection speech by reminding his audience that his power comes from the lowly *peuple* and that he must descend into it to assure his power:

> Je ne viens point ici ceindre le diadème,
> Mais retremper mon titre au sein du peuple même,
> Rajeunir mon pouvoir, renouveler mes droits.
> L'écarlate sacrée était teinte deux fois.
> Cette pourpre est au peuple, et, d'une âme loyale,
> Je la tiens de lui.—Mais la couronne royale!
> Quand l'ai-je demandée? Et qui dit que j'en veux?

But if in this speech Cromwell rejects the throne, he does not go so far as to give sovereignty to the people. His Parliament is still a rubber stamp, as the Roundhead Carr reminds him at the end of this non-historical "historical" play:

> . . . remets l'état en équilibre;
> Rends-nous le parlement. Ensuite, nous verrons. (p. 432)

Carr goes even farther, insisting that Cromwell humble himself before God if he is to receive divine approval:

> Tu viendras avec moi; tous deux courbant nos fronts,
> Tous deux ceints d'une corde, et nous souillant la face,
> Nous irons à sa [God's] barre implorer notre grâce. (p. 432)

Cromwell, too, had used similar language before receiving the trappings of royalty:

> Mais pour que le Seigneur sur nous se manifeste,
> Il faut courber le front et plier les genoux. (p. 404)

Only Carr is really sincere. But even so, by refusing the crown, Cromwell has, as Milton predicted, gained in glory. One embittered conspirator exclaims: "Nos efforts n'ont servi qu'à le placer plus haut" (p. 435).

And yet, Cromwell has not learned the value of his lesson, for his last longing words are "Quand donc serai-je roi?" This final regret seems surprising in such an astute mind, for through the action of the play he has not only learned of the dangers of climbing, but the practical value of lowering himself. We remember that when in Act IV he disguised himself as an ordinary soldier, he found out the last details of the conspiracy and arrested the culprits. He discovered also that his son Richard, whom he had thought to be a traitor, was in reality faithful to him. Even the change in uniform had its psychological effect, leading him to appreciate the lot of the humble who do not have to worry about matters of state. Cromwell had sighed, thinking of his exalted position: "Quelle pompe au dehors! au dedans quelle plaie" (p. 292).

The theme of humility gives rise to the issue of clemency, which is a noble and practical means for assuring political equilibrium and success, for clemency lifts up the fallen in relationship to the one who grants it and thus places the grantor in a seemingly lower position that, paradoxically, serves only to exalt him. Earlier in the play, in Act II, scene v, an aide comes in to ask Cromwell what to do with the remaining Irish that have not as yet been exterminated.

THURLOË

> Faut-il de cette race
> Epargner ce qui reste?

41

CROMWELL

> Et pourquoi? Point de grâce
> Aux papistes! Soyons dans ce peuple troublé
> Comme une torche ardente au sein d'un champ de blé!

In the same scene, Thurloe reminds him of a prisoner who has been forgotten and is seeking a pardon.

> Voilà neuf mois qu'il gît dans un cachot terrible
> Sur la paille oublié. . . . Et mourant de besoin,
> Le pauvre homme est resté, durant ce long espace,
> Seul, nu, glacé.

Cromwell seems horrified: "Neuf mois! Dieu! comme le temps passe" (p. 131), he exclaims, but then passes on to other matters, forgetting all about his victim.

But by the end of the play he has learned much. Now he is willing to pardon the conspirators, even after Lord Ormond told him that if their positions were reversed, he would not spare Cromwell. The Cavaliers are overwhelmed by this generosity. One says: "Cet homme est un problème!" (p. 423), and another says ruefully: "D'un mot il a brisé nos armes" (p. 424). And when one Royalist tries after the pardon to kill Cromwell, he is seized by an outraged mob and hurled into the Thames (p. 541). Thus Cromwell has proof of the value of clemency. But he can see only its practical value, not its inherent nobility: "La clémence est, au fait, un moyen comme un autre" (p. 434), he remarks, and with this cynical thought falls short of true grandeur. One can contrast his practical attitude with the idealism of Pierrot in *Bug-Jargal,* and even more instructive for the sake of comparison is Corneille's *Cinna,* where Auguste's deep clemency is not only practical, but resolves all the tensions, artistic, psychological, and political. Hugo's play closes, however, without any true resolution of the problem. We must conclude from this final ambiguity in *Cromwell* that Hugo was intending to portray an ambivalent character. The fact that his own political allegiances were at that time in a state of uncertainty probably has something to do with the hesitation manifest in the play, but of this one can never be sure. With the passage of time, Hugo's conclusions were to become more clear-cut as his own position became more clear in social and political matters.

With two prose romances and two plays behind us, we are in a position to examine the famous *Préface* to the play with the purpose of comparing Hugo's theoretical statements with our own findings. We are not concerned here with Hugo's theory of periods of literature, nor even with his development of the concept of the grotesque, but rather with the patterns of vertical imagery that have been visible in all the works that we have studied so far. To summarize our findings in their most reduced form: a hero must turn downward if he is to have any hope of rising to a great height. In *Han d'Islande*, Ordener succeeds; in *Bug-Jargal*, there is a partial success (the hero and heroine are saved even if Pierrot dies); in *Cromwell*, the "hero" succeeds, but he has a moral flaw as hero; in *Amy Robsart*, Leicester tries to go directly upward and his effort fails. In the *Préface de Cromwell*, Hugo tries to explain what these heights and depths represent in his cosmos. Although the passages are familiar, we must quote at some length because of their importance. Hugo proposes a dualistic idea of Christianity, which he calls at this stage of his life, "vraie" and "complète."

> Une religion spiritualiste, supplantant le paganisme matériel et extérieur . . . dépose le germe de la civilisation moderne. . . . Elle enseigne à l'homme qu'il a deux vies à vivre, l'une passagère, l'autre immortelle. . . . Elle lui montre qu'il est double comme sa destinée, qu'il y a en lui un animal et une intelligence, une âme et un corps. (p. 11)

Man, he adds in a reference to the Great Chain of Being that anticipates the Bouche d'Ombre, is the mid-point of the ladder that starts with the stone and ends in God. This dualism, Hugo continues, did not exist with paganism, which "donne forme et visage à tout, même aux essences, même aux intelligences. Tout chez elle est visible, palpable, charnel" (p. 12). But in the Christian era, man recognizes his duality and the consequence of his awareness is important. The domain of the soul is "le monde idéal," that of the body "le monde réel." Drama results from the tension between the two:

> Du jour où le Christianisme a dit à l'homme: "Tu es double, tu es composé de deux êtres, l'un périssable, l'autre immortel, l'un charnel, l'autre éthéré, l'un enchaîné par les appétits, les besoins et les passions, l'autre emporté sur les ailes de l'enthousiasme et de la rêverie, celui-ci toujours courbé vers la terre, sa mère, celui-là sans

43

cesse élancé vers le ciel, sa patrie;" de ce jour le drame a été créé. Est-ce autre chose en effet que ce contraste . . . entre deux principes opposés qui sont toujours en présence dans la vie, et qui se disputent l'homme depuis le berceau jusqu'à la tombe. (p. 23)

The astute critic will observe that the images in the above passage are reduced to the figure of the mother and the father and support Baudouin's approach to an understanding of Hugo. But the Oedipal problems of the author disappear with the displacement into literature, and the language becomes more mythical than psychological. In this rather Manichean view of Christianity, the general directions of up and down are given substance by associating with the upward direction, *ciel,* not only *âme,* but also *sublime, lumière, bien* and conversely with the downward *corps,* the words *terre, grotesque, ombre, mal.* The above-quoted paragraph states that there is a struggle in opposite directions, clearly in the hope that man can escape his material form or prison and soar to Heaven.

But Hugo's actual fictional patterns show that man should not strain upward directly to escape the limitations of the body. To succeed he must turn downward into *la terre,* as concretized by the various caves in the prose romances. In so doing, he is also turning down toward death and Hell. Reality and death go together. When Ordener risks death, it is to find the reality not only of love but also of the political intrigue. Léopold in *Bug-Jargal* goes toward death trying to save Marie, his reality of love, and in so doing finds out another reality: the truth of his uncle's murder. But if the Way is down, the ultimate goal is, as Hugo makes clear in the *Préface,* still upward. Léopold made this clear to Marie before leaving her:

—Marie, repris-je, . . . je vais te quitter en effet; il le faut; mais nous nous reverrons ailleurs.

—Ailleurs, reprit-elle avec effroi, ailleurs, où? . . .

—Dans le ciel! répondis-je, ne pouvant mentir à cet ange. (p. 506)

On the other hand, in *Cromwell* the sense of descending into death, though a fixed idea of the conspirators, is not strong in the titular character himself. One finds an occasional weariness with the problems of government, but normally Oliver is preoccupied with reality, as is natural when the pattern is transposed to the world of politics. Here *le peuple,* or as Hugo subtitles Chapter V, "Les Ouvriers," constitutes the political reality on which reposes the superstructure of government. We remember that Cromwell did not feel free to ignore popular attitudes. Thus the downward turn can be into many different things: into matter (body), death, the lower classes, earth, shadow, and reality. This set of choices is somewhat chaotic and in subsequent works Hugo will try to give it a clearer expression than he had up to this point.

A final question must be raised: To what extent are the heroes free to choose their path? Are they already victims of fatality as they will be in *Hernani* and *Notre-Dame de Paris?* First, we remarked in the previous chapter that *Han d'Islande* contains many predictions that come true, and that the hero at times, instead of dominating events, is led by them. Yet despite this suggestion of fatality, no clear message emerges. Ordener apparently chooses death freely rather than marry Ulrica d'Ahlefeld. The same uncertainty prevails in *Bug-Jargal.* Not until *Cromwell* does Hugo even face the problem openly. In the earlier romances the predictions of the future were never truly supernatural, but in this play there is an ancient Jew, Manassé, a money-lender who serves also as a soothsayer. By reading Cromwell's hand (p. 284), he tells of a coming assassination attempt of which he, Manassé, is really ignorant. More interesting yet is Cromwell's soliloquy on the subject when Manassé assures him of his power of divination:

> Se pourrait-il?—Lever le rideau du destin;
> Lire au loin dans le ciel un avenir lointain;
> Déchiffrer chaque vie et chaque caractère;
>
> . . . .
> Dieu marque un but unique à chaque créature. (p. 277)

But although this play poses the question of fatality, it does not answer it, adopting a hesitant "Que sait-on? Tout est mystérieux" (p. 278). Further, it is difficult in a play for an author to speak directly. All thoughts must be uttered through the characters, and as a consequence the attitude toward palmistry and destiny itself may only reflect that of a character situated in the seventeenth century. We must turn to the prose narrative *Notre-Dame de Paris* to determine the relationship between an omnipotent fatality and the imagery of rise and descent. In this novel fatality itself will be expressed in the language of imagery and thus it can combine with the other images and create an artistic whole.

THE TRIUMPH OF
IMAGERY

NOTRE-DAME DE PARIS

T HE MONTHS and years following the completion of *Cromwell* were busy ones indeed for the young author. Hugo turned his attention to lyric poetry, and *Les Orientales* was published in January, 1829. We know that he wanted to write a novel and by 1828 had taken some notes. By November of that year he had even gone so far as to sign a contract with Gosselin calling for a completed manuscript by mid-April of 1829. At the same time, he was continuing his exploration of the theater, this time hoping to write a play short enough to be produced. He completed *Marion de Lorme* in June, 1829, after only a few weeks of writing, but the royal censor refused to let it be performed because of its hostile portrait of a weak monarch. To replace it, he wrote *Hernani* in August and September of that year. With such pressing interests, Hugo seemed unable to free himself to return to his historical novel until the middle of 1830, and then in five months of hard work, he revised his outline and completed the manuscript of *Notre-Dame de Paris*.[1]

These well-known facts reveal that the two plays and the novel were conceived at about the same period in Hugo's life, with the result that it is dangerous to try to determine any clear evolution of form or thought from one to another. The novel was actually written last, but who can say how much of it Hugo was carrying in his head from the earlier plot outline? It is wiser to state that these three works (*Les Orientales* being outside the scope of this study) represent one moment of their creator's vision and, despite generic differences, bear remarkable similarities. It is for the purpose of convenient grouping that we will postpone study of the plays until the next chapter. In this one, we intend to show that Hugo's first prose triumph is an extraordinary achievement of stylistic intricacy, that its essential unity derives from its imagery in co-ordination with its

1. See *Historique du livre*, E.I.N., Roman-II, 445–50.

action, its setting, and its characters. There is another reason as well for postponing discussion of the plays: *Marion de Lorme* and *Hernani* have at their center "fatal" Romantic couples (Didier and Marion, Hernani and Doña Sol), but in *Notre-Dame* this duo is absent, and thus the novel (if we may continue to use that imprecise word) follows somewhat better those earlier efforts that also lacked this particular center. Finally, with what we learn from this work, we will be in a better position to judge the plays.

From the moment of its publication, critics and reviewers were struck by the vast scope of this work. In the 1830's, the *Revue des Deux Mondes* called Hugo's knowledge as revealed in the novel "une science que l'existence de quatre hommes suffirait à peine à amasser."[2] Later, more scholarly observers such as E. Huguet at the turn of the century demonstrated that Hugo's erudition was second hand, even if he did frequently cite Sauval, Du Breul, Mathieu, and others. More recently, it has been learned that the novelist's topographical knowledge of Paris was derived from one map.[3] Yet despite our legitimate suspicions concerning Hugo's historical expertise, we cannot deny that *Notre-Dame* does provide the reader with a rich and varied tableau that seems to stress innumerable details of fifteenth-century social history. So great is this impression upon first reading that we do not have a sense of tight construction. When we add to the local color *à la* Scott Hugo's concern for Gothic architecture and the printing press, and when he throws in a Romantic melodrama, we may well understand why M. F. Guyard concluded:

> Mais on peut déplorer la longueur de cette exposition qui accapare un tiers de l'œuvre, même si elle nous a valu des pages admirables: morceaux d'anthologie précisément, plutôt qu'éléments nécessaires d'une construction romanesque.
>
> L'absence d'unité architecturale manifeste l'absence d'une réelle unité d'inspiration. Entre le roman historique, le roman à idées, le roman poème, Hugo n'a pas su choisir. Il a tenté de fondre des intentions diverses; et la présence, en partie involontaire, de ses soucis les plus intimes, ne devait pas aider à cette tentative."[4]

2. Avril, 1831, p. 188. Cited by Max Bach, "Le Vieux Paris dans *Notre-Dame: Sources et resources de Victor Hugo*," *PMLA*, LXXX (1965), 321.
3. *Ibid.*
4. Preface to *Notre-Dame de Paris* (Paris, 1959), xxiv.

But one should be more wary than is Guyard in accusing a powerful imagination of failure to create an artistic center for his work. We have already seen in previous chapters that even Hugo's minor efforts have a basic solidity of construction and imagination, despite their defects. It should therefore come as no surprise that the same is true for *Notre-Dame*. But to find this unity requires that one cease looking at the work as a literary historian, from without, and substitute for this point of view a more organic, inner vision of literary criticism.

Although we cannot agree entirely with his thesis, J.-P. Weber has already made an interesting attempt along these lines.[5] He claims that Hugo's imaginative center was psychologically inspired from a chance event in the young boy's life: there was a print that hung in his bedroom at Les Feuillantines that inspired the pattern of his literary form. This picture came complete with a story told to him by a servant. This tale that Hugo recounts in *Le Rhin* (1842) concerns one Hatto,[6] an evil archbishop who, in a year of famine, bought all the wheat in order to sell it for a large profit. The people of Mainz begged him for food. When he refused, the population surrounded the episcopal palace. The irate Hatto had them rounded up, locked in a barn, and burned to death. Suddenly, a swarm of rats emerged from the ashes and attacked his palace. Hatto fled, chased by the rats to an island in the Rhine where he built a tower (the Mäuserthurm) in which he hid. The rats swarmed across the water, nibbled through the defenses, and ate the culprit, who was cowering in a *basse fosse*. Hugo recalls the effect that this drawing and its story had on him: "Le soir après avoir prié Dieu et avant de m'endormir, je regardais toujours ce tableau. La nuit je le revoyais dans mes rêves, et je l'y revoyais terrible. . . . Quoi qu'il en soit . . . la Mäuserthurm avait toujours été une des visions familières de mon esprit."[7] Hugo then added, in language that looks forward to *William Shakespeare* and *Promontorium Somnii:* "Vous le savez, il n'y a pas d'homme qui n'ait ses fantômes, comme il n'y a pas d'homme qui n'ait ses chimères." It seems clear, as

5. *La Genèse de l'œuvre poétique* (Paris, 1960) chap. II. Albouy, *La Création mythologique chez Victor Hugo* (Paris, 1963), is more than hesitant, calling Weber's thesis "insoutenable" (p. 248) and of "très fragile construction" (p. 363).
6. In the original legend, Hatton. See J.-B. Barrère, *La Fantaisie de Victor Hugo,* I (Paris, 1949), 277.
7. *Le Rhin,* pp. 176, 178.

Weber claims, that the picture did have a powerful impact on the child's imagination.

Having outlined the legend, Weber then disengages from it four main themes that dominate the picture and its story, and supposedly all of Hugo's work. First, "le thème du ciel embrasé," which he finds easily in *Les Orientales* in descriptions of nature. He shows further that this theme has its political form with "le thème du ciel de fête impériale," whose blaze of glory is evil and doomed to failure. Second, Weber finds "la thématique de la tour des rats," with the tower associated with the church in particular. Third, "le thème de la naissance monstrueuse" of the rats, which Weber connects to actual monstrous childbirth. Finally a fourth theme is "the face in the cathedral," formed by the bishop making an appearance from the interior of his dwelling. Being suspicious of mono-causality, we cannot accept Weber's thesis that this picture and story alone caused Hugo to generate his literary patterns, but we must agree, despite the wary hostility and studied indifference with which most critics have treated his monograph,[8] that he has isolated four important motifs in Hugo's work, and one would have little difficulty in exploring *Notre-Dame* in the light of this theory. The background of a *ciel embrasé* is a frequent motif, the evil bishop in the cathedral is obviously Claude Frollo, the monstrous birth of the rats is easily equated to the army of beggars who swarm against the façade of Notre-Dame, which is itself analogous to the Mäuserthurm.[9] But it is our contention that the novel cannot be explained by this interesting rapprochement, valuable as it is in showing something other than an historical approach to the text. At best, Weber's suggestion can provide a stimulus for a more systematic critical effort that will reveal a more complex literary creation.

Our point of departure must be the prologue to the work, for it sets as central the theme of fatality that had become visible in *Cromwell* and that is also at the heart of *Marion de Lorme* and *Hernani*. Imagining that some unknown medieval hand (fatality is in a sense anonymous) has

8. Weber tries to invalidate Baudouin's psychoanalysis, claiming that his own views are based on Hugo's texts, whereas Baudouin is using psychoanalytic theories that are at best dubious. But as Weber seems at times to outdo his rival in Freudian interpretation, his essay serves mainly to indicate the limitations of biographical criticism. Yet if used with care, they give insight into Hugo and his work.

9. *Notre-Dame de Paris*, p. 354.

carved the word Anankè on the wall of one of the towers, Hugo speaks of this word as having a "sens lugubre et fatal," and he uses the word "renfermer" not only to refer to "sens" but (as our analysis will show) also to the "lugubre et fatal" prisons that dominate the landscape and whose role is to enclose various characters. Hugo himself concluded the preface on Anankè or Fatality with the words: "C'est sur ce mot qu'on a fait ce livre." This theme hardly needs any examination here, for it is by now a platitude of Hugo criticism. But the form that Hugo gave it, the many elaborations of the "sens lugubre et fatal" enclosed within it, needs more careful treatment. Two passages from Book VII merit extensive quotation. The scene is Claude Frollo's monastic cell in one of the towers of Notre-Dame. "Le rayon de jour qui pénétrait par cette ouverture traversait une ronde toile d'araignée, qui inscrivait avec goût sa rosace délicate dans l'ogive de la lucarne, et au centre de laquelle l'insecte architecte se tenait immobile comme le moyeu de cette roue de dentelle" (p. 220). Here Frollo is seen observing the spider's web.

> Dom Claude, abîmé en lui-même, ne l'écoutait plus. Charmolue, en suivant la direction de son regard, vit qu'il s'était fixé machinalement à la grande toile d'araignée qui tapissait la lucarne. En ce moment, une mouche étourdie qui cherchait le soleil de mars vint se jeter à travers ce filet et s'y englua. A l'ébranlement de sa toile, l'énorme araignée fit un mouvement brusque hors de sa cellule centrale, puis d'un bond elle se précipita sur la mouche, qu'elle plia en deux avec ses antennes de devant, tandis que la trompe hideuse lui fouillait la tête.—Pauvre mouche! dit le procureur du roi en cour d'église, et il leva la main pour la sauver. L'archidiacre, comme réveillé en sursaut, lui retint le bras avec une violence convulsive.
> —Maître Jacques, cria-t-il, laissez faire la fatalité!
> Le procureur se retourna effaré. Il lui semblait qu'une pince de fer lui avait pris le bras. L'œil du prêtre était fixe, hagard, flamboyant, et restait attaché au petit groupe horrible de la mouche et de l'araignée. (pp. 231–32)

The intensity of the above passage more than suggests its importance, but in order to make the meaning absolutely clear, Frollo goes on to say: "Voilà un symbole de tout." He then proceeds, as he speaks of the fly, to suggests to the reader the heroine, Esmeralda:

50

Elle vole, elle est joyeuse, elle vient de naître; elle cherche le printemps, le grand air, la liberté; oh! oui, mais qu'elle se heurte à la rosace fatale, l'araignée en sort, l'araignée hideuse! Pauvre danseuse! pauvre mouche prédestinée! Maître Jacques, laissez faire! c'est la fatalité!—Hélas! Claude, tu es araignée, tu es la mouche aussi! Tu volais à la science, à la lumière, au soleil . . . au grand jour de la vérité éternelle, en te précipitant vers la lucarne éblouissante qui donne sur l'autre monde . . . tu n'as pas vu cette toile d'araignée tendue par le destin. (p. 232)

Now, gripped by a wild and hopeless passion for the gypsy girl, he struggles helplessly in the grasp of the "antennes de fer" of fate.

Victor Brombert has noted that "les nombreuses araignées et leurs hideuses toiles où se débattent les mouches effarées"[10] are the "prétexte" for innumerable metaphors, and it has long been observed that the image of the spider is an important one in Hugo. Critics have cited not only the above passage but also the poem of *Les Contemplations,* "J'aime l'araignée et j'aime l'ortie." But the image needs to be examined in its function in the pattern of narrative, rather than merely being referred to as a symbol of fate. First, however, one might well pause to ask the question: Where did this spider come from? We have seen the development of the theme of fatality little by little until it became an important one. But spiders? If we search Hugo's earlier efforts in prose and verse, if we check through *Han d'Islande* and *Bug-Jargal,* there seems to be nothing but an occasional bit of local color that has no symbolic function. There is a mention in *Han* that the monster seizes his victim with a "bras de fer," and in *Bug-Jargal* Habibrah is described in arachnoid terms, but the yield is slim indeed. One cannot refrain from wondering why this image developed in Hugo and why it developed at this time. The question seems to be important, for Hugo's subsequent literary career shows a continuation and evolution of this image, which we shall explore in later chapters.

Baudouin has proposed a psychoanalytic interpretation that the spider and its various changing forms in Hugo represent the author's obsession with the female sexual organ, and given the psychological problems

10. "Victor Hugo, la prison et l'espace," *Revue des Sciences Humaines,* CXVII (Jan.–Mars., 1965), 61.

with sexuality and parental rivalry that were a part of Victor's life, this could be true. Henri Guillemin in his *Hugo et la sexualité* has surmised that it was at about this time, not in 1833, that Hugo was first unfaithful to his wife, and if so, there might be a connection.[11] But perhaps the question is unanswerable and perhaps too it is unimportant, after all, that it be answered. It suffices to say that we have the image and that it is the basis for the whole fabric of the novel. By means of the image, the concept of fatality is added to the earlier idea that the way up is the way to destruction. But as image it is not as yet complete, for Claude Frollo continues:

> Et quand tu l'aurais pu rompre, cette toile redoutable, avec tes ailes de moucheron, tu crois que tu aurais pu atteindre à la lumière! Hélas! cette vitre qui est plus loin, cet obstacle transparent, cette muraille de cristal plus dur que l'airain qui sépare toutes les philosophies de la vérité, comment l'aurais-tu franchie? O vanité de la science! que de sages viennent de bien loin en voletant s'y briser le front! que de systèmes pêle-mêle se heurtent en bourdonnant à cette vitre éternelle! (p. 232)

In short, the original pattern of the rise to destruction has been amplified to include not only the spider but a *double* barrier between man and his ideal, this latter obstacle as impenetrable as it is invisible.[12]

The image may be summarized as follows: A person (fly) in a dark recess, flying up toward the light (knowledge, truth, love, or any transcendent ideal), is caught in a spider web of fatality and devoured. But beyond this web which might possibly be broken through lies the invisible pane of glass that blocks all human efforts. The web and spider are within the realm of the finite, but the second barrier seems infinite. If we may anticipate for a moment and look at *Marion de Lorme*, we find the same idea. Didier (the hero), trapped by the cunning villain, says coldly to Saverny, who is trying to save him:

> A quoi bon? Je voulais mourir
>
> . . . .
>
> Autrement croyez-vous qu'il m'eût pris à son piège,

11. (Paris, 1954), pp. 14–17.
12. Brombert has observed, p. 63, this double barrier in the incomplete *Les Jumeaux* (1837), where a man is inside an iron mask and then within a cell.

Et que je n'eusse pas rompu de l'éperon
Sa toile d'araignée à prendre un moucheron?
La mort est désormais le seul bien que j'envie. (pp. 80–81)

This idea will find its ultimate dramatic and theological expression in *Dieu*, where in order to see the One, "Dieu me toucha du doigt le front, et je mourus." Therefore, death, or the barrier between finite man and infinity, seems to be the "meaning" of the image of the pane of glass. But as any meaning comes from its form, as the form and situation change, the meaning may change also. The one constant is the sense of the double trap: even if the fly breaks through the first barrier, the second one will block it.

To return to *Notre-Dame*, we said earlier that the whole novel is an intricate working out of the image of spider and fly, thematically and formally. We saw that Claude Frollo associated himself both with killer and victim, and Esmeralda with the fly. But there is much more. Let us start with the heroine who, as Frollo had said of her, "vole, elle est joyeuse, elle cherche le grand air, la liberté." Her dark recess is in a sense a sociological one. She lives with that vast army of *truands* in the *cour des miracles*, but she is not of it nor is she contaminated by its evils, either in appearance, speech, or morals. She is a prisoner, having been kidnapped in infancy. Her chance for escape comes, she thinks, when she sees the vulgar military officer, Captain Phœbus de Châteaupers, whom she loves at first sight and toward whom she goes. It is certainly no coincidence that his name is Phœbus, the sun. That he is thoroughly unworthy of her adoration changes none of the patterns of action. The irony merely reinforces the bitterness of fatality. Her first sight of him occurs when he rescues her from Quasimodo in the dark labyrinthine streets of Paris, and with the memory of his heroic action in her mind, she is willing to leave the *parvis* of Notre-Dame, where she is performing for a crowd, and climb (the upward image) to the apartment where Phœbus and some aristocratic girls have invited her to perform with her pet goat. She seems to be escaping from the milieu of the *truands* to a finer life, but her amorous rendezvous with Phœbus in a house of assignation brings out the truth of the matter. Frollo, the spider, had accosted the impecunious Phœbus in the street. The priest is described in terms that suggest the lurking predator: "une espèce d'ombre qui rampait derrière lui" (p.

53

240), and who clutched the captain by the arm. The text refers to "la tenaille qui l'avait saisi" (p. 241), a suggestion both of the *antenne de fer* of the spider and the grip of fate. Frollo offers Phœbus money with which to pay the proprietress of the house so that Frollo can watch from a hidden recess. When the captain arrives there, the sun image finds an ironic reprise, as he "se hâta de *faire dans un écu reluire le soleil*."[13] All the elements of the image are now assembled: the dark recess, the fly, the watching spider, and the sun. The proprietress throws the coin in a drawer. Later a child steals it and replaces it with a dry leaf. This act not only provides "evidence" at the trial for witchcraft but suggests as well the real value of the false sun, money. Up in the room Esmeralda learns that Phœbus has no intention whatever of marrying her, and then, accepting this cruel fact in humility, lets Phœbus make love to her. At this moment the spider comes out of his hiding place and, like an arachnid, pounces on his victim. Frollo stabs the sun-god Phœbus, Esmeralda faints and, almost unconscious, she feels "un baiser plus brûlant que le fer rouge du bourreau" (p. 251). Frollo manages to make his escape from this hovel with its "toiles d'araignées à tous les coins" (p. 243). Shortly afterward, she is arrested and tried for the attempted murder of the soldier.

With her trial the imagery is transferred from the erotic to a social context, befitting the experience. The hall of justice is now the dark recess "vaste et sombre," night is falling and the windows "ne laissaient plus pénétrer qu'un pâle rayon qui s'éteignait" (p. 254), as if once in the grip of that fatality, Justice, the sun itself disappears from view. Here Esmeralda pleads innocent to the murder of Phœbus but is not believed. Taken below to a torture chamber, she finds herself in a room with no opening onto the transcendent: "Pas de fenêtre à ce caveau" (p. 261). The illumination is provided by a hellish glow from the coals heating the instruments of torture. Here we find "des tenailles, des pinces"—which recall the spider's legs and Claude Frollo's grip. Esmeralda is trussed gently upon a table, like a fly in a web, and strapped down: "il lui sembla voir se mouvoir et marcher de toutes parts vers elle, pour lui grimper le long du corps et la mordre et la pincer, tous ces difformes outils de la torture, qui étaient, parmi les instruments de tout genre qu'elle avait vus

13. P. 243. Italics Hugo's.

54

jusqu'alors, ce que sont les chauves-souris, les mille-pieds et les araignées parmi les insectes et les oiseaux" (p. 262). Like most of the Romantics, Hugo is explicit in his imagery. He even adds: "Si l'archidiacre eût été présent, il se fût souvenu en ce moment de son symbole de l'araignée et de la mouche" (p. 263). After brief torture, she confesses to whatever they wish, and "elle retomba sur le lit de cuir . . . pliée en deux, se laissant pendre à la courroie bouclée sur sa poitrine" (p. 264). Hanging by the leather strap, she is like a fly in a web, even bent in half like the fly cited in the original statement of the image.

After her conviction, she is incarcerated in a black dungeon cell which is located, apparently, beneath the torture chambers. This double level of the cave somehow reflects in a descending order the double barrier of web and window of the ascending imagery of the episode in Frollo's cell. Above are the "lumière" and the "cloches," symbols of a glorious ideal; here below, on the other hand, are "zones où s'échelonnent les nuances de l'horreur" (p. 268). In this medieval setting, Hugo calls upon Dante for his chapter title: "Lasciate ogni speranza." The way up to the sun of Phœbus has indeed led to disaster. The imagery which we have seen before is repeated: "Pauvre mouche qui n'eût pu remuer le moindre de ses ailes" (p. 268), and again she is described as "brisée en deux" like the fly.

But Esmeralda's experience with fatality is not yet completed. Saved from execution at the last moment by Quasimodo, she finds asylum in Notre-Dame, only to be removed from sanctuary in the cathedral by Gringoire the poet and Frollo during the attack by the *truands*, who have come to save her. As she is dragged off to the gallows by the mad priest, we are told that the ominous clouds above are "noirs, lourds, déchirés, crevassés, pendaient comme des hamacs de crêpe sous le cintre étoilé de la nuit. On eût dit les toiles d'araignées de la voûte du ciel." Fatality has been projected into nature. Arriving at the gibbet, Frollo announces to her, "Choisis entre nous deux" (p. 396), as he holds her in his powerful grip.

Her response to this command is to wrench herself from his grasp and fall at the foot of the gibbet, "en embrassant cet appui funèbre." Is she not in this act repeating the original image? She breaks through the grasp of the spider only to find herself before death itself, the ultimate barrier. As a matter of fact, even the gallows with its "bras décharné" (p. 300) recreates the black arm of the spider. When she later dies at dawn on these gallows, "la corde fit plusieurs tours sur elle-même" (the wrapping image again) and "Claude contemplait ce groupe épouvantable . . . l'araignée et la mouche" (p. 562). This final touch had been prepared when the executioner climbed the ladder to the noose with the body of the unconscious girl who hangs over his arm "gracieusement pliée en deux" (p. 414).

But her death is to be postponed for a few moments, in the best tradition of the novel of suspense. In order to be free to seek the watch, Claude for a moment hands Esmeralda over to a religious recluse, Sœur Gudule, who inhabits near the gibbet a cell called the Trou aux rats, and who has sworn vengeance on all gypsies who years ago had kidnapped her infant child. By this device Hugo introduces the theme of fatality in the context of the family, for although at first neither realizes the fact, Gudule is Esmeralda's long-lost mother. Earlier, still full of hatred for gypsies, when she heard that Esmeralda was to be executed, she had run to her barred window "avec le brusque soubresaut de cette araignée que nous avons vue se jeter sur une mouche au tremblement de sa toile" (p. 281). When Claude now hands her over, "c'était un bras décharné qui sortait d'une lucarne dans le mur et qui la tenait comme une main de fer" (p. 399), which recalls the *antenne de fer*. Esmeralda tries to pull free: "Elle se tordit, elle fit plusieurs soubresauts d'agonie et de désespoir, mais . . . les doigts osseux et maigres qui la meurtrissaient se crispaient sur sa chair et se rejoignaient à l'entour."[14] A spider's technique. "C'était plus qu'une chaîne, plus qu'un carcan, plus qu'un anneau de fer, c'était une tenaille intelligente et vivante qui sortait d'un mur" (p. 400). The recluse spider announces: "Je vais manger de l'égyptienne" (p. 400).

The recognition scene (managed by a slipper) between mother and daughter seems to save the heroine. The mother breaks down the bars of the window by sheer strength born of love and drags the girl inside the cell as the watch approaches. This act of destroying the bars certainly fits the basic image announced by Claude: "Et quand tu l'aurais pu rompre, cette toile redoutable . . . tu crois que tu aurais pu atteindre à la lumière?" (p. 232). At first it looks as if this gloomy prediction will not

14. The idea of enveloping appeared earlier when Frollo attacked her in her cell: "Elle sentit le long de son corps un contact qui la fit frémir." The priest "l'entourait de ses deux bras," and his kisses are "morsures" (p. 324).

56

come true. The watch disappears to seek Esmeralda elsewhere. But just when all is saved, the silly girl hears Captain Phœbus' voice and rushes toward the opening in the cell crying: "Phœbus! à moi, mon Phœbus!" (p. 408). Alas, "Phœbus n'y était plus." The web had been broken and the fly had escaped, but she had been stopped by a second barrier. The watch hears her voice, returns, and seizes her, and she dies soon afterward. Here the meaning of the second barrier seems to anticipate what Hugo would state in his preface to *Les Travailleurs de la mer* (1866): that beyond the fatalities of dogma, laws, and things, there is the "anankè suprême, le coeur humain." At any rate, her reaching out to the sun of her life destroys her.

We have seen that Esmeralda encounters spiders in the form of Claude Frollo, Justice, and Sœur Gudule, although in the latter case the spider becomes beneficent. But there is yet another: Quasimodo. First his lair, the cathedral itself. One immediately calls to mind the large central *rosace* of Notre-Dame and the fact that in the central image the spider's web was called a "rosace fatale," thus providing an admirable link with the Gothic architecture of fifteenth-century Paris. The main *rosace* lets light into the cathedral just as the light from the outside streams through the web in Frollo's cell. The lacy quality of the architecture is captured in an early description in which Hugo likens a *rosace* to "une étoile de dentelle" (p. 5), and this latter word appeared in the original image. To make the comparison explicit, we need only to turn to the first appearance of Quasimodo at the Fête des fous. During the celebration, a pane of glass in a *rosace* is broken and the competitors for the ugliest face put their heads through the hole. The malformed Quasimodo wins, his countenance "rayonnait" (p. 36) in the aperture, exactly where a spider would be positioned. When Hugo describes him physically, he suggests something resembling a spider: "Une grosse tête hérissée de cheveux roux; entre les deux épaules une bosse énorme dont le contre-coup se faisait sentir par devant; un système de cuisses et de jambes si étrangement fourvoyées qu'elles . . . ressemblaient à deux croissants de faucilles qui se rejoignent par la poignée; de larges pieds, des mains monstrueuses; et, avec toute cette difformité, je ne sais quelle allure redoutable de vigueur, d'agilité et de courage" (p. 37). The bell-ringer rarely leaves the cathedral, just as a spider is imagined rarely to leave its web. To be sure, the imagery that Hugo uses to describe the hunchback is multiple, for he is a "reptile," a

57

"lézard," and particularly a snail living in its shell, the cathedral (pp. 119–20). Thus, the building itself becomes something of a Quasimodo in stone, for Hugo insists on its architectural irregularity and composite nature. Quasimodo even resembles the church in other ways: he is stone deaf and his one eye repeats the one central *rosace* of Notre-Dame. Hugo speaks of the deafness architecturally, for his ability to hear is "la seule porte que la nature lui eût laissée toute grande ouverte" and it is now "brusquement fermée" (p. 120). Now Hugo shifts back to the image of the eye: "En se fermant, elle intercepta l'unique rayon de joie et de lumière qui pénétrât encore dans l'âme de Quasimodo." His soul is now in a "nuit profonde" and he is "séparé à jamais du monde par *la double fatalité*[15] de la naissance inconnue et de sa nature difforme, emprisonné dès l'enfance dans ce double cercle infranchissable" (pp. 119–20). The double barrier of fatality has appeared again.

The picture presented here is that of a soul that is prisoner inside a body, just as the body is prisoner inside the cathedral.[16] With this preparation accomplished, Hugo can then show us this soul as if he were taking us on a guided tour through Notre-Dame:

> Si maintenant nous essayions de pénétrer jusqu'à l'âme de Quasimodo à travers cette écorce épaisse et dure; si nous pouvions sonder les profondeurs de cette organisation mal faite; s'il nous était donné de regarder avec un flambeau derrière ces organes sans transparence, d'explorer l'intérieur ténébraux de cette créature opaque, d'en élucider les recoins obscurs, les culs-de-sac absurdes, et de jeter tout à coup une vive lumière sur la psyché enchaînée au fond de cet antre, nous trouverions sans doute la malheureuse dans quelque attitude pauvre, rabougrie et rachitique comme ces prisonniers des plombs de Venise qui vieillissaient ployés en deux dans une boîte de pierre trop basse et trop courte. (p. 121)

The language is significant. The psyche is in chains, "ployé en deux." One cannot doubt that we have here yet another—more subtle—elaboration of the spider-fly fatality image transferred to a psychological plane.

15. Italics mine.
16. Charles Baudouin, *Psychanalyse de Victor Hugo* (Genève, 1943), points out this phenomenon, p. 231. Hugo's text makes it explicit, stating that Quasimodo "arriva à lui ressembler, à s'y incruster, pour ainsi dire" (p. 119).

The relationship between Quasimodo and the cathedral has sexual overtones, curiously enough. The bell-ringer's favorite *cloche* is called Marie (p. 122), and their contact is erotic: "Tout à coup la frénésie de la cloche le gagnait; son regard devint extraordinaire; il attendait le bourdon au passage, comme l'araignée attend la mouche, et se jetait brusquement sur lui à corps perdu" (p. 123). This passage becomes frankly sexual with the addition of the phrases: "la cloche monstrueuse hennissait toute haletante sous lui" and "elle était possédée et remplie de Quasimodo" (pp. 123–24). Finally, "donner la grosse cloche en mariage à Quasimodo, c'était donner Juliette à Roméo" (p. 125). Hugo rarely leaves one in doubt.

With this concept of Quasimodo as spider established, it is easy to see that like Claude Frollo he pounces on his prey. When Esmeralda first encountered the hunchback in the darkened labyrinth of Paris (the web image), he carred her off "ployée sur un de ses bras" (p. 58). But if he is acting out the role of an evil spider at this moment under Frollo's direction, Hugo assures us that "la méchanceté n'était peut-être pas innée en lui" (p. 121), for he had, because of his deformities, been ostracized by society. Like Sœur Gudule who has changed from hating to loving, he also is changed. When much later he finds himself strapped to a pillory to be scourged, now a fly in society's web, he cries out "A boire!" in a wild fusion of Gargantua and Christ (p. 190). Esmeralda offers him water, and, almost as if baptized, he dies to evil and is reborn to good. Henceforth, although he continues to be a spider, he is now a beneficent one. Although there is occasionally imagery derived from other animals, the key scenes show the center of Hugo's vision. When Esmeralda finishes her "amende honorable" on the steps of Notre-Dame, Quasimodo slides down a rope from the balcony, seizes her, and bounds into the church crying out "Asile" (p. 402). There is here something of the spider lowering itself by a drag-line. The heroine is of course unaware of his transformation. Conditioned by a series of disasters and confused by the total experience, she shows fright the next morning when the hunchback appears at her cell in Notre-Dame. The image is—eternally—the same: "Un joyeux rayon du soleil levant entrait par sa lucarne [= rosace] et venait lui frapper le visage. En même temps que le soleil, elle vit à cette lucarne un objet qui l'effraya, la malheureuse figure de Quasimodo" (p. 310). She expects the evil spider to pounce, only to hear him say gently:

"N'ayez pas peur." He even agrees to stay out of her sight because of his ugly appearance. It is not the least of the bitter ironies of this book, incidentally, that given his moral beauty, all his efforts to help her lead to her death. His only consolation will come with her death. His skeleton is found wrapped around hers in the charnel house. The beneficent spider could achieve no more. Fatality willed in his case that the heroine would prefer the false Phœbus, whom Hugo describes as cracked crystal, to the humble sandstone of the hunchback (pp. 320–21).

Esmeralda is not the only fly. Claude Frollo had cried out: "Claude, tu es la mouche aussi," and the central image fits the priest as well as it does the gypsy. Claude's dark recess is the very cell in which the spider image was first explicitly elaborated. He too tries to fly toward the sun. For him, the light is—ostensibly—that of pure philosophical truth. He is not only a priest but an alchemist seeking to make gold, not for earthly gain, but because "L'or, c'est le soleil, faire de l'or, c'est être Dieu" (p. 138). But for the priest, the pure light of the sun is corrupted. Speculating on how to extract gold from fire, he quotes the alchemists of the past: "Magistri affirme qu'il y a certains noms de femme d'un charme si doux et si mystérieux qu'il suffit de les prononcer." And one Manou says: "Où les femmes sont honorées, les divinités sont réjouies. . . . La bouche d'une femme est constamment pure; c'est une eau courante, c'est un rayon de soleil" (p. 222). The transformation from the purity of light to evil sexuality is completed as Frollo murmurs: "Maria, Sophia, La Esmeral . . . —Damnation! toujours cette pensée." One might observe the transition of the feminine names from the divine, through the more secular but still abstract Wisdom (or knowledge) to sexuality. Esmeralda replaces God, or the Virgin, and becomes Claude's "soleil." Ironically, she is in fact a sort of patron saint of the *truands* of the Cour des miracles: "toute sa tribu . . . la tient en vénération singulière, comme une Notre-Dame" (p. 212). And again: "Elle était d'une beauté si rare qu'au moment où elle parut . . . il sembla qu'elle y répandait une sorte de lumière qui lui était propre" (p. 201), and when she is about to be hanged, "on eût dit une sainte Vierge au pied de la croix" (p. 396). And indeed, she is virtue incarnate, as we see from her humane rescue of the poet Pierre Gringoire about to die on the beggars' gallows, as well as from her giving Quasimodo a drink on the pillory. In the benighted court of "Justice" after her conviction, she is the only light left in darkness: "Les ténèbres y enveloppaient tous les objets d'une sorte de brume. Quelques faces apathiques de juges y ressortaient à peine. Vis-à-vis d'eux, à l'extrémité de la longue salle, ils pouvaient voir un point de blancheur vague se détacher sur le fond sombre. C'était l'accusée" (p. 265). By her very presence she stands in judgment on man's Justice.

But for Claude Frollo, she cannot be a true sun, for he is a priest and she is both a gypsy (a non-Christian group) and a desirable woman. He knows that it is blasphemy to cry as he does that Esmeralda is "une créature si belle que Dieu l'eût préférée à la Vierge" (p. 273). Claude's resolution of his intolerable tension is at least logical. She can come only "du ciel ou de l'enfer" (p. 274). But precisely because she is a desirable gypsy girl, he must conclude: "C'était un ange! mais de ténèbres, mais de flamme et non de lumière" (p. 274). Of course, his logical conclusion is incorrect. She is not a true gypsy but a stolen Christian. Her true name, Agnès, is more reminiscent of the paschal lamb than of a sorceress. Yet for the priest she is "sombre, funèbre, ténébreuse comme le cercle noir qui poursuit longtemps la vue de l'imprudent qui a regardé fixement le soleil" (p. 275). Hugo's imagery has here anticipated Nerval's *Desdichado*. Frollo is explicit in his interpretation when he said in the passage quoted earlier in this chapter that "Tu volais à la science, à la lumière, au soleil," but the shining sun was really a dark one, and as a result he says of himself "tu te débats, la tête brisée et les ailes arrachées entre les antennes de fer de la fatalité!" (p. 232). If he is a fly, then Esmeralda must be the spider for him. Here the imagery becomes obscured, for it is hardly possible to portray the lovely girl directly as a grotesque predatory insect. The only hints that we have are first, that in his mind she is transformed from a luminous to a black sun, whose dark rays would form something of a black body and legs. This suggestion is barely sketched here but will be more visible in the later poetry of exile. The other hint is her ability to torture Claude Frollo by repeating to him: "c'est Phœbus que j'aime, . . . c'est Phœbus qui est beau" (p. 399). Just as Esmeralda had felt the priest's burning kisses on her, "il poussa un cri violent, comme le misérable auquel on applique un fer rouge," and we remember the arachnoid images of the torture instruments used on her. Beyond these tiny hints, Hugo apparently was unwilling to go. Here again, fatality is ironic, because Esmeralda, whose name signifies "emerald," the precious stone which in medieval lore was effective in calming lust, does not calm Claude Frollo's passion, but on the contrary inspires it and unwittingly brings about his destruction.

Claude, with his fly's gossamer wings of virtue stripped off, resolves—boldly—to go in the other direction, toward the black arts, toward Hell. Immediately the imagery adjusts itself to fit the changes. Because of his baldness and his flapping sleeves, he is referred to as a *chauve-souris* (one recalls *Musdœmon*). He also appears at times as a specter; his eyes are glowing coals, etc. He becomes a demonic character from melodrama in the tradition of Lewis' Monk. This change in Frollo's direction from up to the light to downward, forces us to face up to a seeming contradiction. We have shown in the previous works of Hugo that the way down was the way to salvation, and yet Frollo is not saved by his descent, falling, like Habibrah or Musdœmon, with a cry of "Damnation" from the balcony of Notre-Dame. Yet there is no question of the descent. He describes his own progress in these terms: "Je n'ai pas rampé si longtemps à plat ventre et les ongles dans la terre à travers les innombrables embranchements de la caverne sans apercevoir, au loin devant moi, au bout de l'obscure galerie, une lumière, une flamme, quelque chose . . . où les patients et les sages ont surpris Dieu." (p. 137). To this he adds, "je rampe encore; je m'écorche la face et les genoux aux cailloux de la voie souterraine. J'entrevois, je ne contemple pas" (pp. 138–39). Why does he not succeed, why is he destroyed if avoiding direct ascent preserves one from destruction?

The answer must lie in the moral qualities of the "hero." In contradistinction to Ordener or to Léopold d'Auverney, Claude is anything but a virtuous man. His own obsessions with sex keep him, like Lancelot, from finding any Grail. Further, his goal is blasphemous. "Faire de l'or, c'est être Dieu" and "saisir Dieu" show a demonic mode of thought, and in 1831 Hugo was not ready to take the next step and redeem the totally wicked, as he would many years later in the analogous situation of *La Fin de Satan*. If we must seek an explanation for Hugo's attitude, it is likely that in 1832 the *faune*, if he was, as Guillemin claims, already guilty of marital infidelity, was not ready to forgive himself as he would later. Not only will *La Fin de Satan* reflect this concern, but the same image will appear in highly developed form in *La Légende des siècles*, where we observe a Titan, Phtos, who like Claude Frollo is crawling through underground passages trying to find the light, "à plat ventre, grinçant des dents, livide." Phtos succeeds in his quest, as we shall show in a later chapter, but Frollo does not. To conclude: When the priest tries to ascend to the pure light, he is blocked first by the web of lust and even if he were to break through it, he would know "la vanité de la science." In desperation trying the demonic arts, he feels somehow that he can seize God, or the Ultimate. Like Lucifer, his fall is as prodigious as his pride. Unlike Hugo's Lucifer, it is permanent. To succeed in reaching God requires unselfishness or humility.

Esmeralda and Frollo are not the only victims of the dazzling light of the absolute. Even Sœur Gudule, the recluse, is a fly as well as a spider. She lives in a dark recess, from which she is separated by the barred window of her cell. Her "sun" is her daughter whom she hopes to find. If she can locate her, she plans that the two will leave Paris and go off to Rheims, which she idealizes as a Paradise. She does break through the web of the barred window to save her daughter, but she cannot do anything about the ultimate fatality, the "ananké suprême" of the human heart. Esmeralda will die for Phœbus rather than live for her mother. In this case, the web was a self-imposed claustration, but it was there nonetheless.

Even the carefree Jehan Frollo, Claude's insouciant and irresponsible brother, is touched by this image. At first a reader might suppose that this idler would have no sun, no transcendent ideal for which he would be willing to die. Yet he risks scaling Notre-Dame (going up) during the *truands'* attack on the cathedral to serve his god of pleasure and adventure (p. 359). As he put it, "je veux être mon frère l'archidiacre si cela m'empêche de jouer le jour, de jouer la nuit, de vivre au jeu et de jouer mon âme après ma chemise" (p. 158). Quasimodo, no longer beneficent because he is protecting Esmeralda, pounces on him, plucks off his armor, as the spider in the image pulled the wings off the fly, spins his victim around, and kills him, hurling him to his death, where inevitably, he hangs dead in the web (near the *rosace* of the cathedral) "plié en deux," "le crâne vide" (p. 359), as if sucked empty.

Only Pierre Gringoire and Phœbus de Châteaupers escape the web of fatality. The former constantly flies into the web, but only by accident, never because he is trying to reach an absolute beyond. His first experience comes when he is following Esmeralda through the darkened streets of Paris which form a labyrinth or maze or web in which Quasimodo seizes the girl, as we showed above. When the spider pounces, Pierre is faced with the decision whether to try to save her. He neither advances nor retreats. The reason for his indecision is that he is not following her with any sense of absolute passion, like Claude, but rather because he is looking for food and warmth, and his only reason in following her was the negative "Pourquoi pas?" (p. 56). He himself realizes that the heights of the ultimate hold no attraction for him; he realizes that he "hésite éternellement entre le haut et le bas, entre la voûte et le pavé, entre la chute et l'ascension, entre le zénith et le nadir" (p. 56). In theological terms, neither in Heaven nor in Hell; in Limbo. In contrast, Frollo enjoys stronger sensations. When Gringoire tells him on another occasion: "Je viens de l'échapper belle! Je manque toujours d'être pendu. C'est ma prédestination," the priest answers in disdain: "Tu manques tout" (p. 386). To return to the earlier incident, Pierre becomes lost in this web of dark streets. Here he begins to see forms, described as "lourds insectes." A legless man is referred to as an "espèce d'araignée à face humaine." Soon he is trapped in the Cour des Miracles of the underworld. Three beggars hold him "comme par trois tenailles" (p. 66). Saved by Esmeralda, he fulfils Hugo's earlier prediction concerning him: "Véritable éclectique . . . Gringoire était de . . . [cette] race précieuse . . . de philosophes auxquels la sagesse, comme une autre Ariane, semble avoir donné une pelote de fil qu'ils s'en vont dévidant depuis le commencement du monde à travers le labyrinthe des choses humaines" (p. 21). To extend Hugo's own image, Gringoire is a fly content to avoid the dazzling window and crawl around inside the room eating crumbs of food. Hence he escapes. His reasonableness is neatly captured by his charming phrase: "Oh! que volontiers je me noierais, si l'eau n'était pas si froide" (p. 44). He prefers to bask in the real sun for its real warmth than to fly toward it (p. 333). Even when in the clutches of Louis XI, his luck holds and he is released. As for Phœbus, he did not die when stabbed by the priest, and later, although Hugo calls it "une fin tragique" (p. 422), he ends by getting married. He doesn't even know what an absolute is.

The individual fates of the separate characters are all expressed with the same images interlocked in intricate patterns. But the novel (or romance) is not only personal; it has political overtones which continue the note first sounded in *Han,* then in *Bug-Jargal* and in *Cromwell,* where rebellious miners, slaves in revolt, and grumbling populace (the last act of *Cromwell* is called *Les Ouvriers*) provide a disturbing backdrop to the actions of the protagonists. In *Notre-Dame,* the *peuple* is presented in the fifteenth century as a future political force that will some day destroy the monarchy. The early pages of the tale are built around a series of antitheses: classic against romantic, old against young, rectors against students, aristocracy against the people, who are in turn symbolized by the artisan Jacques Coppenole.

In 1830, Hugo's attitude toward the masses had already arrived at the point where he sided with them, provided that they fitted his social (and Romantic) concept of a noble working class. As he was to define it a few years later in *Le Rhin,* there is the *peuple* (noble, worthy) and the *populace* (the rabble). Both positive and negative aspects of the lower class are captured in *Notre-Dame* by the image of the sea, which makes an early appearance here in Hugo's fiction. The ocean can be calm, beautiful, and co-operative at one moment, and uncontrollably violent the next. Hugo uses the image for both groups. He calls the vile beggars "populace" (p. 347) and a "flot irrésistible" (p. 64) which is "hurlant, beuglant, glapissant, . . . se ruant." The more sedate crowd that has come to see Gringoire's play is called the *peuple* having "l'aspect d'une mer, dans laquelle cinq ou six rues, comme d'autant d'embouchures de fleuves dégorgeaient à chaque instant de nouveaux flots de têtes" (p. 2). Hugo adds to this maritime imagery words like *ondes, courant, vagues.* This is the lower class for which Coppenole speaks. "Ajoutons que Coppenole était du peuple, et que ce public qui l'entourait était du peuple. . . . L'altière algarade du chaussetier flamand, en humiliant les gens de cour, avait remué dans toutes les âmes plébéiennes je ne sais quel sentiment de dignité encore vague et indistinct au quinzième siècle" (pp. 26–27). Strong in his class consciousness, Coppenole later announces in his conversation in the Bastille with no less a personage than Louis XI, that in 1482 "l'heure du peuple n'est pas venue" (p. 381), and then in an obvious anachronism predicts the fall of the Bastille: "Quand le beffroi bourdonnera, quand bourgeois et soldats hurleront et s'entretueront, c'est l'heure qui sonnera" (p. 382). Is the change of political structure inevitable? Hugo seems to think so, generalizing: "Toute civilisation commence par la théocratie et finit par la démocratie" (p. 144), and Hugo explores the problem further through imagery as Louis XI visits the prison cells of the Bastille.

The monarch is spending the night in his *chambrette* in this fortress, which we may safely take as a symbol of pre-Revolutionary France. From here he leaves to inspect his cages, special cells in which political prisoners hope in vain for liberation. Their cages are barred: "Il y avait aux parois deux ou trois petites fenêtres, si drument treillissées d'épais barreaux de fer qu'on n'en voyait pas la vitre" (p. 367). One prisoner, who has been inside a cell for fourteen years, pleads for mercy. The King pretends not to hear his desperate plea for clemency, and as he moves away, "le misérable prisonnier, à l'éloignement des flambeaux et du bruit, jugea que le roi s'en allait. Sire! sire! cria-t-il avec désespoir. La porte se referma" (p. 369).[17] The image is clarified shortly afterwards as Pierre Gringoire gives a lesson in statesmanship to his monarch. "Sire," he cries, "vous êtes le soleil" (p. 376), and "la clémence est la seule lumière qui puisse éclairer l'intérieur d'une grande âme. La clémence porte le flambeau devant toutes les autres vertus. Sans elle, ce sont des aveugles qui cherchent Dieu à tâtons" (p. 376). Thus, to shift to the prisoner's point of view, the average citizen is in a cage, blocked from the light by the cage with its spider web of bars. This recess is the creation of Louis' political caprice, we are led to understand, but even if he could break out of the dark cage, he would still not be free, for he would find himself still inside the Bastille, symbol of France of the *ancien régime*. Again we see the double barrier, the second more formidable than the first. And by walking off with his light, the King abdicates his central position as sun, leaving mankind in darkness. In the essay "Ceci tuera cela," which forms an integral part of the whole work, Hugo intervenes to explain that royalty is medieval and passé. The imagery used here is important: "le soleil du moyen âge est tout à fait couché" (p. 149), and with the invention of the printing press after the "dark" Middle Ages, "des nouveautés vont se faire jour" (p. 145). If the monarchy is a setting sun, what will be the new center of light? If we remember Hugo's idea that all civilizations begin as theocracies and end as democracies, the new light can only be the *peuple* itself. This image is not clearly developed in *Notre-Dame* because revolutionary ideas expressed in theoretical terms of the sovereignty of the masses were not really possible in the fifteenth century, but the following passage is suggestive:

17. The parallel with the scene in *Cromwell* between Thurloe and the Protector is obvious.

66

> L'invention de l'imprimerie est le plus grand événement de l'histoire. C'est la révolution mère. C'est le mode d'expression de l'humanité qui se renouvelle totalement. . . . Sous la forme imprimerie, la pensée est plus impérissable que jamais. . . . De solide qu'elle était [expressed through architecture], elle devient vivace. Elle passe de la durée à l'immortalité. On peut démolir une masse [e.g., the Bastille], comment extirper l'ubiquité [e.g., books, but also the masses].

If we add to this comment another phrase: "L'attention populaire, comme le soleil, poursuivait sa révolution" (p. 34), we get yet another hint, even if "révolution" in the immediate context means only the orbit of the sun.

Marion de Lorme contains two passages that help make this matter clear. Even more than *Notre-Dame*, the play stresses the importance of royal clemency (l. 1483) and should the monarch fail to exercise it, the political consequences can be serious. A nobleman tells the king:

> Sire! le sang n'est pas une bonne rosée;
> Nulle moisson ne vient sur la grève arrosée
> Et le peuple des rois évite le balcon
> Quand aux dépens du Louvre, on peuple Montfaucon. (p. 102)

Should it be necessary to add that the Grève and Montfaucon play a prominent role in *Notre-Dame?*

But this king can still play a role, if he will only do so:

ROCHEBARON

> A quoi sert le roi?

BRICHANTEAU

> Les peuples dans la nuit
> Vont marchant, l'œil fixé sur un flambeau qui luit.
> Il est le flambeau, lui. Le roi, c'est la lanterne
> Qui le sauve du vent sous sa vitre un peu terne. (p. 37)

Despite the grammatical confusion of the sentence, the antecedent of "Il" can only be *le peuple*. The king's role is reduced to that of protector of truth, which keeps the masses from burning too intensely or from going out as a source of truth altogether. Hugo as early as 1830 has cast the

67

common people in the role of the new sun, an association that will swell in size and force until its apocalyptic expression in "Plein Ciel" of *La Légende des siècles.*

This transference of light to the people creates, on the political plane, a radical transformation of the image. The fly and the sun are no longer opposite. The fly (*peuple*) becomes the sun (also *peuple*), with the result that if the imprisoned masses can only break through their bonds, they have, in a sense, but to fly toward themselves! In short, the luminous ideal is no longer unattainable in political terms. We may then expect that henceforth fatality will operate most strongly in the primarily non-political works. Surely *Hernani* and *Les Travailleurs de la mer* show the grip of fatality, whereas *Les Misérables* and *Quatrevingt-treize* stress man's ability to overcome it, although, as we shall show in subsequent chapters, the matter is much more complex than this.

Up to this point, we have viewed *Notre-Dame* as an artistic entity whose center is not a hero, nor even as some critics have suggested, the cathedral itself, but an image that unites the novel and permits one to counter Guyard's complaint that Hugo couldn't choose between the historical, ideological, and poetic novel. The historical evocation of the Middle Ages permits the development of the cathedral-recess with its *rosace* as spider web and its monolithic architecture symbolic of feudalism. These forms are linked to Hugo's themes: preoccupation with architecture as such, liberalism as manifested by the democratizing possibilities of the printing press and the hope of future revolution, the plea for a better judicial system. The themes are in turn linked via the imagery to the characters in the grip of various passions. As Hugo himself said in *Notre-Dame:* "L'idée mère, le verbe, [était] dans la forme" (p. 221). The novel is profoundly unified, and within this unity, we arrive at a restatement of an important image already elaborated in his earlier efforts.

The many recesses or "antres" that were a stock motif of *Han d'Islande* and other works are repeated in *Notre-Dame,* as we have seen. Do they have some association with evil religious cults, like the druidical altar of the grotto of Walderhog or the evil mass of Biassou? The answer must be a resounding affirmative. The first "cave" is the Palais de Justice, where Pierre Gringoire's morality play is to be presented. An innocent place in this scene, it is yet one in which we find under a vaulted arch (1) stone statues of all the early kings of France, (2) an elevated marble slab on which the play is acted out in behalf of royalty, with Greek gods figuring among the characters on the stage. The patterns are there already, even if no important meaning seems to emerge from them at this point. The next scene is more important. In the hidden Cour des Miracles where (as in *Cromwell*, almost) there is a king, albeit a beggar king, upon his throne, there is also a stone statue of God to whom Pierre can pray before his execution (p. 69), and various other "religious" motifs. One of the leaders of the *truands* is "empereur de Galilée" (p. 68); the king, Clopin Trouillefou, speaks like a pope (p. 69), but all these trappings are of course demonic, a kind of witches' sabbath (p. 66), where even the place name—La Cour des Miracles—plays a role. The bewildered Gringoire asks: "Où suis-je?" (p. 65). When answered "Dans la Cour des Miracles," Pierre counters wittily: "Je vois bien les aveugles qui regardent et les boiteux qui courent; mais où est le Sauveur?" They answer "par un éclat de rire sinistre."

The Cathedral of Notre-Dame poses a special problem. It is not demonic in itself, providing asylum to the virtuous Esmeralda, and Hugo insists on its genuine religious atmosphere:

> Les lignes solennelles de cette architecture, l'attitude religieuse de tous les objets qui entouraient la jeune fille, les pensées pieuses et sereines qui se dégageaient . . . de tous les pores de cette pierre, agissaient sur elle à son insu. L'édifice avait aussi des bruits d'une telle bénédiction et d'une telle majesté qu'ils assoupissaient cette âme malade. (p. 314)

But on occasion, the cathedral can become demonic. During the attack by the beggars, it belches forth molten lead from its devilish stone gargoyles. Hugo comments on these fantastic creatures: "Leurs innombrables sculptures de diables et de dragons prenaient un aspect lugubre" (p. 354). Referring to one portal, he adds: "cette grimoire écrite en pierre par l'évêque Guillaume de Paris, lequel a sans doute été damné pour avoir attaché un si infernal frontispièce au saint poème que chante éternellement le reste de l'édifice" (p. 128). But the demonic quality of the church is most visible at the moment of Esmeralda's "amende honorable" on its very steps, prior to her execution as a witch. Claude Frollo, the priest of the cathedral, eager to destroy the girl,

69

perverts the truth of Christianity into something ominous and evil. "Tout au fond, dans l'ombre de l'abside, on entrevoyait une gigantesque croix d'argent, développée sur un drap noir" (p. 291). The religious procession includes a "croix d'or" with Claude lurking behind it (pp. 291–92). When the priest then appears under the Gothic portal "enveloppé d'une vaste chape d'argent barrée d'une croix, il était si pâle que plus d'un pensa . . . que c'était un des évêques de marbre agenouillés sur les pierres sépulcrales du chœur" (p. 292). Picking up the motif of the first scene, Hugo has Jehan Frollo refer to "cette rangée de statues" of the early kings of France. When Claude returns to the cathedral that night, the imagery is repeated: "Aux grandes ombres qui tombaient de toutes parts à larges pans, il reconnut . . . les tentures de la cérémonie du matin. . . . La grande croix d'argent scintillait au fond des ténèbres," in a "nuit de sépulcre" (p. 313). Surely there is an aura of horror here. Hugo is already showing in this double vision of the church that when it represents love, man, the people, the sanctity of the individual, and the ineffable God, it is beneficent. But to Victor Hugo Christianity in its medieval Roman Catholic form tended to exalt the priest rather than the humble masses (p. 145). When Frollo, a priest, tries to kill in the name of God, under the silent but approving glances of past royalty, and spurns Quasimodo crying for water at the pillory, the church and its cross become demonic.

Another use of the demonic cave is the torture chamber beneath the Hall of Justice. The fires heating the instruments suggest of course the flames of Hell, a stone monster is sculptured overhead, and in the corner hovers Claude Frollo, an evil religious symbol watching Esmeralda on the slab, the demonic altar of "Justice." Similarly, the recluse's cell has a suggestion of the diabolic. The bars are in the form of a cross and the mother's adoration of her lost daughter is so excessive as to be blasphemous. Inside her cell is the remaining slipper of her infant child, in the mother's mind a religious fetish. Finally, the image reappears in the final pages of the work at the Montfaucon charnel house, "un édifice de forme étrange, qui ressemblait assez à un cromlech antique, et où il se faisait aussi des sacrifices."

"Qu'on se figure . . . un gros parallélipipède de maçonnerie, haut de quinze pieds, large de trente, long de quarante. . . . Sur cette plate-forme seize énormes piliers de pierre brute," from which skeletons dangle.

There is a stone cross and underneath, "on y avait pratiqué une vaste cave" for the bones (p. 423). There Quasimodo rejoins Esmeralda.

We might do well to quote again for comparison's sake the description of the grotto of Walderhog:

> Trois pierres longues et massives, posées debout sur le sol, en soutenaient un quatrième. . . . Sous cette espèce de trépied gigantesque s'élevait une sort d'autel. . . . Ordener reconnut une de ces colossales constructions druidiques . . . [qui] avait bu profondément le sang des victimes humaines.

All this is contained in a "salle oblongue et ovale, creusée à moitié dans la roche et terminée par une espèce de maçonnerie cyclopéenne."[18] Thus there is a real connection, through imagery, between Han and his cave and the evil practices of the church and the monarchy. Lest it be considered an exaggeration to claim that in 1830 Hugo interpreted the monarchy as an evil cult, we cite here Pierre Gringoire's diatribe against the rule of Louis XI, which is given within a larger context of favorite Hugolian ideas:

> C'est une éponge à prendre l'argent posée sur le peuple. Sous ce doux sire dévot [the connection with the church is deftly inserted here], les fourches craquent de pendus, les billots pourrissent de sang, les prisons crèvent comme des ventres trop pleins. Ce roi a une main qui prend et une autre qui pend. (p. 393)

This analysis has tried to show a total artistic unity to *Notre-Dame de Paris*. What seems to have been a rather chaotic historical novel turns out to be an elaborate piece of artistry. Its center is the idea of fatality and its method of elaboration is the set of images that we have examined. One can see from the above that J.-P. Weber was correct in seeking another way of looking at Hugolian fiction, but the simple story of Hatto cannot

---

18. In *La Légende des siècles*, in a poem entitled "Montfaucon," Hugo also compares the evil place to the tabernacle of demonic religions:

        ses piliers bruts, rune d'un dogme atroce,
Semblent des Irmensuls livides, et ses blocs
Dans l'obscurité vague ébauchent des Molochs;
Baal pour le construire a donné ses solives

· · · · · · · · · · · · · · · · ·
Saturne ses crochets, Teutatès ses menhirs. . . .

suffice to explain such a rich tapestry as this. One final remark seems in order: The earliest romances had strong overtones of myth to them, but first in *Cromwell* and now here, this dimension disappears nearly entirely. We know from the work of Albert Py[19] and Pierre Albouy that in the 1820's Hugo had rejected in the name of Romanticism the Greek myths in their classical form but had not yet achieved his own expression of the cosmic. But if *Notre-Dame de Paris* remains a romance and is not expanded to the dimensions of myth, in its wealth of images elevated to symbols, it is nonetheless a masterpiece of nineteenth-century art.

19. Albert Py, *Les Mythes grecs dans la poésie de Victor Hugo* (Genève, 1963), pp. 45–47.

THE THEATER OF
THE THIRTIES

W ITH THE exception of *Notre-Dame de Paris,* Hugo concentrated primarily on poetry and drama in that period spanning the years 1829–1843. During these fourteen years, he wrote several volumes of lyric poetry and completed seven plays. The lyric poetry clearly falls outside the scope of this study, as was explained in the Introduction, but these seven plays present a problem. Only *Hernani* and *Ruy Blas* are of high quality and in such plays as *Marion de Lorme* imagery is infrequent and much of it secondary, that is, not fused with the action of the play. It would, therefore, be tempting to omit consideration of these plays altogether, for in some cases any analysis would have to point to the inadequacy or poverty of texts that do not appear to develop Hugo's imagery further. But what we have learned from the patterns of language in the earlier works does on occasion shed light on the major plays and sometimes it is in the minor plays that we can see that the form does evolve, developing the image of the demonic figure in the cave on the one hand, and the themes of fatality and social conflict on the other. Therefore, without trying to make an exhaustive study of each play, we will try to follow only the principal images and themes.

The first of them was of course *Marion de Lorme,* written in June of 1829. When Hugo read it to a circle of admiring friends, including Balzac, Delacroix, Musset, Dumas, and Vigny, it was warmly received. Baron Taylor of the Théâtre Français was eager to produce it, but royal censorship interfered. Given the instability of the regime of Charles X, the censor decided that the idea of portraying on the stage an indecisive king like Louis XIII was a poor one. As it turned out, Hugo was probably fortunate. The "bataille romantique" could be waged over the far superior *Hernani,* which he wrote immediately upon the rejection of *Marion de Lorme.* Set in neutral Spain, it passed the censors' watchful eye.

Yet even if this play is inferior to *Hernani,* it is worth the critic's time. As in the case of *Notre-Dame,* we are dealing with a somber hymn to fate.

In the preceding chapter, we found that this theme was given substance by imagery based on the spider and the fly. It appears in *Marion de Lorme* as well (again, we must emphasize that we consider it unwise to try to establish any chronological sequence of influence from one to the other), but whereas we showed in the previous chapter that the theme of clemency was important to this play, the spider imagery is only occasional, and more important, it is unconnected to any physical objects. There are no real spiders, webs, *rosaces,* labyrinths of streets, and so forth, which give vigor to the imagery of the novel, probably because in a play, these objects cannot easily be conjured into being. In their stead, we have somewhat lengthy expositions of local color that have little or nothing to do with the action and thus weaken the dramatic unity and impact. But on the positive side, we find at the center of the play our first true "fatal" Romantic couple, Didier and Marion, of that type that we have come to recognize in Hernani and Doña Sol.

Didier is an orphan, a common device of drama that prepares for a recognition scene. But for Hugo, the orphan represents not only the theatrical convention but a more serious personal problem: his earlier estrangement from his father. Transferred from the author's psychology to art, Didier's absence of family results in no recognition scene (we never do learn who he is), but rather, by his isolation, in an intensification of the self. So, shrouded in an aura of mystery, he appears before us as sensitive, noble in demeanor, and apparently well educated. Although naturally energetic, for he saves another man from thieves by his fine sword-play, he nonetheless continues Hugo's passive hero, content to strike a series of dramatic poses, describing himself as "funeste et maudit" (p. 19), in contrast with his "pure" Marie who is—inevitably—"un ange de lumière" (p. 19). That he considers himself a victim of fatality is obvious:

> Hélas, ma destinée
> Marche, et brise la vôtre à sa roue enchaînée. (p. 61)

Marie is his only hope:

> Moi, fatal et méchant, m'as-tu pas, faible femme,
> Sauvé de mon destin, hélas! et de mon âme?

But out of consideration for her, he begs her to leave him to his fate.

74

> Mais je dois t'avertir, oui, mon astre est mauvais.
> J'ignore d'où je viens et j'ignore où je vais.
> Mon ciel est noir.—Marie, écoute une prière.
> Il en est temps encor, toi, retourne en arrière.
> Laisse-moi suivre seul ma sombre route; hélas!
> Après ce dur voyage, et quand je serai las,
> La couche qui m'attend, froide d'un froid de glace,
> Est étroite, et pour deux n'a pas assez de place.
> Va-t'en! (pp. 63–64).

In this lamentable verse, Hugo has none of the original imagery of *Notre-Dame*. He uses instead a trite restatement of the voyage to death within a context of grim fatality. To express this domination of fate through the plot, Hugo contrived a heroine who is a courtesan incognito. It is her fate to fall in love with a hero athirst for purity, who likes to refer to the courtesan (unaware of her true identity) as a "vile créature, impure entre les femmes!" (p. 24). There are other ways in which fatality operates with the plot: (1) Didier finds himself duelling just when Richelieu has outlawed it under pain of death, (2) the king who wishes to pardon him for duelling is weaker than his prime minister, (3) the only way that Marion can save him is by giving herself to the evil Laffemas, but in so doing, she destroys any desire to live in her beloved's mind. Didier, learning of the last-mentioned episode, exclaims:

> Oh! pourquoi ma nourrice,
> Au lieu de recueillir le pauvre enfant trouvé,
> M'a-t-elle pas brisé le front sur le pavé!
> Qu'est-ce que j'avais fait à ma mère pour naître? (p. 124)

At the play's end, our Romantic hero is executed under the edict forbidding duelling. As a minor character put it earlier to the king:

> Sire, être mort ou pas né,
> Voilà le seul bonheur. Mais l'homme est condamné. (p. 107)

But is the grip of fatality really all-powerful? Is existence totally bleak? In this connection, one must remember that there was originally a different ending from the one we know today. Not only did the hero die, but he refused to pardon Marion at the end for her infidelity. Moved by the protests of his friends that the play was too grim to be tolerable, Hugo

75

had Didier pardon Marion and he even went so far as to suggest a transcendent happiness that sounds as if it came from *Les Contemplations:*

> Que le bec du vautour déchire mon étoffe,
> Ou que le ver la ronge, ainsi qu'il fait d'un roi,
> C'est l'affaire du corps; mais que m'importe à moi!
> Lorsque la lourde tombe a clos notre paupière,
> L'âme lève du doigt le couvercle de pierre,
> Et s'envole. (p. 127)

Hugo has reverted to the idea announced in *Han d'Islande* and in *Bug-Jargal* that descent into death can lead to ultimate joy. Within the context of the play, it is Marion's pleas for clemency (pp. 135, 140) that motivate the hero's change in attitude and his final pardon, thus suggesting a link with the theme of clemency in politics, which is also developed here in much the same language as in *Notre-Dame,* as we saw in the previous chapter.

But the novelty and interest of *Marion de Lorme* lie not in the manner in which its various images or themes are handled but in its center of the passionate "fatal" love of hero and heroine. In Hugo's earlier works, whenever a love rivalry appeared, three distinct types of rivals were visible. There were first, of course, the traditional, pure, virtuous heroes—Ordener and Léopold, but they soon faded out and would rarely reappear in Hugo's work in such conventionalized form (Otbert in *Les Burgraves* is perhaps the only example of this type in the later works). The others can be grouped into (1) the comic character not to be taken seriously as a lover, (2) the evil seducer, and (3) the noble, but somehow grotesque or taboo, or, more generally, "fated" hero.

Hugo's first comic hero was Frédéric d'Ahlefeld of *Han d'Islande,* the young *précieux* steeped in Mlle de Scudéry and oblivious to the horror about him. He chatters amiably about transforming the Gothic novel in which he finds himself into a pastoral tale. The passage is genuinely entertaining:

> Il me semble, et je serais heureux que ma charmante compagne
> partageât mon avis, que les aventures de Han pourraient fournir un
> roman délicieux, dans le genre des sublimes écrits de la damoiselle
> Scudéry, l'*Artamène* ou la *Clélie,* dont je n'ai encore lu que six

volumes, mais qui n'en est pas moins un chef d'œuvre à mes yeux. Il faudrait, par exemple, adoucir notre climat, orner nos traditions, modifier nos noms barbares. Ainsi Drontheim, qui deviendrait *Durtinianum*, verrait ses forêts se changer, sous ma baguette magique en des bosquets délicieux, arrosés de mille petits ruisseaux. (pp. 67–68)

Ethel Schumacher responds to this idiocy by ignoring his suit, and the young *étourdi* is suitably punished later by being eaten by Han. This comic "rival" theme is repeated in *Cromwell* by Rochester, who aspires to the hand of Francis Cromwell. In the midst of the conspirators' meeting, his only thought is for an elegy he has composed. The scene surely owes something to Molière:

ROCHESTER

> . . . je vous tiens pour un juge excellent
> Et, pour vous le prouver, à votre seigneurie,
> Je vais lire un quatrain nouveau.

> *Il se drape et prend un accent emphatique*

> "Belle Egérie. . . .

> *Il s'interrompt*

Devinez, je vous prie, à qui c'est adressé.

Rochester's ultimate fate is to be forced to marry a comic crone with the comic name of Dame Guggligoy. As for Francis, she is merely amused by the foppish young aristocrat.

In *Notre-Dame,* Pierre Gringoire follows in the tradition of Frédéric and Rochester. Like the other two a composer of pretentious literature, he has no idea of true passion and prefers the friendship of Djali, the goat, to the beauteous Esmeralda. There is no love on either side in their marriage, which remains unconsummated. In *Marion de Lorme*, it is Saverny who considers love but an idle pastime. The comic character is thus a frequent one in Hugo's imagination at this time but in later works will tend to disappear. Opposite these frivolous characters are the evildoers bent on lustful seduction. Richard Varney in *Amy Robsart* is the only clear case prior to *Marion de Lorme,* but between this second category of evil seducer and the third, the noble but taboo hero as exemplified by

77

Pierrot, we can find intermediate types: Quasimodo is noble and taboo, but hardly a lover in the normal sense. Claude Frollo is an evil seducer, but is also taboo, as he is a priest.

In the earliest works, there was a rivalry between two men only: Ordener and Frédéric, Léopold and Pierrot, Varney and Leicester; but with the late 1820's the number grows. *Notre-Dame de Paris* has Quasimodo, Frollo, Phœbus and Gringoire hovering about the heroine. This pattern is similar in *Marion de Lorme*. The fated hero is Didier, of course. He is not without his faults, for in the first version he refused to pardon the woman who had sacrificed all for him, and even in the more compassionate final text, he is still blind, arrogant, and cruel:

> J'aurais pu,—pour ma perte,—aussi, moi, naître femme.
> J'aurais pu,—comme un autre,—être vile, être infâme,
> Me donner pour de l'or. . . . (p. 136)

We mentioned above the Marquis de Saverny, who plays the role of the frivolous lover. He has the same attributes as his predecessors. A "tout jeune homme blond, vêtu à la dernière mode de 1638," he is a fop who is willing to share Marion with any number of others and whose main interest, again like the others in his category, is literary:

> On ne parle à Paris que *Guirlande d'amour*,
> Et c'est, avec *le Cid*, le grand succès du jour. (p. 18)

One can gather that Saverny, like Gringoire, has no sense of passionate absolute. His "Mais, diable! être pendu, voilà ce qui m'ennuie!" (p. 126) resembles Gringoire's refusal to let himself be hanged because he loves life and his *boutade:* "Oh! que volontiers je me noierais, si l'eau n'était pas si froide" (p. 44). Unlike Gringoire however, Saverny does not avoid death, but for him it is no absolute but merely an adventure like any other, a nobleman's pastime. He is so calm that he naps prior to his execution.

The third category of suitor is the magistrate Laffemas, the typical villain of the Varney stripe, described by Didier with the usual diabolical attributes:

> Démon! j'ai dans tes yeux vu la sinistre flamme
> De ce rayon d'enfer qui t'illuminait l'âme! (p. 78)

When Laffemas makes his offer to release Didier if Marion will but be complaisant, we find the theme of lust once again united to villainy. Laffemas is a "tentateur" with a "ricanement" (p. 88). One can see parallels with Claude Frollo, but a difference is also visible: Laffemas has none of the sense of the absolute that possesses Frollo. To conclude: *Marion de Lorme* shows typical Hugolian characters, themes, and images. The plot, themes, and characters are reasonably unified, but the imagery has not yet been adequately worked out for the needs of the stage. *Hernani* will be more successful.

In this famous play, the three rivals return under the names of Hernani, Ruy Gomez, and Don Carlos as fated hero, demonic villain, and "comic" lover respectively. Like Didier, Hernani is not flawless, for he doubts the fidelity of Doña Sol far more than is reasonable, and he is perhaps overly bent on vengeance. Like Didier, his "fatal" aura is disquieting, but otherwise he belongs to the heroes of romance. Although his identity is at first unknown, like that of Ordener, he reveals himself at the proper moment to be of a properly pedigreed aristocratic family, and thus acceptable to the feudal canons of romance. Ruy Gomez is the demonic and taboo lover. The taboo is not so much the fact that he is the girl's uncle but that he is an old man. To the youthful Hugo, his lechery is unthinkable. Like Esmeralda at the gallows crying out to Claude Frollo that the gibbet "me fait encore moins horreur que vous," Doña Sol carries a dagger on her person, intending to commit suicide rather than belong to the old man. Hernani calls him a demon (p. 648). At the end, like Frollo, he is "damné." As for Don Carlos, because he has royal power, he is not a frivolous character like Saverny or d'Ahlefeld, but he has the essential attribute: he considers wenching an amusement. No absolute lover could declaim:

> J'offre donc mon amour à madame.
> Partageons. Voulez-vous? J'ai vu dans sa belle âme
> Tant d'amour, de bonté, de tendres sentiments
> Que madame, à coup sûr, en a pour deux amants. (p. 540)

Nor is the comic foppish element lacking entirely. Emerging from his *cachette* in Act I, he remarks:

> Mais j'entendais très mal et j'étouffais très bien.
> Et puis je chiffonnais ma veste à la française.
> Ma foi, je sors! (p. 540)

This obvious utilization of the patterns of the other works of the 1820's should lead a critic to suspect that *Hernani* will show parallels that create an artistic unity as did the others. But as Guyard did with *Notre-Dame,* critics have claimed the contrary. It is perhaps unfair to the profession of theatrical criticism to reach back to Francisque Sarcey's *Quarante ans de théâtre,* but he is not alone in crying out: "Y a-t-il rien de plus étrange que le quatrième acte d'*Hernani,* si l'on y cherche une œuvre sérieuse de théâtre? C'est une suite de scènes insensées, qui tombent les unes par-dessus les autres, sans lien comme sans raison." Georges Lote continues this view more recently in his *En Préface à Hernani,* commenting on Sarcey's remarks: "Tout ceci est très judicieux."[1] He outdoes Sarcey in agreeing with the critics of 1830 that at the end of Act IV, "il semble donc que tout soit achevé. Ici les parodies ont signalé le défaut de la cuirasse" (p. 100). He alludes to one parody, *N,I,NI,* which at the end of Act IV urges the spectators, who would surely think the play was finished, to keep their seats for "le second et *seul* dénouement de l'ouvrage." Lote calls the technique of Ruy Gomez' horn an "artifice misérable." His more general conclusion is: "Ce quatrième acte finit comme font ordinairement les mélodrames, et le cinquième selon le mode usité dans les tragédies. Ainsi la pièce se ressent de ses doubles origines. Ces deux dénouements montrent que l'auteur n'a pas su choisir: il a procédé par addition" (p. 168). Lote prefers to approach the play from the point of view of Hugo's sources and has no trouble exposing the inadequate history and imitations of Pixérécourt's melodramas. Having like so many others shown the logical absurdities of *Hernani,* Lote tries to salvage something by making laudatory remarks about the lyric poetry it contains. "*Hernani* . . . est l'expression déjà complète d'un grand poète, qui s'appelle Hugo. Tout le reste ôté, cela du moins demeure et illustre le drame malgré toutes les faiblesses qu'on peut lui découvrir: c'en est assez pour le faire vivre" (p. 189). Although this "salvaging" of the play is more condemnation than eulogy, it would be an error to overcompensate and claim the play to be perfectly balanced and constructed. But it is our contention that it is a more coherent creation than has often been thought.

The play starts with the centrality of the hero and heroine, fated to love each other, even if they are oddly unaware of each other's circumstances. Hernani, the outlaw, hides his true identity from Doña Sol, and he seems

1. *En Préface à Hernani—cent ans après* (Paris, 1930), p. 151.

to have no idea why she is being forced to marry Ruy Gomez. As each of them is threatened by some aspect of society's injustice (the exiled nobleman, the unwanted marriage), this situation provides Hugo with the opportunity to have spiders pounce on the hapless flies. But again, as was the case with *Marion de Lorme,* because the stage makes impossible the literal presence of these insects, Hugo eliminated them, at least as concrete images, reducing them to a more acceptable abstraction. He manages this change more ably than in his previous effort. For instance, Doña Sol, like Phœbus, is named for the sun, and Hernani is the victim in the toils of fate, but the spider is replaced by some vague form, deadly and dark:

> Ange! Ah! dans cet instant
> Où la mort vient peut-être, où s'approche dans l'ombre,
> Un sombre dénouement pour un destin bien sombre. (pp. 567–68)

This pattern constitutes the recurring motif of the play. In Act I, the sudden emergence of the king from his hiding place to surprise the lovers is a comic use of the idea. The sudden seizing of the king by Hernani in Act II, "surgissant tout à coup derrière lui" (p. 561) "dans l'ombre" is the dramatic center of the act. Don Ruy Gomez surprises the lovers in Act III; the king pounces on the conspirators in the labyrinthine underground of Act IV, and of course, Ruy Gomez returns (dressed in black) to bring death in Act V. All of this takes place in a world of fatality ("La fatalité s'accomplit," we learn in Act V), and we can see that each act is an elaboration of the basic motif to which Hugo has returned: the way to light is blocked by some fatality, crouched and lying in wait. Can one descend and be saved? Again, if one descends into death, yes; otherwise, no. After trying vainly to stop Hernani from taking poison, Doña Sol exclaims:

> Calme-toi. Je suis mieux.—Vers des clartés nouvelles
> Nous allons tout à l'heure ensemble ouvrir nos ailes.
> Partons d'un vol égal vers un monde meilleur. (p. 655)

The theme of reuniting beyond the grave is restated in terms that make clear that the tomb is but a gateway to a better life. The heroine cries:

> Mort! non pas! nous dormons.
> Il dort. C'est mon époux, vois-tu. Nous nous aimons.
> Nous sommes couchés là. C'est notre nuit de noce. (p. 656)

81

As important as the tradition of the lovers reunited in death beyond the reach of fatality is the political dimension of the play. Charles V offers an interesting contrast to the irresponsible monarchs of *Notre-Dame de Paris* and *Marion de Lorme*. Don Carlos, the insouciant libertine of the first three acts, suddenly changes and learns, as Louis XI, Louis XIII, and Richelieu did not, the high wisdom of clemency. How did he learn where the others failed? A comparison with *Notre-Dame* is illuminating. Both monarchs are menaced, Louis XI by the *truands* attacking "his" cathedral, Charles V by would-be assassins. These threats take place in a setting of massive stone, Louis in the Bastille with its vaulted arches and underground corridors, Charles at the tomb of Charlemagne. Here is Hugo's stage description for Act IV: "De grandes voûtes d'architecture lombarde. Gros piliers bas. . . . Il est nuit. On ne voit pas le fond du souterrain; l'œil se perd dans les arcades." In *Notre-Dame*, Louis goes through the stone corridors bearing a torch, observes the prisoners, refuses them clemency, and leaves them in darkness. Charles V proceeds differently. He is in an underground passage, but he is not on a casual visit. His purpose is to seek guidance and to understand his role in politics. To gain enlightenment, he goes into an even deeper recess—the tomb of Charlemagne himself (again, the concept of a double barrier). By coming here to meditate, he is turning downward, away from any abstract speculations, toward the lived history of man, toward the finitude of man who becomes dust: "Voyez la poussière/ Que fait un empereur." In this famous monologue, Charles discovers the Truth that transforms:

Dans l'ombre, tout au fond de l'abîme,—les hommes.
—Les hommes! c'est-à-dire une foule, une mer. (p. 614)

This Truth that the other monarchs had ignored, Charles finds despite the menacing terms of "foule" and "mer." His descending quest leads him not to night but to light. He cries out before entering the inner recesses of the tomb:

. . . s'il est vrai qu'en son lit solitaire
Parfois une grande ombre au bruit que fait la terre
S'éveille, et que soudain son tombeau large et clair
S'entrouvre, et dans la nuit jette au monde un éclair. (p. 615)

Then he supposes that this tomb is "pleine de clarté" and enters. Upon emerging he asks the shades of the Emperor: "Ai-je bien à ta flamme

82

allumé mon flambeau?" (p. 630) He then completes the cycle of imagery by associating, as does Hugo in *Notre-Dame*, the "flambeau" with clemency, the word that closes this important act. To recapitulate: whereas Louis XI removed light from the people, Charles V lighted his torch down in the darkness where both Truth and the masses are found. The imagery is repeated: the way down is, for the man of good will, the way to light and salvation. Thanks to this experience, Charles V is transformed (a change understandable in mythic if not in psychological terms, for it is a commonplace of mythology that the perilous descent has this effect), Hernani is restored to his rightful social position as Jean d'Aragon, and the lovers are united in marriage. But in *Hernani* the human possibilities of optimism are limited to the political success of the state. The lovers, thanks to the hero's sense of honor, are doomed to die. Or, to word it differently, Hernani has broken through the finite barrier or web. But there is the second one that stops him as it did the fly. Here it is the "ananké suprême, le cœur humain" in the form of Ruy Gomez' bitter jealousy and Hernani's sacred Spanish oath that turn joy into tragedy. Viewed in this manner, the final two acts mean that man may overcome much, but there is always some ultimate defeat. The play is no slapping together of disparate sources, or even merely an abuse of melodramatic techniques of the day (gloomy caves and poison were stock devices), but at this period in Hugo's life, a consistent image of the irony of human existence.

The four plays that follow *Hernani* are today virtually ignored by producers and critics alike. Written, except for *Le Roi s'amuse* (1832), in lackluster prose, *Lucrèce Borgia* (1833), *Marie Tudor* (1833), and *Angélo, Tyran de Padoue* (1835) merit the oblivion into which they have fallen. They repeat the characters and the many Hugolian devices of melodrama with which we are familiar. As a consequence we will, like other critics, treat them more as a group, singling out any new patterns of imagery as they appear. If observed from an over-all perspective, they tend to demonstrate that Hugo is beginning to move away from a tone of dominant tragic fatality to one of greater optimism. Pierre Albouy, commenting on the second and less chilling ending of *Marion de Lorme*, states that "la rédemption tend à devenir le principal ressort des drames de Hugo" (p. 266). By this he means that the evildoers are somewhat redeemed, usually by some form of love, frequently parental love. Albouy reminds us that this theme was visible as early as *Han d'Islande* in which the d'Ahlefelds are both wicked and punished for their evil, and yet are made less totally monstrous because of their love for their son Frédéric. In like fashion, in this group of four plays, Triboulet, the jester of *Le Roi s'amuse,* deeply loves his daughter Blanche, and in *Lucrèce Borgia,* the evil titular heroine loves her son Gennaro. In these two creations the tone is still one of black fatality. In the former, the outraged father plans the assassination of the king for having seduced his daughter, and it seems as if indeed the king will die and Triboulet and his daughter escape. But despite certain knowledge of the king's fickleness, Blanche gives her life for her faithless lover's, and it is her body in a sack that Triboulet throws into the river. In this series of events a second barrier, the "anankè suprême, le cœur humain," operates again to frustrate human plans. One can see a parallel with the scene in *Notre-Dame* where Esmeralda frustrates her mother by calling out desperately to Phœbus and thus brings destruction upon them both. In *Lucrèce Borgia* it looks as if Gennaro will succeed in fleeing Ferrara, but it turns out that he delays his flight to attend a party where his mother is ignorant of his presence. She has arranged to have the whole company of young men poisoned, and so Gennaro dies too. Thus the pattern of *Hernani* is repeated: a penultimate act that ends hopefully for the central characters, but a final one that brings destruction. And in these two plays, the evil-doers are punished by being themselves the killers of their children.[2]

The imagery of *Notre-Dame de Paris* appears on occasion in these plays, but only sporadically and more in a decorative than in a functional manner. Some examples of this imagery are: As the hero is Lucrèce's son by her own dead brother Jean, Gennaro is understandably kept ignorant of his incestuous lineage, and further, he cannot understand why he is constantly under the surveillance of this evil woman. Concerning this ominous situation, his friend Maffio observes uneasily: "Il faut tirer mon frère Gennaro de cette toile d'araignée" (p. 460), but he does not succeed. The imagery also provides a suggestion of a sun toward which

---

2. In the preface to *Lucrèce Borgia,* Hugo claimed that "*Le Roi s'amuse* et *Lucrèce Borgia* ne se ressemblent ni par le fond ni par la forme" (p. 441) but admits that they do have similar themes: "la paternité sanctifiant la difformité physique, voilà *Le Roi s'amuse,* la maternité purifiant la difformité morale, voilà *Lucrèce Borgia.*" Despite the accuracy of the comment, to this critic it seems that the failure of the human effort is more significant.

the hero can soar. There is a certain "Fiametta," supposedly the sweet-heart of Gennaro, but she never appears on stage and the hero seems little interested in her (p. 461). She is for Hugo a "little flame," a small light of no significance. Actually, Gennaro is much more eager to determine the identity of his long-lost mother. She is a more intense sun, albeit an evil one. Picking up the image he had used in *Notre-Dame* with the *écu* as a sun, Hugo has Maffio say of her: "C'est un ducat d'or à l'effigie de Satan" (p. 474). But if Gennaro is a fly struggling in the web, Lucrèce must serve as spider, just as Gudule was briefly one for Esmeralda. Her black clothing suggests the creature and she tries to turn into a beneficent figure, but she is also a victim of fate, and she fails. The absence of sustained imagery here in a play written after *Notre-Dame* suggests that its absence in *Marion de Lorme* was not only due to the earlier composi-tion of this latter play, but also to the difference in genre.

In the climax of *Lucrèce Borgia*, where the true identities are revealed, we find that the play does more than repeat in banal form a few leftover images. Here there is the first really explosive use of the diabolical religious motif in the cave. In the final scene, penitents dressed in black and white robes bear a silver cross (against a black background) into the locked room where all the youths have been poisoned. They bring, too, five coffins draped in black and sing dirges to the dead. The scene, more hideously spectacular than Esmeralda's *amende honorable*, indicates Hugo's horror for the demonic aspects of the Roman Catholic church, an attitude that will be even further intensified in his last play *Torquemada* (1869). But is it only the church that provokes the horror of the scene? Baudouin has made clear Hugo's attitude toward the mother figure, and with the poet's growing disaffection with religious orthodoxy, he can mingle the two in the same scene.

But is the evil mother to be totally condemned? Is she redeemed by her love for her son? Hugo treats this question by using his well-established theme of clemency, although in this case the technique is superficial and unconvincing. We learn that she decides to exercise clemency on certain political prisoners, telling her evil servant: "Je n'étais pas née pour faire le mal. . . . C'est l'exemple de ma famille qui m'a entraînée" (p. 453), and she asks him: "Est-ce que tu n'en as pas assez du crime?" (p. 455). She senses a dual pull in her, explaining that "deux anges luttaient en moi, le bon et le mauvais; mais je crois que le bon va enfin l'emporter"

(p. 456).[3] But her clemency is in vain. She comes to realize fully that she is a "damnée du ciel" (p. 456), and like Cromwell she uses clemency as a tactic only, "un moyen de me faire aimer de votre peuple" (p. 487). *Lucrèce Borgia* is a melodrama, but it is not merely a repetition of hackneyed motifs which were used more imaginatively in *Notre-Dame de Paris* and *Hernani*. Although the play does continue the fated hero motif and has an ending that snatches disaster from the jaws of triumph, the final gruesome scene marks by its prominence an "advance" in Hugo's technique: the monster lurking in the cave has now become an attractive but evil female figure.

The low quality of this play is matched by that of *Marie Tudor* (1833), for Hugo took even less care here in giving plausibility to his *coups de théâtre*. The fate of documents proving Jane Talbot's noble birth, the ancient Jew, the impossible last-minute substitution at the execution of the villain for the hero, etc., etc., would make a Pixérécourt envious. Such as it is, however, the world of the play is governed by fatality on the philosophical level and by the Queen of England on the social level. Therefore, during the play, the monarch operates as a kind of spider. Referring to her favorite with whom she is disenchanted, she exclaims: "Je veux le voir plié en deux . . . mains liées . . . manié par le bourreau . . . j'y veux mettre une corde" (pp. 57–58). Also, with her diabolical laughter and evil smile (pp. 54, 91), she provides, like Lucrèce, a gloomy setting for the conclusion with its hooded figures, black sheets, and white crosses. Again the lurking monster is a female figure. But in this play, at the last moment, the grip of fatality is broken, the Queen thwarted, and a happy ending provided.

The action is more complex than in the two preceding efforts, reverting to the *Tres para una* pattern of 1829–1831. Jane Talbot, "vêtue de blanc" (p. 79), finds herself the center of attention of a profligate rake (Fabiani, the Queen's favorite), a partial satanic figure (the Queen herself), and a noble lover (the artisan Gilbert). This trio would seemingly evoke only Hugo's well-tested and indeed overused devices until we realize that for

3. Auguste Vacquerie after the reprise of 1881 stated that Lucrèce's appeal, "Gennaro, Gennaro ayez pitié des méchants, vous ne savez pas ce qui se passe dans leur cœur" (E.I.N., p. 463), was a concept dear to the author. See E.I.N., pp. 571–72. This detail reveals Hugo's growing desire to redeem the fallen, including himself.

the first time, the noble hero is not a nobleman and the girl is actually seduced.

One would suppose that in this royal drama, a humble worker like Gilbert would have no role to play. As the Tower Keeper warns him: "Tu es amoureux. Tu es du peuple. Et qu'est-ce que cela te fait les intrigues d'en haut, à toi qui es heureux en bas?" (p. 15). But chance, or rather Hugo's lack of concern for historical exactness,[4] wills otherwise. When Gilbert vows revenge upon the court favorite for having seduced Jane, he is able to come into contact with different classes. And he arrives in their midst seeking revenge not only as a man, but as the social represent-ative of the people: "L'homme du peuple se venge aussi" (p. 61). So not only does a commoner become a hero but the *peuple* itself becomes one. Outraged at the Queen's refusal to have her favorite executed, the wily Simon Renard mutters: "Essayons du peuple" (p. 70). Soon crowds swarm around the Tower demanding Fabiani's head. Renard warns the Queen: "Il faut que votre majesté prenne un parti sur-le-champ, madame. Le peuple veut la mort de cet homme. Londres est en feu. La Tour est investie. L'émeute est formidable. . . . Les partisans de madame Eliza-beth sont mêlés au peuple. . . . Tout cela est sombre" (p. 80). The Queen counters with a different term, calling them "populace" (p. 81) and "canaille." Simon Renard reacts to these words like Hugo himself: "Vous pouvez encore dire la canaille, dans une heure vous serez obligé de dire le peuple" (p. 81). The scales tip in favor of the latter. Jane Talbot has meanwhile been begging the Queen to spare Gilbert. Upon her refusal, the girl cries out: "Ah! je perds mes peines! Ah! vous ne m'écoutez pas! Eh bien, si la reine ne m'entend pas, le peuple m'entendra! Ah! ils sont bons, ceux-là, voyez-vous" (p. 94). Jane has made her irrevocable decision, and she and Gilbert are united at the end of the play. It seems, too, as if Hugo has made his choice. He has Gilbert pardon Jane even though she is "fallen." This clemency stands in marked contrast to the attitude of the aristocrats. Richelieu, Ruy Gomez, even Hernani are inflexible. This class struggle is actually captured by the

4. More generally, because Hugo turns the rather chaste Queen into a frenzied female in love, various critics have felt that Hugo strayed too far from what was permissible. See Paul de Saint-Victor, *Victor Hugo* (Paris, 1892), pp. 90–93, and Marc Blanchard, *Marie-Tudor: Essai sur les sources de la pièce avec des notes inédites de Victor Hugo* (Paris, 1935).

subtitles of the three acts, or "Journées" as they are called here: I, "L'homme du peuple"; II, "La reine"; III, "Lequel des Deux?" The larger meaning seems clear: Is one to choose the monarchy or the common people? In the context of the play Simon Renard manages to achieve a precarious synthesis that reconciles opposing class interests. He arranges for Fabiani to be substituted for Gilbert (as he is bound, gagged, and hooded, none can tell the difference), and so can announce in the final line: "J'ai sauvé la reine et l'Angleterre" (p. 96). But any reconciliation of monarch and the *peuple* in Hugo cannot be permanent.

The political aspect of *Marie Tudor,* the theme of *Tres para una,* and the final scene with demonic hoods and crosses in the Tower show that Hugo has not abandoned his recurring motifs. The saving of the hero and heroine is a radical break from the previous efforts and heralds a new direction in Hugo's theater, but of these important matters, Hugo himself seemed uninterested or unaware. The essence of the play, he claimed, "la pensée qu'il a tenté de réaliser dans *Marie Tudor,*" is "une reine qui soit une femme. Grande comme reine. Vraie comme femme" (p. 6). Although Hugo's remark is perhaps valid, it misses the real heart of the action.

This series of dramas closes with another effort, *Angélo, Tyran de Padoue* (1835), which seems to be and in truth is a tedious compilation of devices and themes taken from melodrama. However, the value of the play is real for our understanding of Hugo's imagery. The wife of the tyrannical *podestà,* Catarina, has secretly loved the heroic Rodolfo, but their love has remained pure. The secret police of the Conseil des Dix of Venice arranges for a jealous rival, Tisbe, an actress of the people, to sneak into her bedroom when her lover is hiding there and to raise the alarm, thus intending to cause the death of the "faithless" wife and her lover. This room, another of Hugo's demonic caves, is entered by means of three secret locked doors and is a place of mystery. On its walls hangs a crucifix (the religious motif) which turns out to be a recognition device that saves Catarina, for Tisbe had sworn to give her life for the person owning it, this person having saved her mother years previously. This room, dominated by "un lit magnifique sur une estrade et sous un dais porté par des colonnes torses. Aux quatre coins du dais pendent des rideaux cramoisis qui peuvent se fermer et cacher entièrement le lit" (p. 163), is an idyllic but fearsome spot, as one of the characters makes clear: "Il y a dans Padoue une chambre, chambre redoutable, quoique pleine de fleurs, de parfums et d'amour peut-être, où nul homme ne peut pénétrer, quel qu'il soit, noble ou sujet, jeune ou vieux, car y entrer, en entr'ouvrir la porte seulement, c'est un crime puni de mort" (p. 166).

What appeared attractive is really deadly because of the husband's jealousy. The latter dramatizes his attitude for the spectators by placing an executioner's ax and block on his wife's bed. Within the plot of the play, the danger is adultery. The obsessive motif of cave and demonic altar have been given an explicit erotic content: the altar is now a bed of love, and the key with which the locked doors to the room must be opened is not hard to understand.[5] If we seek an explanation in Hugo's unconscious, the crime may well be more than adultery. The theme of the evil mother of *Lucrèce Borgia* suggests the taboo of incest,[6] but the literary critic must limit himself to the text of the play with its themes of politics and adultery. Seen in this light, we find *Angélo* to be only another stale melodramatic plot. Its only real interest is that it provides a stage in the transformation of the cave and altar motif that will become even clearer in the later *Les Travailleurs de la mer* and finally comes out into the open in *L'Homme qui rit,* as we shall show in subsequent chapters.

But despite the danger and horror of the room, Hugo contrived a happy ending. The actress-with-a-heart-of-gold sacrifices herself to save the lovers and dies blessing them. This ending shows Hugo's continuing interest in contriving an optimistic final vision, and it also shows in its triteness the paucity of his invention at this moment. His dramatic career by 1835 resembles a match that has flared up brightly, burned lower and lower, and is about to go out. As sometimes happens, however, there is a final burst of light prior to darkness. For Hugo, it was *Ruy Blas,* first played at the Théâtre de la Renaissance on November 8, 1838.

This play is distinguished from those that preceded it by its versification, for Hugo had abandoned verse in the plays that followed *Le Roi s'amuse.* He also exercised much greater care with his language and the improved style makes for a much better play. But otherwise, the spectator is on familiar ground. There is first a repetition of the *Tres para una* device. The heroine is besieged by three men, the first of whom is the

5. Henri Guillemin, *Hugo et la sexualité* (Paris, 1954), quotes a note of Hugo's that dates from about 1828: "L'homme a reçu de la nature une clef avec laquelle il remonte sa femme toutes les vingt-quatre heures" (p. 13).
6. See Charles Baudouin, *Psychanalyse de Victor Hugo* (Genève, 1943), chap. VI, for the role of the mother in Hugo.

villainous Don Salluste, whose antecedents can be traced back to Richard Varney, Claude Frollo, and Laffemas. Salluste chortles happily:

> Oh! Mais je vais construire, et sans en avoir l'air,
> Une sape profonde, obscure et souterraine. (p. 338)

The same idea recurs frequently throughout the five acts, with "piège," "trappe," "creuser," "glu," being typical vocabulary. The queen is alarmed by this man's ominous presence:

> L'enfer est dans cette âme,
> Devant cet homme-là je ne suis qu'une femme.—
> Dans mes rêves, la nuit, je rencontre en chemin
> Cet effrayant démon qui me baise la main;
> Je vois luire son œil d'où rayonne la haine;
> Et, comme un noir poison qui va de veine en veine,
> Souvent, jusqu'à mon cœur qui semble se glacer,
> Je sens en longs frissons courir son froid baiser! (p. 366)

The parallel between Salluste and the queen, and Frollo and Esmeralda is obvious. Like the gypsy girl, too, the queen is a prisoner, although in a more subtle way. Marie is a captive of court protocol. She tries repeatedly to do things by herself, to have women attendants come in and play cards, to eat with her maid-in-waiting, but is not permitted to do so. The latter legitimately calls the royal chambers "une prison bien austère et bien sombre" (p. 371). The queen even envies the washerwomen singing of love on the way to work.

Another of the three is Don Guritan (we may safely exclude the king from this group, for he is off hunting wolves), an aged courtier, jealous, like Ruy Gomez, of the queen. The comic or foppish claimant has disappeared, or rather, has taken on a different role in the play, and we shall examine him shortly. The third man is of course Ruy Blas himself. It is obvious that in this tale, all three of the men are taboo: Salluste by his evil, Guritan by his age, and Ruy Blas, the commoner, by his class. For the second time, or the third if we include Tisbe from *Angélo*, the *peuple* is involved in the love intrigue. Ruy Blas is naturally the one for the queen to love, for the taboo is not of the hero's (or nature's) making. The distinctions of class can only be for the liberal Hugo false barriers that need overcoming. So the valet and the queen fall in love and he, by the contrived artifice of Salluste's plan of revenge, passes as a Grandee of Spain, becomes her favorite and for a time virtual head of the government. But he and the queen are like flies heading toward the sun, unaware of the nearly invisible web set to catch them. The hero exclaims ecstatically:

> Devant moi tout un monde, un monde de lumière,
> Comme ces paradis qu'en songe nous voyons,
> S'entrouvre en m'inondant de vie et de rayons! (p. 402)

The sun is of course Marie, whom he calls "cet ange."

Before too long, however, the joy fades, as Ruy Blas begins to realize that Salluste has been setting a trap. He declares to the villain:

> Vous m'entraînez vers un gouffre invisible.
> Oh! je sens que je suis dans une main terrible!
> Vous avez des projets monstrueux. J'entrevoi
> Quelque chose d'horrible. . . .—Ayez pitié de moi! (p. 407)

But a cry to a sadistic villain only serves to increase the torture. Ruy Blas realizes the futility of his plea and senses disaster approaching, although the imagery has now become more mechanical than arachnoid.

> Bâtir une machine effroyable dans l'ombre,
> L'armer hideusement de rouages sans nombre,
> Puis, sous la meule, afin de voir comment elle est,
> Jeter une livrée, une chose, un valet,
> Puis la faire mouvoir, et soudain sous la roue
> Voir sortir des lambeaux teints de sang et de boue. (p. 409)

But at the end of the play, although Ruy Blas confesses to the villain that he is "tout garotté dans vos complots hideux" (p. 452), he still has enough freedom to bolt the door of the secret house and to crush the "serpent," in a scene somewhat reminiscent of Gennaro's killing of Lucrèce Borgia. There follows a final love scene between hero and heroine just before his death by suicide.

Does the repetition of images and motifs stop here? Far from it. The "mythe du peuple" as a rescuing force that was visible in *Marie Tudor*, although muted now because of the Spanish setting, has a certain role in *Ruy Blas*, not only in the obvious case of the hero, but also with Don

César who, though technically noble, is more Bohemian (under the name of Zafari). These two characters meet early in the play and seal a pact. Ruy Blas says (unaware that Zafari is a nobleman): "Tous deux nés dans le peuple!" and calls Zafari "Frère"[7] three times, in a manner that reminds one of Léopold and Pierrot in *Bug-Jargal*. Recalling earlier days of freedom, Ruy Blas exclaims: "Nous chantions dès l'heure où l'aube naît" and comments: "C'était l'aurore" (p. 350). This association of the *peuple* and the sunrise repeats the imagery of *Notre-Dame*. And so the sun rises. This lowly man, a "ver de terre" in love with an "étoile," conscious that the masses have been victimized by governmental corruption for twenty years, cries out: "Sauvons le peuple" (p. 405). In his famous tirade to the venal ministers (III, ii), he explains that the former sun of Charles V "s'éteint," or rather its "rayons" have been turned into piastres, an interesting reprise of the sun-money imagery. The queen unites herself to Ruy Blas not only in love but in politics, agreeing that Ruy Blas must "Sauver l'état qui tremble, et retirer du gouffre/ Le peuple qui travaille . . ." (p. 401). Alas, because of the historical moment in which the play takes place, there can be no renewal of national energy. Spain has lost its vitality, and Ruy Blas's cry to save the people falls on the deaf ears of Don Salluste, just as Gringoire had pleaded in vain with Louis XI.

There are other echoes of Hugo's earlier plays as well. Someone hides in a *cachette* (III, iii) and one even finds a suggestion of the *scène des portraits* of *Hernani* in Guritan's placid recital of the fate of earlier dueling opponents (II, iv). The cumulative impression of all these repetitions would seem to be that *Ruy Blas* has nothing much new to offer. Yet, there is a significant difference between this play and those that preceded it, a difference that is concentrated in the comedy of Act IV, in which the most central motifs of Hugo's previous work are brilliantly parodied. Satire is normally the end of a form, although in Hugo's case he would revert to it, for it was too important to his creative patterns to disappear.

The setting is familiar: the darkened "cave" ("Une petite chambre somptueuse et sombre"). It is the demonic Salluste's hideaway, guarded by "deux noirs muets," also of diabolic mien (perhaps a reduction of the two thugs Orfeo and Gaboardo of *Angélo*). The sole window has bars of iron like the "croisées des prisons." The villain has planned to lure the

7. César reciprocates, p. 355.

heroine to her doom in this room. The familiar web imagery is suggested by Ruy Blas's decision to "rompre cette trame," cliché though this phrase be. The villain can run in and out at will, like a spider in its web. He has all the keys to all the locks: "Il peut entrer, sortir, dans l'ombre approcher." In contrast, Ruy Blas is a prisoner of his love and of his lack of understanding of all the machinations of Salluste.

Suddenly into this cave bursts Don César, the picaresque Bohemian, a comic Ordener plunging into the recesses of Han's cave. He slides down the chimney and by so doing recalls the earlier idea that a hero descends into Hell in order to gain ultimate salvation. But here the context is irresistibly comic, or at least non-heroic, evoking *The Three Little Pigs* or Santa Claus more than rituals of romance or myth. Appearing in the room, rather than brandishing a sword and braving the ogre, he apologizes for his presence saying: "Pardon! ne faites pas attention, je passe" (ii), only to find that he is speaking to an empty room. With the comic tone definitely established (and César's appearance in Act I was comic enough to lead us to expect this humor), he can then proceed to use the language of the hero, both Classic and Romantic. "Recueillons-nous. La solitude est bonne," he soliloquizes. This sounds like the point of departure for a classic tirade as well as for the meditative introspections of a René. But as this phrase is uttered with an "Ouf" after he has flopped into an armchair, the appropriate dignity is somewhat lacking. Next, draping himself in clothing he finds there in order to hide the rags he is wearing (the mock hero), he swears vengeance against his foe but does not even know where his enemy is. The heroic quest is quickly abandoned, however, as he finds himself before a sumptuous feast. He eats and drinks with Rabelaisian gusto and finally provides us with the missing motif of a religious symbol in the cave: he kneels down and embraces the table loaded with food, and then comically calls the table an "autel," and his imitation of the classical custom of asking hospitality is converted into a gastronomic parody of the Communion, as the directions state: "Il boit" and "il mange."

The "hero," "purified" by this "religious" ritual, is then tested. Various lackeys of this land of enchantment, mistaking him for Don Salluste, enter to offer him gold (he grabs it by the handful) and to make cryptic utterances, arrange his clothes, etc. Don César concludes light-heartedly: "Je suis chez Belzébuth." Then there follows the temptation by the "siren," as an old *entremetteuse* arrives to offer him an amorous rendez-vous. The anti-hero is quick to accept. Next he is challenged to a duel by Don Guritan and proves that he is no coward by accepting the challenge and then killing the old (but still formidable) warrior. But the duel is pointless and genuine heroes do not kill without reason. Finally, the chief villain, Don Salluste, arrives to find his plans seemingly thwarted by Don César's intrusion. César at first laughs triumphantly, unafraid of Hugo's spider of fatality:

> Depuis toute la matinée
> Je patauge à travers vos toiles d'araignée.

Now he tries to turn into a real hero. He drops his banter to announce with solemnity:

> D'ailleurs, dans ce palais-prison,
> Je sens quelqu'un en proie à votre trahison.
> Toute intrigue de cour est une échelle double;
> D'un côté, bras liés, morne et le regard trouble,
> Monte le patient; de l'autre le bourreau.
> —Or vous êtes le bourreau nécessairement.

His conclusion is that "Je prétends sauver ceux qu'ici vous perdez." But César cannot qualify as a real hero, since for all his ritual of purification before the test, it was nothing but comic parody. Therefore, he is totally unprepared and is quickly outwitted by the villain and led off to prison by the police, who think him an escaped outlaw. The act is over.[8]

Most critics have agreed that *Ruy Blas* is a well-constructed play. The Glachants concluded years ago: "Il semble que la pièce ait atteint vrai-ment . . . à la perfection des qualités dramatiques compatibles avec ses théories et son tempérament."[9] Albouy tries to establish a triple level of unity, "une réalité historique, une notion morale, une forme d'art."[10] Léon Emery came closest to the center of the play when he described Ruy

8. Jean Gaudon, *Victor Hugo, dramaturge* (Paris, 1955), sees this act as important but takes it perhaps too somberly when he calls it "la victoire de la fatalité" (p. 94). This gloomy view is corrected by J.-B. Barrère, *La Fantaisie de Victor Hugo*, I (Paris, 1949), 334–40.

9. Paul and Victor Glachant, *Essai critique sur le théâtre de Victor Hugo* (Paris, 1902–1903), I, 297.

10. Pierre Albouy, *La Création mythologique chez Victor Hugo* (Paris, 1963), p. 182.

Blas as a man who unconsciously carries the wishes of the people as a divine mission,[11] but none of these critics has made clear that Act IV is no interlude or irrelevancy but that it has a real function. It is essential to understand the difference between Don César's and Ruy Blas's failure to overcome those who are ruining the nation. The true hero faces an evil social structure too strong for him to overcome, but his self-sacrifice is a ritual act that can prepare the future liberation of the nation. Don César's attempt to play the hero riding to the rescue, however, fails because he lacks the redemptive qualities needed. The wider lesson is clear: if the *peuple* is frivolous, like César, it will remain disreputable *populace* and be called Zafari. Only if it achieves a genuine and pure nobility can it be redemptive. This is why the final act reverts to a noble tone. Ruy Blas is showing the true way to the ideal. Despite the hero's death, the conclusion does maintain some sense of optimism for the future, in that the queen pardons the lackey for his love and his deception. This conclusion suggests that in symbolic terms the *peuple* may legitimately aspire to something better and that Hugo is continuing to move slowly in the direction visible in *Marie Tudor* and *Angélo*. He is groping to express his idea that there must be some reconciliation or synthesis between the masses and the pinnacle of power.

To summarize: When Hugo turned to the theater, in his best plays he successfully adapted to the stage the same quest-motifs and images that made the success of *Notre-Dame*. In his poorer dramas, the forms deteriorated in quality, but they are still visible, and they keep the critic's interest by their continuing evolution toward something new. But having by this time exploited the theater as fully as he could, Hugo needed a new medium of expression. On the one hand, he would continue prose fiction in the later novels from *Les Misérables* to *Quatrevingt-Treize* and, in addition, he would try epic poetry. Both of these could liberate him from the confines of the stage and permit the freer play of the imagination. It would also permit him to reintroduce the theme of descent to salvation which had become weakened since the fourth act of *Hernani*. But Hugo liked the theater and he was to make one more attempt at it during these years. He would try to combine it with the epic and so he created that famous "failure," *Les Burgraves*.

11. *Vision et pensée chez Victor Hugo* (Lyon, n.d. [1939]), p. 31.

CHAPTER V

TOWARD EPIC AND MYTH

FROM THE EARLY POETRY
TO *LES BURGRAVES*

CRITICS ARE in unanimous agreement that Hugo's vision pushed him steadily in the direction of the epic and mythic in his literary expression, but much still needs to be done in order to show exactly how this transformation took place. As the origins of this development lie in Hugo's formative years, it is necessary at this point to go back in time and study Hugo's earliest poetic efforts. We make no pretense here of any encyclopedic exhaustiveness but will select those passages that can shed light on the poet's developing patterns of imagery as they lead to *Les Burgraves*. We shall discover that Hugo's early Classicism is not so far removed from his later mythmaking as might at first be supposed.

In the young Victor's "Trois cahiers de vers français" (1815–1816),[1] an early poem, "Bonaparte," likens the dictator to those early usurpers, the Titans of Greek mythology. This parallel is obviously made within the tradition of French Neoclassical doctrine, but as the struggle between Zeus and the Titans is the image on which *Les Burgraves* will be based many years later, and as more generally it shows Hugo's desire to transform man into myth, this verse (one hesitates to call it poetry) takes on special significance:

> Telle on vit des Titans la troupe audacieuse
> Elever jusqu'au ciel sa tête ambitieuse:
> Trois fois, traînant des rocs, sa fureur entassa
> Péléon sur Olympe, Olympe sur Ossa,
> Trois fois, le dieux vainqueur, d'un coup de son tonnerre,
> De leurs corps renversés couvrit au loin la terre. (p. 23)

Within the framework of this struggle, Hugo starts to use images that will have a long career. One of these, mentioned above, is the displaced rock.

1. As the E.I.N. is not fully satisfactory for Hugo's early works, all references to the lyric poetry prior to *Les Burgraves* are from the fine edition of Pierre Albouy, *Œuvres poétiques de Victor Hugo* (*Avant l'exil, 1802–1851*), (Paris, 1964), in the Pléiade edition.

In another part of the poem, it appears again, this time in a natural setting:

> Tel, quand, du haut des monts blanchis par les frimas,
> Entraîné par les vents, un roc avec fracas,
> Se détache, et, roulant sur des gouffres de glace,
> Bondit, tombe, et s'accroît: son horrible masse,
> Faisant voler au loin d'horribles tourbillons,
> Va bientôt de sa chute engloutir les vallons. . . .(p. 22)

In both passages, there is associated with the rock the idea of a fall. We are now in a position to recall that Han made use of rocks against the insurgent miners, and that the rebellious slaves acted similarly against pursuing troops in *Bug-Jargal*. It is likely that the beam thrown and the lead poured by Quasimodo from Notre-Dame fit the same pattern, although more distantly. In verse, of course, there is no need for verisimilitude. The rocks can "submerge valleys" without any sense of absurdity.

Another image pattern that one should certainly expect to find, and does, is the cave. When Hugo translated fragments of the *Aeneid*, he selected the lair of the Giant Cacus whom Hercules overcomes in the course of his labors:

> Là, dans un antre immense, au jour inaccessible,
> Vivait l'affreux Cacus, noir géant, monstre horrible.
> A ses portes pendaient des crânes entr'ouverts,
> Ses meurtres, chaque jour, faisaient trembler la terre. (p. 83)

This text dates from early 1817 and appears to be part of Hugo's inspiration for *Han d'Islande*. But in trying to fit this language to a scene set in time and space, Norway of 1699, Hugo had to exercise care. Han cannot be of giant size, even if the simple miners imagine him to be, for biological monstrosities belong to pure legend or science fiction. But in poetry Hugo could soar as far as he liked into the mythical. Indeed, most of the translations of the classics that he did at this period show this interest. Of these, "Achéménide" is of particular interest:

> Encelade, dit-on, sous ces rocs obscurcis
> Cache ses vastes flancs, que la foudre a noircis;
> Le poids du mont l'écrase, et sa brûlante haleine
> Chasse au loin les rochers qu'il soulève avec peine. (p. 123)

97

The rocks are now linked specifically to the legends of the Titans, although in the most traditional fashion. A slightly more novel poem, "Promenade nocturne," also of 1817, associates the Titans with nature:

> Ici, se déployant en longs amphithéâtres,
> Des rochers menaçants, confusément épars,
> Obscurcissent les dieux de leurs cimes grisâtres,
>   Que chargent d'éternels brouillards.
> Des pins, au noir feuillage, aussi vieux que les mondes,
> Hérissent leurs sommets neigeux;
> Sous les replis obscurs de leurs voûtes profondes,
>   Mugissent les vents orageux;
> Et, sous leurs sombres flancs, des lacs marécageux
> Balancent lentement leurs limoneuses ondes.
>   Leur aspect inspire horreur . . .
> On croit voir ces Titans. . . . (p. 86)

Here the rocks, "voûtes," and forests are accompanied by fog; all will appear later in *Les Burgraves*.

Ogres or Titans, however, do not exist without a hero who appears to overcome them. In the case of Cacus, the avenger is Hercules; with the Titans, it is Zeus. The idea of vengeance permits a political dimension when Hugo transposes these motifs to modern history. In "La Mort de Louis XVII" the avenger is a divine angel sent by God to punish Anarchy and Revolution. The political dimension in no way reduces the transcendent imagery. Phrases like "glaive éternelle," "résonnait de chaînes et d'épées," "agita trois fois son armure terrible" accompany "l'Eternel" who crushes the "hydre" of revolution, described as Cain and Prometheus rolled into one (p. 144). One must not forget that Prometheus was a Titan.

All these images of struggle, Titans, rocks, forests, with a political dimension added, appear in the poem "Les Derniers Bardes." The tyrant Edward invades Scotland:

> Les bataillons épais en colonnes s'allongent,
> Ils marchent; et leurs cris, que mille éclairs prolongent,
>   Se mêlent au long bruit des vents.
> Tout-à-coup, sur un roc dont la lugubre cime
> S'incline vers l'armée et menace l'abîme,

Debout, foulant aux pieds les ténébreux brouillards,
    Agitant leurs robes funèbres,
Aux lueurs de l'éclair qui perce les ténèbres,
    Paraissent de sombres vieillards.
    Tels sur ces roches nébuleuses,
On a vu s'élever, dans les nuits orageuses,
    Les tristes géants de l'hiver.

The chief bard,

    Un vieux héros des temps déjà passés.
Dans ses yeux brille encore l'éclair de sa jeunesse,

curses the invaders, likening their army to a wild torrent whose "fougue"
undermines a mountainside.

Mais qu'au sommet des monts sa fureur turbulente
Ait miné d'un vieux roc la base chancelante;
Des neiges, des glaçons, pressant l'énorme amas,
    Le rocher déraciné roule,
Et dans sa vaste chute entraînant les frimas,
    Grossit quand le torrent s'écroule.
Le mont dont il descend s'ébranle et retentit,
Masse immense! il bondit de montagne en montagne,
    Et tombe enfin dans la campagne
    Sur le torrent qu'il engloutit. (pp. 166–69)

The images, constantly repeated in a context of chaos and judgment of
the wicked, concretize the idea that evil brings about a mighty collapse
that buries the guilty. This idea will recur in more sophisticated form in
Les Burgraves, not to mention *La Légende des siècles.*

Yet even with the liberation provided by the poetic form, in a sense
Hugo was still limited by space and time. The story of Edward is a
narrative set in something resembling a real place, and Hugo seems to
have felt cramped by this restriction. In the preface to the 1822 edition of
his *Odes,* he longs for more freedom: "Au reste, le domaine de la poésie
est illimité. Sous le monde réel, il existe un monde idéal, qui se montre
resplendissant à l'œil de ceux que des méditations graves ont accoutumés
à voir dans les choses plus que les choses" (p. 265). This is not a novel

aesthetic concept. What is of interest for us is the manner in which Hugo moves back and forth with his images from the *monde réel* to the *monde idéal,* thereby enriching each from the other's domain. He puts natural imagery into the "sky" and "celestial" imagery on earth, while he elaborates thematically the fundamental pattern that we have seen in the previous chapters: that the thrust upward fails, individually or politically, and that like the rocks of the mountain, some great edifice falls. Hugo's technique will become clear if we analyze parts of a few typical poems.

The early ode "La Bande noire" (1824), a plea for the conservation of the ancient ruins of France, describes real castles but adds to them words like "flamme," "Dieu," "voilées de mystères," "rayon," "ciel," "ailes," "régions nouvelles." We quote part of the text:

> Parvis où notre orgueil s'enflamme!
> Maisons de Dieu! manoirs des rois!
> Temples que gardait l'oriflamme,
> Palais que protégeait la croix!
>
> . . . .
>
> Murs voilés de tant de mystères
> Murs brillants de tant de splendeurs!
>
> Oui, je crois, quand je vous contemple,
> Des héros entendre l'adieu.
> Souvent, dans les débris du temple,
> Brille comme un rayon du dieu
>
> . . . .
>
> Souvent ma muse aventurière
>
> . . . .
>
> Ceignit la cuirasse guerrière
> Et l'écharpe des paladins;
> S'armant d'un fer rongé de rouille
>
> . . . .
>
> Et, vers des régions nouvelles,
> Pour hâter son coursier sans ailes,
> Osa chausser l'éperon d'or.
>
> J'aimais le manoir dont la route
> Cache dans les bois ses détours,

Et dont la porte sous la voûte
S'enfonce entre deux larges tours.

Aujourd'hui, parmi les cascades,
Sous le dôme des bois touffus,
Les piliers, les sveltes arcades,
Hélas, penchent leur front confus;
Les forteresses écroulées

. . . .

Courbent leur tête de granit.

In a later strophe, the poet concludes:

Si ce ne sont plus que des ombres,
Ce sont des ombres de géants!

The concrete imagery of the castles is blended with vocabulary from an ideal world, or, to put it differently, Hugo has projected the "real" castles out of reality into the transcendent, but the verse does not lose the sense of association with a social class, the feudal aristocracy. Thus as the buildings disappear into the heavens, the social class crumbles at the same time.

Hugo later used this technique to warn against the ambition of Napoleon Bonaparte, toward whom he was still somewhat hostile in 1825:

Montez donc, et tentez ces zones inconnues!
Vous croyiez fuir aux cieux . . . vous vous perdez aux nues!
Le mont change à vos yeux d'aspect et de tableaux;
C'est un gouffre, obscurci de sapins centenaires,
        Où les torrents et les tonnerres
        Croisent des éclairs et des flots. ("Les Deux Iles")

Again Hugo has started in the real world and projected his vision into the empyrean, even if in this case his metaphors become mixed. The sense of political and moral judgment is clear, too, again in a context where the upward soaring leads to disaster. Hugo makes the judgment explicit later in the poem:

Voilà l'image de la gloire:
D'abord un prisme éblouissant,

101

Puis un miroir expiatoire,
Où la pourpre paraît du sang.

But the interesting part of this section is that Hugo imagines the heavens in terms of natural imagery right out of "Les Derniers Bardes," with its "sapins centenaires" and its "torrents et tonnerres." Here he has enriched the celestial with the earthly.

The reference to Bonaparte (and there are others) provides a link between myth and history. Earlier the Corsican was described as a Titan, as Prometheus, and as Cain. But as a historical figure, he is of this world. Hugo therefore was in a position to transfer his imagery once again back into the real world. He did this in "La Mort de Louis XVII," so it comes as no surprise to find in *Cromwell,* within a context of "reality," the protagonist musing on his power in this language:

Au moindre vent qui change, qui vibre au moindre bruit,
L'édifice effrayant s'écroule, et, dans la nuit
Un trône, un peuple, un monde ainsi s'évanouit.

In contrary fashion, language referring to a feudal social structure occasionally appears in an otherwise purely "poetic" description:

Mon bonheur s'éleva comme un château de fées
Avec ses murs de nacre, aux mobiles couleurs,
Ses tours, ses portes d'or, ses pièges, ses trophées . . .
Puis soudain tout fuyait. . . .
Un tombeau dominait le palais écroulé. ("Ode Dixième," 1822)

The constant reworking of the imagery leads to a beautiful creation in "Soleils Couchants" of *Les Feuilles d'automne.* Space permits citing only those passages that clearly continue the imagery in question. The subject matter is the clouds in the sky, but the language or imagery is that of our earth, of buildings on earth and feudalism, a reversal of the pattern of "La Bande noire." We have italicized the words that we have been following:

J'aime les soirs sereins et beaux, j'aime les soirs,
Soit qu'ils dorent le front des *antiques manoirs*
  Ensevelis dans les feuillages;

102

Soit que la *brume* au loin s'allonge en bancs de feu;
Soit que mille *rayons* brisent dans un ciel bleu
    A des archipels de nuages.
Oh! regardez le ciel! cent nuages mouvants,
Amoncelés là-haut sous le souffle des vents,
    Groupent leurs formes inconnues;
Sous leurs flots par moments *flamboie un pâle éclair,*
Comme si tout à coup quelque *géant de l'air*
    Tirait son glaive dans les nues.

Puis se dresse un *palais;* puis l'air tremble et tout fuit.
L'édifice effrayant des nuages détruit
    S'écroule en *ruines* pressées;
Il jonche au loin le ciel, et ses cônes vermeils
Pendent, la pointe en bas, sur nos têtes, pareils
    A des *montagnes renversées.*[2]

Ces nuages de plomb, d'or, de cuivre, de fer,
Où l'ouragan, la trombe, et la foudre, et l'enfer
    Dorment avec de sourds murmures,
C'est Dieu qui les suspend en foule aux cieux profonds,
Comme un guerrier qui pend aux poutres des plafonds
    Ses *retentissantes armures.*[3]

The poet then urges: "regardez à travers ses voiles," and he concludes: "un mystère est au fond de leur grave beauté," both expressions found in "La Bande noire." The poet-narrator seems eager (as was Bonaparte in "Les Deux Iles") to fly to the heights of Heaven:

Et l'œil épouvanté, par delà tous nos cieux,
Sur une île de l'air au vol audacieux,
    Dans l'éther libre aventurée,
L'œil croit jusqu'au ciel monter, monter toujours,
Avec ses escaliers, ses ponts, ses grandes tours,
    Quelque Babel démesurée!

2. Cf. "Les Derniers Bardes."
3. Cf. "A. M. Alphonse de Lamartine" (1825):

    Soyons comme un soldat qui revient sans murmure
    Suspendre à son chevet un vain reste d'armure. (*Odes et Ballades*)

One hardly need add that the Tower of Babel was destroyed, that the colossal edifice fell, like Bonaparte, because of something evil in its nature. Hugo's patterns are running true to form.

Conversely, a poem from *Les Feuilles d'automne* that has only recently received any serious attention,[4] "La Pente de la rêverie," makes explicit what we have been deducing from the narrative patterns: the way from the *monde réel* to the *monde idéal* is not up but down. In the 1822 preface to the *Odes,* Hugo had already suggested this by saying that the ideal world lay under ("sous") the real world. But the way is perilous, as is any descent into an underworld:

> La spirale est profonde, et quand on y descend,
> Sans cesse se prolonge et va s'élargissant,
> Et pour avoir touché quelque énigme fatale,
> De ce voyage obscur souvent on revient pâle.

Hugo undertakes the quest anyway:

> Mon esprit plongea donc sous ce flot inconnu,
> Au profond de l'abîme il nagea seul et nu
>
> . . . .
>
> Soudain il s'en revint avec un cri terrible,
> Ebloui, haletant, stupide, épouvanté,
> Car il avait au fond trouvé l'éternité.

A few years later, in 1839, his poem "Puits de l'Inde" (*Les Rayons et les Ombres*) develops the idea even further, uniting the theme of dangerous descent, massive stone, and the spider with a frightful religious experience:

> Puits de l'Inde! tombeaux! monuments constellés!
> Vous dont l'intérieur n'offre aux regards troublés
> Qu'un amas tournoyant de marches et de rampes,
> Froids cachots, corridors où rayonnent des lampes,
> Poutres où l'araignée a tendu ses longs fils,
> Blocs ébauchant partout de sinistres profils
>
> . . . .

---

4. See J.-B. Barrère, *Victor Hugo, l'homme et l'œuvre* (Paris, 1952), pp. 74–75, although the poem was briefly admired by Charles Renouvier, *Victor Hugo, le poète* (Paris, 1900), Chap. XI, p. 208.

Cryptes qui remplissez d'horreur religieuse
Votre voûte sans fin, morne et prodigieuse!

This language is that of the past in that it echoes the corridors of the
Bastille of *Notre-Dame,* but it is more that of the later *La Légende des
siècles,* and were it to be transferred to the stage, it would suggest the
Caveau Perdu of the last act of *Les Burgraves* into which the frightened
characters must descend to find the Truth and to attain salvation. More
generally, as we shall see shortly, these patterns of imagery permeate the
entire play.

Hugo grew toward an epic and mythic vision not only through poetry
but through prose as well, and we shall go back in time once more to
follow this development. We mentioned in an earlier chapter that Hugo
was in conscious rebellion against the mythological language of the
Classical epics. After his early imitations, or rather translations, of Virgil,
tired of the banality of neoclassical imagery, Hugo made a real attempt to
avoid it. This negative attitude helps explain why one finds little sympathy for these traditional forms in *Notre-Dame.* Through Pierre Gringoire's morality play which opens the narrative, with its heavy allegory
and official Jupiter and Venus, Hugo gently makes fun of Classicism:
"C'était en réalité un fort bel ouvrage, et dont il nous semble qu'on pourrait encore fort bien tirer parti aujourd'hui, moyennant quelques arrange-
ments. L'exposition, un peu longue et un peu vide, c'est-à-dire dans les
règles, était simple" (p. 19). The anachronism is amusing. But despite
his hostility to any Classicism, there is discernible even here, perhaps
unknown to the author himself, some suggestion of turning back to it.
Hugo openly associates Quasimodo with Haephestus, who was a hunchback, limped, and was greeted by the laughter of the gods. Quasimodo is
the subject of "un rire tellement inextinguible qu'Homère eût pris tous
ces manants pour des dieux" (p. 34). Later he is seen portrayed as a
smith at his forge, melting the lead that he then pours upon the assailants
of the cathedral. Now this Haephestus loves Esmeralda, the "goddess" of
the *truands,* who are thought in the popular mind to worship Jupiter (p.
175), a fact which combined with her beauty makes her a sort of Venus.
She in turn loves the soldier Phœbus, a fusion of Apollo (pp. 84, 211)
and Mars. Indeed, in the novel's central image, the fly soars toward "le
soleil de mars" (p. 232). Thus there is a delicate suggestion of the rivalry

105

between Mars and Vulcan for Venus, to use the Latin names. But even if this is the case, the possibilities of myth remain superficial and undeveloped in *Notre-Dame*. They are even to some extent contradictory, for Quasimodo is a cyclops as well (pp. 39, 190) and Esmeralda is purer than any Venus.

Hugo's more profound attempt at aggrandizement into myth was not through the individual, even a semi-mythic one like Han, but through the masses whose grandeur and power could create an epic tone without losing human or even historical verisimilitude. The swarms of rebellious slaves in *Bug-Jargal* and the beggars of *Notre-Dame* solve this problem (well before Zola) very neatly, for the heroes can not only be of normal size, but also reasonable in their actions. And if there are individual heroes distinguished from the average man, their epic stature is derived from the grandiose quality of their passions or sense of honor. But a special problem exists if we consider the restrictions of the stage. Epic passions are excellent here, but crowds are clumsy in a proscenium box, and the play can last only three hours, which gives little time to develop epic sweep. In *Cromwell,* Hugo's impatience with these limitations led him to burst apart the time span. In *Marie Tudor,* we recall, the *peuple* is a character that nearly appears on stage en masse, and the scope of the action is at times epic. The play would no doubt be more successful as a film. While Hugo submitted more tamely to the restrictions of the theater in the other plays of the 1830's, he would try to fuse them in one final effort. As he put it in the preface to *Les Burgraves:* "commencer par l'épopée et finir par le drame" (p. 494).

The development of an epic tone in prose is most visible, prior to 1842, in Hugo's account of his trips along the Rhine, which he had visited in 1838, 1839, and 1840, and published under the title *Le Rhin.* It is in these letters that he reveals his fascination with the atmosphere and legends of the area that unite the epic and the fantastic. A fine example of Hugo's imaginative method of transforming even humdrum reality into some fantasy of horror is found in his description of a humble fishing net in the Rhine:

> De temps en temps on entrevoit, à demi cachée sous les épines et les osiers et comme embusquée au bord du Rhin, une espèce d'immense araignée formée par deux longues perches souples et courbes, croisées transversalement, réunies à leur milieu et à leur point

culminant par un gros nœud rattaché à un lévier, et plongeant leurs quatre pointes dans l'eau. C'est une araignée en effet.

Par instant, dans cette solitude et dans ce silence, le levier mystérieux s'ébranle, et l'on voit la hideuse bête se soulever lentement, tenant entre ses pattes sa toile, au milieu de laquelle saute et se tord un beau saumon d'argent. (Lettre XVII, pp. 140–41)

Giving another example of the transformation of the reality, referring to a castle, Hugo writes: "Ce n'est plus un donjon . . . c'est un énorme madrépore que pénètre et que remplit inextricablement de toutes ses antennes, de tous ses pieds, de tous ses doigts . . . la végétation, ce polype effrayant" (pp. 321–22). We have chosen these two examples among many to show that the spider imagery of *Notre-Dame* is not dead but just beginning a rich transformation that would lead to the wilder creations of *Les Travailleurs de la mer* and to "Le Vautour" in *Dieu*.

It is also in *Le Rhin* that Hugo told the tale of the Mäuserthurm. Can *Les Burgraves* be a disguised dramatic rendition of this story? The question is pertinent, for the name Hatto appears in the play as well as in the legend. Oddly enough, J.-P. Weber makes rather little use of Hugo's theater in his essay, pleading the limitations of space. Professor Russell is content to note the obvious connection: "Ce burgrave possède la cruauté de l'archvêque Hatto de la Tour des Rats à Bingen. Le burg d'Heppenheff est pénétré de l'atmosphère d'horreur et de réprobation qui plane sur la Mäuserthurm."[5] One can show additional parallels. The barons on the heights dominate the local population as brutally as had the archbishop of legend. The play's Hatto callously orders men hanged, cities pillaged, merchants ambushed (pp. 526–27). Though not a priest, he does violate an oath sworn on the Bible (p. 528). The theme of fire, the "ciel embrasé," is present, too, if only in imagery. The heroine, watching the sunset, exclaims:

> Oui, le couchant s'enflamme.
> Nous sommes en automne et nous sommes au soir.
> Partout la feuille tombe et le bois devient noir.
>
> . . . .
>
> Les vitres du hameau, là-bas, sont tout en feu. (p. 516)

5. Olga W. Russell, *Etude historique et critique des "Burgraves" de Victor Hugo, avec variantes inédites et lettres inédites* (Paris, 1962), p. 174.

The theme of the "naissance monstrueuse" of the avenging rats of the legend is expressed through Frédéric Barberousse, who has been sleeping in a cave under the village. This sleeping giant awakens, penetrates into the castle, and reduces the burgraves' power. The other part of Weber's thesis, the face in the cathedral, is somewhat less clear but may find a counterpart in Job, who haunts the castle as Quasimodo haunts Notre-Dame. At any rate, the play does incorporate elements of the legend and in so doing adds to the mythical tone of Hugo's creation. The dramatic element of poetic justice inherent in legend and play provides the necessary motivation for the action.

But Hugo's immense assimilative powers do not stop here. There is still another legend that Hugo tells in *Le Rhin*, "La Légende du beau Pécopin et de la belle Bauldour," which comprises forty-three pages in the E.I.N. The story as Hugo tells it is already transformed from its original sources,[6] and because of its role in forming *Les Burgraves*, we summarize it here:

Pécopin and Bauldour are in love and betrothed. They have all the traditional virtues of romance heroes, except that the former loves hunting to excess. One day, he passes an old man who asks him whether he hears what the birds are saying. Pécopin makes fun of him. Now of course it is very dangerous for any questing hero to refuse to listen to little old men who appear to give aid. More alarming still is his indifference to his failure to achieve oneness with nature and understanding the birds' songs. This failure to pass the test bodes ill. Soon Pécopin is swept off into many adventures that need not detain us here. Yet all during this time he yearns for Bauldour. Toward the climax of the narrative, we learn that "un soir, [il] arriva à l'entrée d'un bois" (p. 203) near the Rhine. He enters the woods and after a while, "le sentier qu'il suivait se perdit." He wonders where he is and as he vainly seeks his way out, a flock of wild ducks passes overhead in ominous presage. Then he hears the dread song of the dwarf Roulon. Pécopin has stumbled into the fatal "bois des pas perdus," from which no traveler ever emerges. This dwarf inhabits the summit of a mountain and takes pleasure in causing the destruction of passers-by. But hope appears when a lordly though disturbing figure ("il y avait je ne sais quoi d'étrange, de vague et de lumineux dans ce visage pâle qui souriait, éclairé de la dernière

6. J.-B. Barrère, *La Fantaisie de Victor Hugo*, I (Paris, 1949), 277.

lueur du crépuscule," p. 205) offers him escape and promises his safe return to Bauldour if Pécopin will but hunt with him for the duration of this one night. In a wild hunting ride, suggestive of Hugo's own *Mazeppa* or *L'Aigle du casque* or of Flaubert's *La Légende de St. Julien L'Hospitalier*, they pass through thick fogs ("tout à coup une brume épaisse l'enveloppa," p. 210). The ride finally ends "devant la façade d'un sombre et colossal édifice" (p. 212). "C'était une maison forte comme une citadelle, une citadelle magnifique comme un palais, un palais menaçant comme une caverne, une caverne muette comme un tombeau" (p. 213). Inside the enchanted castle, Nimrod, "un géant d'airain qui était vivant,"[7] sits on a throne surrounded by all the famous hunters of history. As a feast is served, Pécopin defies them:

> Je vous défends de faire un pas; ou par la mort et que Dieu m'aide!
> je vous apprendrai à tous, même à toi, l'homme de bronze, ce que
> pèse sur la tête d'un fantôme le soulier de fer d'un vivant! Je suis
> dans la caverne des ombres, mais je prétends faire à ma fantaisie
> . . . de[s] choses réelles et terribles. (p. 218).

But then the sun rises and the demonic castle and its specters vanish. Pécopin collapses and awakens before the castle of his beloved. Alas, the end is ironic, for the "night's" hunt had lasted one hundred years. Bauldour is now an ancient crone, while Pécopin is still young.

Certain parts of this story seem to have combined with the other strands of the fabric that we have been examining to inspire the composition of the play. This legend is particularly connected with the "Prologue" to the first version of *Les Burgraves*, published in the *Reliquat* of the E.I.N.[8] In this prologue the curtain rises to reveal "une gorge de montagne que couvre en ce moment un épais brouillard" (p. 585). The setting is a forest by the Rhine, where a convoy of merchants has halted at nightfall, and it resembles the locale where Pécopin entered the "bois des pas perdus." The merchants emphasize the presence of the fog: "Le brouillard cache tout," "Quel brouillard!" they exclaim. This theme of

7. The theme of the statue appears frequently with this period in Hugo's life. "La Statue" and "Au Statuaire David" (*Les Rayons et les Ombres*) develop this idea, which will be continued later in *La Légende des siècles* with actual living statues ("La Paternité") and seeming ones (e.g., "Eviradnus"). In *Les Burgraves*, Job and Barberousse will anticipate these later figures and by their commanding presence help in the creation of an epic tone.
8. Pp. 585–95.

the fog is of course nearly impossible to realize on the stage and is absent from the final version of the play. But it will be an important image in the later prose fiction, where its function will be more apparent than it is here, where it serves merely to mask the castle perched on the peak. In the play proper, this castle of Heppenheff is described as standing "inaccessible au milieu des nuées," the fog replaced by clouds to suggest both unreality and a world far removed from our own.

To return to the prologue, after the setting there follows the exposition of the situation which recounts the earlier feuding between Barberousse and the burgraves. Guanhumara, the hag of the play, appears as an aged witch gathering wood. When asked by the travelers where they are, her cryptic answer explains nothing. One asks her "Que regardes-tu là?" to which she replies: "Cet oiseau [cf. the ducks] qui s'envole.—Que nous présage-t-il?—Rien de bon" (p. 589). Soon someone arrives to announce that behind the fog there is a castle described in terms that evoke the enchanted castle visited by Pécopin at the end of his ride (the ride of course cannot be captured on the stage because of the limitations of the theater as well as the exigencies of the plot). The master of Heppenheff is a demonic figure:

> . . . le maître, homme fantasque,
> Ayant changé de nom comme on change de masque,
> Y revint. Depuis lors, du démon possédés,
> Ces murs mystérieux ne sont plus regardés
> Que par des yeux troublés d'horreur et d'épouvante. (p. 590)

The travelers soon learn that they have fallen into a trap set by the burgrave Hatto (who has, interestingly, "les instincts de Nemrod," p. 492) just as the dwarf of legend Roulon takes pleasure in catching the unwary. Even Pécopin's brief illusion of a happy ending is paralleled when a soldier appears to offer to help them escape, but they are caught before they can flee.

If we understand this background to the play, as we leave the prologue and move to the play proper, we can feel more keenly its legendary origins of a demonic nature.[9] First, the legendary castle was described as

9. That this pattern of the prologue is typical of legend and folk tale generally is clear if one reads the opening paragraph of *The Six Swans* in *Grimm's Fairy Tales:* "Once upon a time, a certain King was hunting in a great forest, and he chased a wild beast so eagerly that none of his attendants could follow him. When

citadel, palace, cave, and tomb, and this same descending progression is to be observed in the play. The military motifs and references to Heppenheff's fortress-like nature open the drama, then we are treated, even if briefly, to the orgies of the occupants (the palace motif), and in the last part we descend into the Caveau Perdu, which becomes a tomb. Within the castle itself, the spectral quality is easily felt. The first scene is in a *galerie des portraits*, "un logis par les spectres hanté." Job the centenarian (an echo of the theme of one hundred years) appears as "une figure pétrifiée" (p. 529), somewhat evocative of the bronze Nimrod. But this spectral castle "exists" in the play's reality, and what the spectator sees is a concretization of legend and of Hugo's earlier poetic imagery. From a poem like "Les Derniers Bardes" comes the idea of the old man perched on a crag. The torrent along which the army wended its way reappeared in the torrent of Habibrah's cave and is here the river into which Fosco (Job) threw his half-brother. From an architectural poem like "La Bande noire" with words like *manoir, piliers, forteresse*, we pass to the concrete reality of these objects before our eyes on the stage. And from "Soleils couchants" comes the giant who "tirait son glaive" and whose "retentissantes armures" rang through the poem. In *Les Burgraves*, the décor of Act II describes "Armures complètes adossées à tous les piliers" and in the action, swords are drawn and glitter in the light.

The setting, then, is one where not only is there room for drama but where also the epic and even the mythic can flourish. These larger dimensions are intensified, of course, by Hugo's addition of Biblical references. Surely the key character Job cannot fail to evoke the Old Testament hero even in the most casual reader or viewer, and Olga Russell's study of the sources of the play proves that Hugo refreshed his memory of Scripture from the Genoude translation, incorporating many phrases of it into his play.[10] Not only the names but the themes of the

---

evening drew near he stopped and looked around him, and then saw that he had lost his way. He sought a way out, but could find none. Then he perceived an aged woman with a head which nodded perpetually, who came towards him, but she was a witch. 'Good woman,' said he to her, 'can you not show me the way through the forest?' 'Oh, yes, Lord King,' she answered, 'that I certainly can, but on one condition, and if you do not fulfill that, you will never get out of the forest and will die of hunger in it.' "

10. Russell, chap. VI, *passim*. Later, in *William Shakespeare*, Hugo wrote: "Tout le poème de Job est le développement de cette idée: la grandeur qu'on trouve au fond de l'abîme" (pp. 24–25). This is also the case for Job of *Les Burgraves*.

brevity of human life, the judgment of God on man's pride, the expiation of guilt, and finally of God's favor bestowed on the faithful find some echo in *Les Burgraves*, even though the Biblical Job was not guilty of the murder of his half-brother. Thus these three levels of the play, the dramatic, the epic, and the mythic, merit separate analysis.

The *drame* of this play encompasses the loves, hopes, and jealousies of the principal characters and in this manner creates the type of plot that Hugo had dealt with in *Hernani* and other plays. The hero is another Gennaro, an orphan, a "pauvre capitaine . . . de race incertaine" (p. 517), resembling more or less the typical hero of romance, like Ordener. He loves Regina[11] and dramatic tension arises from the fact that her life is endangered by the hag Guanhumara, who is poisoning her in order to avenge herself, albeit indirectly, on Job. A happy ending seems assured early in the play when Job "adopts" the noble Otbert as his son, to replace his long-lost Georges. In actual fact, Otbert *is* Job's son, although the father does not learn this fact until late in the play. Job gives Otbert a fief or two and promises Regina to him and not to the vicious Hatto who desires her. But to save Regina from poisoning, Otbert has already agreed to kill for Guanhumara. When Job gives his son and his beloved a chance to flee the castle, to be married in a nearby town, Otbert is tempted to head toward this "éden radieux" (p. 549) of happiness, but feeling obliged to honor his promise to the hag, he refuses the direct voyage to Heaven, and like an Orpheus must descend into Hell to save Regina. The Hell is the Caveau Perdu of the third part. Here he discovers that the man he is to kill is his own father, Job. If he refuses, Regina, again in a coma from a magic potion (Hugo does overuse poison as a plot device!), will die.

This dramatic line crosses with the personal loves and hates of Frédéric Barberousse, Job, and Guanhumara, where we encounter the familiar theme of the "frères ennemis." In *Han d'Islande*, there was the rivalry of Orugix and Musdœmon; in *Bug-Jargal*, Pierrot and Léopold called each other "Frère"; in *Notre-Dame* Claude Frollo, thinking of his brother Jehan, says to himself: "Caïn, qu'as-tu fait de ton frère?" (p. 398). In *Ruy Blas*, Don César and the titular hero call each other brothers, and in the unfinished play *Les Jumeaux* (1839), the theme appears so obses-

11. Again the celestial name, renewing Doña *Sol*, and *Marie* de Neubourg of earlier plays. The word Regina suggests "Maria regina coeli."

sively that, if we may believe Baudouin, the play remained unfinished because its author's own feelings of guilt over the insanity of his brother Eugène (who died in 1837) came too near to the surface to be tolerable, and Hugo's eye trouble was a displacement of this psychic disturbance.[12] Perhaps this is so, but certainly the theme of the hostile brothers provides the crime in *Les Burgraves* and with it the need for expiation. In the wildly intricate plot of the play, Job had, when a young man under the name of Donato, tried to kill his half-brother Fosco (who later turns out to be Barberousse) and had thrown him into the river. He did this foul deed out of jealousy over the girl Ginevra, and then revenged himself on her by selling her into slavery. She in her turn has come back unrecognized as the crone Guanhumara. Her revenge is to have Job killed by his own beloved son, whom she herself had stolen years previously and had then reintroduced into the castle as Otbert. Over these many years, Job has returned to the scene of his crime (the Caveau Perdu) each night to pray for forgiveness of his crime.[13] Thus a pattern was set: while he prospered materially and rose to power, he declined morally. The possibilities here for vertical imagery are plentiful. But it turned out that the crime was not absolute. Fosco did not die but recovered, and the two brothers meet and are reconciled in the final scene, in which their antagonism is resolved by Job's complete submission. Guanhumara, hatred incarnate, who has uttered Satanic comments like "Je vais prendre ton âme" (p. 524), is unable to convert her hatred to love again and therefore must die to resolve the tension, after once more rescuing Regina. Hatred yields to love at the final curtain. Fatality is destroyed once more as Hugo continues to develop an optimistic vision of the world.

The second level, and indeed perhaps the most important one, is the epic, one of whose principal characteristics has traditionally been the political drama of national unification, which is precisely the theme of this play. Job and his family represent the regional power of the nobles along the Rhine. In the castle live four generations, "L'aïeul, le père, le fils, le petit-fils; faire de toute cette famille comme le symbole palpitant et

---

12. Charles Baudouin, *Psychanalyse de Victor Hugo* (Genève, 1943), p. 16.
13. Victor Brombert, "Victor Hugo, la prison et l'espace," *Revue des Sciences humaines*, CXVII (Jan.–Mars, 1965), p. 70, observes astutely that on the psychological plane the *caveau* represents remorse, and in a wider context, a jail is the interior of a man. He cites "C'est de son propre cœur qu'il est prisonnier" (*Légende des siècles*, p. 336).

complet de l'expiation; mettre sur la tête de l'aïeul le crime de Caïn, dans le cœur du père les instincts de Nemrod, dans l'âme du fils les vices de Sardanapale," wrote Hugo in his preface (p. 492), predicting that the fourth will be even worse. While the first two generations have grandeur and nobility despite their crimes, the latter two "amoindris par leurs vices croissants, vont s'enfonçant dans les ténèbres" (p. 493). This degeneration is not only familial and personal but also political. What was once great regional power has degenerated and become mere banditry.[14]

The evil burgraves are symbolized by their towering fortress. Job, in his speech of welcome to the "beggar" Barberousse in disguise, sums up their position and their attitude:

> Vous a-t-on dit qu'il est l'asile de tout brave,
> Qu'il fait du riche un pauvre, et du maître un esclave;
> Et qu'au-dessus des ducs, des rois, des empereurs,
> Aux yeux de l'Allemagne en proie à leurs fureurs,
> Il dresse sa tour, comme un défi de haine. . . . (p. 535)

From this mountain fastness the warlords go out to kidnap and pillage. Therefore, this tower of hatred must fall, but Hugo had had enough of any such activity *on the stage* with the flaming tower collapsing in *Amy Robsart*. His solution of this problem was to relegate the event to an earlier occasion when Frédéric had humbled the burgraves in a war. Therefore, destruction of their castles appears only in the exposition, which, free of the limitations of the stage, can mingle the language of politics with that of legend and poetry. Referring to these earlier battles, Hugo recreates his poetic imagery from the earlier years:

> Souvent, dans l'ombre et la fumée,
> Le château, pris enfin, s'écroulait sur l'armée. (p. 513)

The smoke of battle is but a new form of the fog that we found in the legend of Pécopin and in the clouds that surround Heppenheff in the prologue, and all these variations on an image have their antecedents in the Scottish fogs or clouds of sunset of the earlier poems. The castle itself

14. This sense of degeneration, or of shrinking in heroic stature, was one of Hugo's concerns in *La Préface de Cromwell*. In primitive times, Hugo claimed, men were "colosses," then in the ancient, or epic period, they are "géants," and in the modern "dramatic" period they are men like Hamlet or Macbeth (p. 21).

resembles both those rocks which in "Les Derniers Bardes" flattened Edward's army and also the clouds of "Soleils couchants" that collapse in the sky only to create new forms (again it must be emphasized that the images appear in many earlier poems; if we have chosen the last two named on which to concentrate, it is only because they are particularly good examples). In the political dimension, one can evoke here the *écroulement* of *Cromwell*, which becomes a feeling of impending disaster in *Les Burgraves:*

> O souvenirs! ô temps! tout s'est évanoui!
> L'éclair a disparu de notre œil ébloui.
> Les barons sont tombés; les burgs jonchent la plaine. (p. 531)

Then the emperor extends the idea to each individual German and to the "nation" as a whole:

> Chacun veut se dresser de toute sa hauteur.
>
> . . . .
> Abjection—L'empire avait de grands piliers,
> Hollande, Luxembourg, Clèves, Gueldres, Juliers,
> —Croulés! (pp. 537–38)

The burgraves are largely responsible for this calamitous condition, and the agent of their overthrow will be Barberousse, Job's rival in politics as in love. He is an historical personage of the twelfth century who died by drowning during the third crusade. For purposes of the plot Hugo restores him to life and adds the prediction that he will return twice from the dead, after slumbering in a cave until his beard should grow long enough to wrap itself three times around a stone table.[15] Like Don Carlos of *Hernani*, Barberousse had visited the tomb of Charlemagne, but unlike his predecessor he had profaned it by stealing his cross (this becomes a recognition device in the play). In human terms, the act explains Barberousse's penance for so many years in the cave under the village of Heppenheff. But in spite of his almost sacrilegious act, Job and the nation need him badly:

15. The poem "Puits de l'Inde" cited earlier in this chapter contains the following lines:

Dans un caveau . . .
Un vieillard surhumain, sous le roc qui surplombe,
Semble vivre oublié par la mort dans sa tombe.

115

Mais j'entends mon pays qui m'appelle; je sors
De l'ombre où je songeais, exilé volontaire. (p. 552)

Job, appalled by the moral decline of his family, believes that Barberousse is the only one who can overcome the banditry of the local lords
and forge a new national unity. For these political reasons, Job saves his
rival when he is at the mercy of Magnus and Hatto in the castle; only the
emperor can exorcise the "démons dans ma patrie en flamme" (p. 544),
and later the delighted Job proclaims: "J'ai sauvé mon pays; j'ai sauvé le
royaume" (p. 562). In return for this grandeur and vision, the emperor
Barberousse asks Job to reign over the Rhineland under the national
leadership of the former's grandson, who will be elected the new emperor
at the end of the play.

This strong epic motif is nevertheless dominated at times by the
mythological elements, and apparently Hugo's first trip to the Rhineland
itself was the immediate inspiration for this even larger orientation. In
the preface to *Les Burgraves*, he first refers to Aeschylus' Thessalia, "un
lieu sinistre." "Il y avait eu là autrefois des géants; il y avait là maintenant des fantômes," and after a grandiose evocation of the somber gods
who dwelt there, Hugo concludes: "mais, pour Eschyle et ses contemporains, ces plaines ravagées, ces forêts déracinées, ces blocs arrachés et
rompus, ces lacs changés en marais, ces montagnes renversées et deve-
nues informes, c'était . . . l'effrayant champ de bataille où les Titans
avaient lutté contre Jupiter" (p. 489). Hugo then draws a parallel with
the Rhineland: "Ce que la fable a inventé, l'histoire le reproduit parfois.
. . . On devine que nous voulons parler des bords du Rhin. . . . Là, en
effet, il y a six siècles, d'autres Titans ont lutté contre un autre Jupiter.
Ces Titans, ce sont les burgraves; ce Jupiter, c'est l'empereur
d'Allemagne" (p. 490).

There is no doubt that these words should be taken seriously. As Hugo
was to put it some years later in *William Shakespeare:*

Un excès de fréquentation de la mythologie en a fait la surface
banale; toutefois, pour peu que l'on creuse, le grand sens énigma-
tique se révèle. La foule s'amuse tant de la fable qu'il n'y a plus de
place dans son intention pour le mythe; mais ce mythe multiple n'en
est pas moins une puissante création de la sagacité humaine, et

116

quiconque a médité sérieusement sur l'unité intime des religions prendra toujours fort au sérieux ce symbolisme païen. (p. 311)

In these few lines, Hugo establishes himself as one of the wisest critics of the nineteenth century, for official criticism never did see that underlying not only Hugo's work but indeed much of the creation of that century were strong patterns of myth, open or disguised.

According to Classical mythology, the Titans surprised their father Uranus and overthrew him and set one of their number, Cronus, as sovereign of the earth. Cronus then married his sister Rhea and it was foretold that one of their sons should overthrow him. So he swallowed the children Rhea bore him until the angry mother gave birth to Zeus in secret. The infant was hidden in a cave, and when he grew up he led a war against the Titans, who chose the huge Atlas as their leader to replace their aged Cronus. The war lasted for years, but with the aid of the Cyclopes and a thunderbolt, Zeus struck down Cronus, confined the Titans to Tartarus, and then ruled the world.

This legendary world is transferred, with some attempt at disguise, to *Les Burgraves*. The physical and psychological dissolution of the world of common reality permits the flowering of legend and myth. Job had said of his existence:

Et les objets réels, perdus sous un brouillard,
Devant mon œil troublé, qui dans l'ombre en vain plonge,
Tremblent derrière un voile ainsi que dans un songe.

.   .   .   .

C'est que tout a croulé dans ma haute demeure. (p. 561)

The function of the fog (or clouds, or smoke) becomes clearer. It is Hugo's sign of the passage from the real world to the mythic world. And once past the threshold, Job is a "demi-Dieu" (p. 574) and Frédéric Barberousse is not merely a twelfth-century historical figure. His spending years in a cave while his beard grows makes him a legendary being, and his disappearance is put in mythic terms. As he says: "Le monde entier m'a cru descendu chez les morts" (p. 552). His return, like that of Zeus, is motivated by revenge, and Hugo somehow succeeds in suggesting the war between Zeus and the Titans in his expositions of the earlier struggle between Frédéric and the Burgraves. The first version of the play described it as follows:

C'étaient des guerres de géants!

. . . .

Certes, je m'en souviens!—Je puis même à mon tour
Vous conter qu'en son fort nous assiégions un jour
Un burgrave, un bandit levant haut sa bannière,
Comte chez l'empereur, lion dans sa tanière.
On fit brèche. On donna l'assaut. Tout le premier . . .
Barberousse parvint au sommet de la tour.
Tout fuyait. Frédéric, sur cette plate-forme,
Ne trouva qu'un guerrier d'une stature énorme,
Seul. . . .
Il [Frédéric] saisit le géant entre ses poings terribles,
Et l'étreignit si fort sur son corset d'airain
Que son talon fit choir deux créneaux dans le Rhin.

. . . .

Le burgrave, étouffé, vaincu malgré sa taille,
Tomba de sa hauteur. . . . (pp. 586–87, *Reliquat*)

Having succeeded in overthrowing the Titans, Zeus chained them and buried them in Tartarus. This idea is echoed in the play as the vanquished burgraves let themselves be manacled and then go off to fight the barbarian hordes attacking the empire. And on the dramatic plane, the sense of crushing weight that Job experiences over his guilt is neatly tied in to the burial of the Titans, who strained against the weight of the mountains oppressing them. Job speaks:

Quand mon passé, mes maux, toujours appesantis,
Vont retomber sur moi?

A Regina

Car, vois-tu ma colombe,
Je soulève un moment ce poids, puis il retombe. (p. 548)

Now behind the myths of Zeus and the Titans there lies a pattern of even more primitive religion of the Mediterranean area, wherein at the end of one period of reign, a new (solar) god challenged and defeated the old one. Barberousse to some extent reflects this tradition by his very physique in that "sa barbe était d'or" (p. 507). He has in the above version to the first part of the play a certain resemblance to the solar god

Herakles (Hercules), who fought a lion in his first labor, wrestling with it and choking it to death. Is there also a suggestion of Herakles' defeat of Anteus, who could only be defeated by being lifted from the ground? The conqueror's victim in the passage also suggests the old king who is dethroned and hurled to his death in the sea. Of course, the fall is displaced into suggestive imagery, for Job must survive to be a character in the play, but the language calls this ritual to mind: "[il] tomba de sa hauteur" and "son talon fit choir deux crénaux dans le Rhin." But this interesting passage did not survive intact to the final text, probably because it suggests a permanent defeat of Job prior to the start of the play. Hugo decided to break up this speech and scatter its lines throughout the text, omitting the details of the hand-to-hand struggle (the last five lines cited). Even so, enough remains to suggest primitive myth. Frédéric in the final version appeared "couvert d'or du talon au cimier" in the earlier battles, and Job's soliloquy of the last act in which he recognizes that his time has come ("L'un des deux va tomber. C'est moi. L'ombre me gagne.") re-enacts the ancient idea that the old king must consent to his fate (or *moira*) before yielding to his successor. In this play, however, Job and Barberousse are reconciled, a solution that not only can be explained by the political needs of the nation, but even echoes the fact that in some primitive cultures, the new king ruled with his tanist or twin (the motif of the brothers again) at the end of his reign, if we can accept Robert Graves's interpretation.[16] The echoes of the distant past are blurred and far from clear, but one can observe that Job and Barberousse are half-brothers and, further, the general ritual nature of the encounter is suggested by the fact that the old king may not die or be deposed until the end of his reign, often given in terms of one hundred, Job's age. Can this be what Pierre Albouy is suggesting when he concluded: "Au point de vue théâtral, ce drame de centenaires était une gageure intenable. Si on le considère avec nous comme un mythe, cette longue durée est non seulement admissible, mais nécessaire" (p. 267)? Albert Py closes his perceptive study of Greek myths in Hugo's poetry with the suggestion that Hugo, in opposing the official olympians, found himself attracted to the primitive cults that Hellenism had vanquished.[17]

16. *The Greek Myths* (Baltimore, 1955), I, 19.
17. *Les Mythes grecs dans la poésie de Victor Hugo* (Genève, 1963), pp. 259–60.

119

In short, Barberousse emerges as a figure conforming to the age-old pattern of mythic action. Upon his birth there was a presage of descent into Hell and he does indeed go down into the underworld and returns reborn with a sense of wholeness, initiated, reappearing with his own soul saved, perhaps, but with a wider mission as well: that of bestowing the boon of national unity on Germany. Something of a tribal god, he unites salvation and politics, mythology and the epic. In this role, he appears in the final scene of the play as a literal *"deus" ex machina,* thwarting the evil Guanhumara and saving all the others as well.

But before concluding this discussion, it is important to observe that the regular pattern of mythic action is not repeated in one important particular. When Barberousse first comes to the castle disguised as a beggar, he renounces his privileged status as guest and is about to be killed by the angry lords when Job, his arch-enemy, steps in to save him. The hero does not slay the ogre, Satan,[18] rival god, or whatever form the Other may take; the evil one here saves him. In the last scene, the action is reversed when Frédéric saves Job in the Caveau Perdu. This reconciliation is illustrated by a familiar image. We remember the web of fatality and its subsidiary form of a barred grill-work. In this play, it reappears and unlike all the bars in previous caves and cages the "trois barreaux" are "tordus et défoncés." In one sense, the breaking of the steel web was an act of evil, for Job had years earlier hurled his brother out of this window into the torrent. But it would seem that evil turns out to be good, for the broken bars suggest a conquered fatality, and the play closes with the ritual of comedy, the reconciliation of the group, with Guanhumara carried off in a coffin. It is easy to link this outcome with that of the earlier *Han d'Islande* where Ordener, also a suggestion of a solar god, does not slay Han, and with the later *Fin de Satan* where Isis-Lilith is destroyed and God and Satan are reconciled in a universal salvation and where the agency of redemption, "l'ange liberté," is the offspring of Satan himself. Here too, salvation will at least in part come through the efforts of the evil person.

The conclusion of *Les Burgraves* looks ahead to this later poetry through a final *envoi,* spoken by the author:

Suis Barberousse, ô Job! Frères, allez tout seuls.
De vos manteaux de rois faites-vous deux linceuls.

18. Job says: "Je suis le vieux Satan" (p. 578).

Ensemble l'un sur l'autre appuyant votre marche,
De la vieille Allemagne emportez tous deux l'arche!
O colosses! le monde est trop petit pour vous.
Toi, solitude, aux bruits profonds, tristes et doux,
Laisse les deux géants s'enfoncer dans ton ombre!
Et que toute la terre, en ta nuit calme et sombre,
Regarde avec respect, et presque avec terreur,
Entrer le grand burgrave et le grand empereur. (p. 582)

The two "heroes" end as equals, but even more interesting is the remark about the smallness of the world. Surely it applies to the world of Hugo's theater. His stage too small, the tensions of myth and the drama of human existence too great to be successful, henceforth he would revert either to prose fiction where he could combine human drama and cosmic imagery far more successfully, or to poetry where his imagination could soar freely, in such works as *La Légende des siècles* and *La Fin de Satan*, which are the subject of our next chapter. As for *Les Burgraves*, it was a failure in more than the traditional sense implied by some manuals of the history of literature: a failure at the box-office. The play has unified theme and structure, operates on dramatic, epic, and mythic levels, but it was unsuccessful because of the limitations of drama itself, and the consequent necessity to have so much of the play's epic and mythic parts relegated to the exposition.

THE LATER POETRY

LA LÉGENDE DES SIÈCLES
AND *LA FIN DE SATAN*

THE CONCLUDING *envoi* of *Les Burgraves,* which directly anticipates the form of the later epic and cosmic poetry, compels us to ignore chronology for the moment and to skip over *Les Misérables,* on which Hugo had worked hard in the 1840's and had completed in exile in 1862. Although *Les Châtiments* (1853), *Les Contemplations* (1856), and the posthumously published *Dieu* have epic and mythic elements, these essentially lyrical or ideological works, when taken as a whole, lack sufficient narrative progression to be included within this study. But *La Légende des siècles*[1] and *La Fin de Satan,*[2] we feel, have a strong enough plot that they cannot be ignored. Further, they demonstrate the culmination of certain of the images that Hugo had been developing for years, and finally, the two need to be treated together because Hugo himself intended them to be linked, as he explained in his preface to the 1859 series of *La Légende.*

But the critic who approaches the immensity of this latter work faces certain problems that make analysis difficult. First, there is the fact that the various poems which compose this epic were written over a period of many years. For the purposes of this study, which presupposes the artistic unity of the final work, we will ignore chronological differences in dates of composition as well as the fact that it appeared in three series, using as the text the final order given in the E.I.N. There is the even more vital problem of the manner in which one should approach this work. For example, when Paul Berret did his monumental edition of *La Légende,* he was content to make relatively few remarks concerning its structure. He observed that "la critique parle volontiers de la majesté de l'ensemble, et moins souvent de son unité";[3] otherwise he says little more

1. Published in three series: 1859, 1877, 1893.
2. Published in 1886, but parts were written as early as 1854.
3. *La Légende des siècles,* I (Paris, 1921), lv.

122

than Hugo. The poet had written from Hauteville-House in 1859 that his purpose was to show "l'épanouissement du genre humain de siècle en siècle, l'homme montant des ténèbres à l'idéal, la transfiguration paradisiaque de l'enfer terrestre, l'éclosion lente et suprême de la liberté."[4] Berret puts it this way: "Tous les exploits des héros de *La Légende des siècles* sont les degrés d'une ascension: Eviradnus, Roland, l'Ane du *Crapaud,* c'est l'ascension par l'amour; Nuño, Fabrice, c'est l'ascension par la souffrance; le *Satyre* et *Plein Ciel* chantent l'ascension par la science."[5] Berret puts this rise within a general moral framework where "Tout a une responsabilité morale."[6] These perfectly sound conclusions are not fully developed because Berret was more interested in the sources of the individual poems. Other critics like Saurat, Heugel, and Rigal have debated such ideas as pantheism or Illuminism,[7] but as Paul Cormeau put it: "malgré tout, l'œuvre vaut davantage indépendamment de l'idée qu'elle sert."[8] This is why *La Légende* still stands as a major poetic work of the nineteenth century, despite the considerable banality of its moral preachment, and is no doubt why Glauser wished to concentrate on "la poésie pure" of the exile on the Channel Islands. All these scholar-critics, by limiting themselves to one aspect of this vast work (or other of Hugo's mythic poems), were able to avoid becoming bogged down in its very immensity. In our turn we shall be even more selective, trying only to chart the general outline of *La Légende* and *La Fin de Satan* in the light of the structures and images that we have followed up to this point. As brevity is the source of clarity here, we will of necessity omit many citations that could be used, but which might easily turn this chapter into a tedious compilation.

In the prologue to *Les Contemplations,* Hugo had likened his universe to a vast ocean into which the poet must reach down in order to find truth:

> Poète, tu fais bien. Poète au triste front,
> Tu rêves près des ondes.
> Et tu tires des mers bien des choses qui sont
> Sous les mers profondes.

4. *La Légende des siècles,* I, E.I.N., p. 10.   5. *La Légende,* ed. Berret, I, xlv.
6. *Ibid.,* p. xxii.   7. See Introduction and Bibliography.
8. " 'Le Satyre' dans *La Légende des siècles* de Victor Hugo," *French Review,* XXXIX (1966), 851.

This idea of a descent for truth, which we have shown to be a constant in Hugo, is again in *La Légende* a perilous adventure, a fight for life, from which the hero (be he the poet or all mankind) emerges transformed, just as Charles V was transformed in Charlemagne's tomb and Job in the Caveau Perdu. The test is a fearsome one and, speaking as a poet, Hugo knew that "il faut que le songeur soit plus fort que le songe."[9] He knew the nightmarish quality of his own imagination and had in mind as well the horrible example of his brother Eugène, who had cracked under the pressure of his hallucinations. In *La Légende*, Hugo links the descent into the abyss with total chaos and gives to it an overtone of fatality, for the poet is not free to do otherwise. The picture is one of the poet's being hurled against his will over a falls like Niagara:

> Il se cabre, il résiste au précipice obscur,
> Bave et bouillonne, et, blanc et noir comme le marbre,
> Se cramponne aux rochers, se retient aux troncs d'arbre,
> Penche, et, comme frappé de malédiction,
> Roule . . .
> Tordu, brisé, vaincu, rien ne vit, rien ne surnage . . .
> Tout à coup, au-dessus de ce chaos qui souffre,
> Apparaît, composé de tout ce que le gouffre
> A de hideux, d'hostile et de torrentiel,
> Un éblouissement auguste, l'arc-en-ciel;
> Le piège est vil, la roche est traître, l'onde est noire,
> Et tu sors de cette ombre épouvantable, ô gloire![10]

The first half of this passage recaptures Habibrah's desperate struggle over the abyss, but the last part shows that there is some chance that the strong poet may survive the perilous journey. And in the case of a poet, the quest itself creates the poetic universe. Hugo put it well in the titular line of poem XXVII: "Un poète est un monde enfermé dans un homme." Indeed, the entire *Légende* is such a world, enclosed in its creator's mind and following the poet's own pattern of descent and rise from the abyss. It does so in a double cosmos, one evocative of the ideal and real worlds of the 1822 preface to the *Odes* (but with what a difference in technique and

9. *Promontorium Somnii*, ed. René Journet et Guy Robert (Paris, 1961), pp. 31–32.
10. *Les Chutes: Fleuves et poètes* (XXV).

vision!). In a marginal comment on the manuscript Hugo observed: "Les manifestations extérieures de l'invisible sont un fait."[11] The structure of *La Légende* is that of macrocosm and microcosm, a world of myth echoed by a more or less "historical" pattern of action set in the realm of human time.

The mythic vision opens the work in a sort of prologue entitled "La Vision d'où est sorti ce livre." The poet explains his own involvement in language that repeats the idea of the descent:

Et je revoyais là le vieux temps oublié.
Je le sondais.

The world that he contemplates is one of disaster, ruin, and evil:

Tous les siècles tronqués gisaient; plus de lien;
Chaque époque pendait démantelée; aucune
N'était sans déchirure et n'était sans lacune;
Et partout croupissaient sur le passé détruit
Des stagnations d'ombre et des flaques de nuit.

The theme of this vision is the same one with which Hugo had struggled for years. Two spirits pass by:

Ils passèrent. Ce fut un ébranlement sombre.
Et le premier esprit cria; Fatalité!
Le second cria: Dieu! L'obscure éternité
Répéta ces deux cris dans ses échos funèbres.

Which one will dominate? Hugo's sympathies lie with the latter, for he sees the whole history of mankind ("Tout le prodige humain, noir, vague, illimité") as "la liberté brisant l'immuabilité," whereas a less optimistic version—"la liberté mêlée à la fatalité"—Hugo relegated to the *Reliquat*. And by looking ahead in time, the poet forecasts a happy ending:

Seulement l'avenir continuait d'éclore
Sur ces vestiges noirs qu'un pâle orient dore,
Et se levait avec un air d'astre, au milieu
D'un nuage où, sans voir de foudre, on sentait Dieu.

The narrative of the epic begins with two poems intended to fix man's condition prior to the fall in Eden, "La Terre" and "Le Sacre de la

11. *La Légende*, ed. Berret, I, 108.

femme." Then in the section *Entre Géants et Dieux*, the poet presents for the first time the completed mythical expression of his patterns which found an earlier cosmic exposition in those lines from "La Pente de la rêverie," quoted in the previous chapter, and which we give again here:

> Mon esprit plongea donc sous ce flot inconnu
> Au profond de l'abîme il nagea seul et nu,
> Toujours de l'ineffable allant à l'invisible. . . .
> Soudain il s'en revint avec un cri terrible,
> Ebloui, haletant, stupide, épouvanté,
> Car il avait au fond trouvé l'éternité.

To the general framework of these lines the poet adds dramatic narrative structure and a cast of characters, choosing the mythological Giants (for Hugo, "Giant" and "Titan" are interchangeable terms) whom we first see after they have been overthrown by Jupiter. In the classical myth the fall of the Titans was permanent, but Hugo begins where tradition ends. A Titan warns the usurper, Jupiter:

> Prenez garde!
> Laissez-moi dans mon trou plein d'ombre et de parfums.
> Que les olympiens ne soient pas importuns,
> Car il se pourrait bien qu'on vît de quelle sorte
> On les chasse. . . .
> Ah! certes, ces passants, que vous nommez les dieux
> Furent de fiers bandits sous le ciel radieux; . . .
> Non, je ne les crains pas; et quant à leurs approches,
> Je les attends avec des roulements de roches
> Je les appelle gueux et voleurs, c'est leur nom.

It has been many years since the rolling rocks of "Les Derniers Bardes" and *Han d'Islande,* but the language is still recognizable. The Olympians are then presented in all their power:

> L'Olympe est à jamais la cime de la vie; . . .
> Nous sommes tout. Nos coups de foudre sont fumants,
> Jouissons. Sous nos pieds un pavé d'ossement,
> C'est la terre; un plafond de néant sur nos têtes,
> C'est le ciel.

The Titans are buried:

> A cette heure, un amas de roches les écrase;
> Poursuivons, achevons notre œuvre, et consommons
> La lapidation des géants par les monts!

Over all, receiving the full force of Hugo's satire, Olympus "Rayonne; et tout le mal possible est là, divin." But one Titan, Phtos, bound with bronze cord in a "souterrain" (p. 55), suffers because "le mal triomphe" (p. 57). By a mighty effort he breaks his bonds, the first barrier, a distant form of Hugo's old spider web. Phtos

> Se débat. . . .
> Tout à coup, sous l'effort . . .
> Le carcan s'est fendu, les nœuds ont éclaté!
> Le roc sent remuer l'être extraordinaire;
> "Ah!" dit Phtos, et sa joie est semblable au tonnerre.
> Le voilà libre!

But he still has the second barrier, the mountain, over him just as Louis XI's prisoner in *Notre-Dame* would still be in the Bastille even if he could escape from his cage. Phtos begins to crawl, trying to achieve his freedom, but unable to rise, he begins a perilous descent through the darkness back into the "flanc sacré de la terre, sa mère" (p. 73). A "plongeur de l'Ignoré" like his poet-creator, he struggles down to the very bottom—"Plus loin n'existe pas." He pulls out the last stone:

> O vertige!
> O gouffres! l'effrayant soupirail d'un prodige
> Apparaît; l'aube fait irruption.

Phtos looks into numberless skies and stars in whose depths

> O stupeur! il finit par distinguer, au fond
> A travers l'épaisseur d'une brume éternelle,
> Dans on ne sait quelle ombre énorme, une prunelle!

It seems appropriate here to make a comparison of this section with the anthology-piece "La Conscience," whose action unfolds in our earthly world and is situated, as a poem, between the idylls that open *La Légende* and the cosmic adventures of the Titan. Cain, having killed Abel, flees from God and ends in a tomb where the divine eye is still firmly fixed upon him. The idea of the outcast, the motif of entombment, and the divine eye of judgment unite in these two poems the cosmic and the "real" worlds. As "La Conscience" is the first poem of the series that shows evil at work in the world, and as it presents the familiar Hugolian theme of the *frères ennemis,* it is easy to deduce that in the process of creation of the giant Phtos, Hugo identified himself with the outcast, as he must have done with Cain. Still, he gives no clear explanation of how the early Edenic world was corrupted. All the poet seems to know is that evil has become manifest. But let us return to the myth. The Titan stands secure in his knowledge that God is beyond all gods, thanks to his seeing the cosmic eye, thanks to having gone through darkness and imprisonment to the ultimate depths where there is light and truth,

> Le colosse, en rampant dans l'ombre et sous la terre,
> S'était fait libre, était sorti de sa prison,
> Et maintenant montait, sinistre, à l'horizon.

Grave and proud, he cries out to the Olympians, "O dieux, il est un Dieu!" All the familiar patterns are there: the futility of direct ascent blocked by Jupiter's bolts and by the weight of the mountain, the double barrier, and the success by descent.[12] In the following sections of the epic, his struggles underground are played out in our world as battles between good and evil in various cultures, without much regard for sociological exactness or chronological sequence. Perhaps, as Paul Zumthor has pointed out, the darkest moment for the optimistic or good side is to be found in the decadence of the Roman Empire, in "Au lion d'Androclès."[13] At the beginning of the poem, Hugo reminds the reader that these acts that take place in our microcosm are symbolic of something greater ("La Ville ressemblait à l'univers"). The picture is one of undiluted horror:

> Le noir gouffre cloaque au fond ouvrait son arche
> Où croulait Rome entière.

Rome is also called an "immense égout," an image that will be put to good use in *Les Misérables.* But this period of darkness resembles that

12. Pierre Albouy, *La Création mythologique chez Victor Hugo* (Paris, 1963), p. 259, observes that in *William Shakespeare,* there is a fine parallel with Dante: "le fond de l'enfer touché, Dante le perce, et remonte de l'autre côté de l'infini" (p. 38).
13. *Victor Hugo, poète de Satan* (Paris, 1946), pp. 100–1.

128

moment at which Phtos was about to be able to turn back upward toward the light. The poet reminds us that this moment in history is

Cette heure où l'on dirait que toute âme se tait,
Que tout astre s'éclipse et que le monde change.

The early Eden is no more:

Le crime sombre étant l'amant du vice infâme.
Au lieu de cette race en qui Dieu mit sa flamme,
Au lieu d'Eve et d'Adam, si beaux, si purs tous deux,
Une hydre se traînait dans l'univers hideux.

The transformation from evil to good will be slow, and in the next poem, "L'Islam," John of Patmos, the seer and the *mage*, explains God's methods. While his reference is to the growth of a tree, the subsequent nature imagery of "Le Satyre," as well as its general language, permit a wider application:

L'ordre éternel n'a point de ces rapidités;
Jéhovah, dont les yeux s'ouvrent de tous côtés,
Veut que l'œuvre soit lente, et que l'arbre se fonde
Sur un pied fort, scellé dans l'argile profonde;

A bright future is possible only when history is solidly rooted in the clay of earthly reality. The turning down, even into the "cloaque" of Rome seems a necessity for future growth toward the light.

It is surely no coincidence that Hugo chose this nadir of human achievement to step back from history in order to intercalate three poems that reinforce this commentary on God's and man's efforts in the world, and provide a basic framework of interpretation for the details of man's history. The first, "Les Sept merveilles du monde," presents to us the voices of the Seven Wonders of the Ancient World, which speak to mankind in haughty tones of their eternal and lofty domination of time, only to have the minuscule earthworm enter at the end to announce: "Je suis le ver. Je suis fange et cendre. . . ." The worm represents earthly finitude and more specifically death. In language that is curiously reminiscent of "Les Deux Iles" (cf. p. 139), it declares to these arrogant structures:

Edifices! montez, et montez davantage.
Superposez l'étage et l'étage à l'étage,

129

> Et le dôme aux cités;
> Montez; sous votre base écrasez les campagnes;
> Plus haut que les forêts, plus haut que les montagnes,
> Montez, montez, montez!
>
> . . . .
>
> Ne vous arrêtez pas. Montez! montez encore!
> Moi je rampe, et j'attends. Du couchant, de l'aurore
> Et du sud et du nord,
> Tout vient à moi, le fait, l'être, la chose triste,
> La chose heureuse; et seul je vis, et seul j'existe,
> Puisque je suis la mort.

The worm concludes with the now familiar warning:

> La ruine est promise à tout ce qui s'élève.
> Vous ne faites, palais qui croissez comme un rêve,
> Frontons au dur ciment,
> Que mettre un peu plus haut mon tas de nourriture,
> Et que rendre plus grand, par plus d'architecture,
> Le sombre écroulement.

In the second of this group of three poems, "L'Epopée du ver," the worm proclaims his mastery, not only of the haughty edifices previously mentioned, but also of the entire world and all within it, even daring to have the last word on God's creation:

> La création triste, aux entrailles profondes,
> Porte deux Tout-Puissants, le Dieu qui fait les mondes,
> Le ver qui les détruit.

But in the last of the series, "Le Poète au ver de terre," Hugo refutes the claims of death, and holds aloft as a goal the soul which is the "réel." Thus having reminded us of a future hope, the poet returns to the march of history and embarks on the somber period of the Dark Ages, and begins to show within human history man's striving toward the light. At first, the progress seems almost nonexistent, for while we find a few admirable knights-errant, for the most part the poet presents us with a series of triumphant, rapacious feudal barons, all of whom have their castles perched upon some crag, reflecting in the "real" world the gods on

Olympus. In "Le Cycle héroïque chrétien," v "Le Jour des rois," the barons on the heights attack and pillage the plain, like Hatto in *Les Burgraves:*

> La journée était bonne, et les files des lances
> Serpentaient dans les champs pleins de sombres silences;
> Les montagnards disaient: "Quel beau coup de filet!"
> Après avoir tué la plaine qui râlait,
> Ils rentraient dans leurs monts, comme une flotte au havre,
> Et riant, et chantant, s'éloignaient du cadavre.

In the long poem "L'Italie-Ratbert," the elevation of the evildoers is not literally upon a mountain; rather their lofty estate is that of rank, albeit vilely usurped. Ratbert and his henchmen have plundered and murdered, but his flatterers declaim:

> Ta politique est sage et ta guerre est adroite,
> Noble empereur, et Dieu te tient dans sa main droite.

The villains do not notice that a stone statue of Satan smiles at the remark.

So also in "Les Quatre Jours d'Elciis," where there are more evil barons,

> . . . la plupart
> Bandits bien crénelés et droits sur leur rempart,
> Maîtres de quelque place à d'autres usurpée.

In "Gaïffer-Jorge, Duc d'Acquitaine," the evil duke's castle is described as a

> . . . palais de roi, nid de vautour.
> Forteresse où ce duc, voisin de la tempête,
> Habite, avec le cri des aigles sur sa tête.

When this lord digs down to determine on what his castle is built, he finds himself directly over Hell. Similarly in "Masferrer," speaking of the feudal lords, the poet concludes:

> Ils sont maîtres des cols et maîtres des sommets. . . .
> Ils se dressent, chaos de blocs démesurés;

> Leur cime, par delà les vallons et les prés,
> Guette, gêne et menace . . .
> Tous ces géants ont l'air de faire dans la nue
> Quelque exécution sombre qui continue.

But whereas in the decadent period of Rome the decent soul of mankind took refuge in Androcles' lion (no human being meriting the honor), here men do appear to judge the wicked. In "Le Jour des Rois," the one who stands in judgment is a beggar, but one "mythologized" in a way impossible on the stage of *Les Burgraves*. He is an obvious Phtos-figure in human form:

> Alors, tragique et se dressant,
> Le mendiant, tendant ses deux mains décharnées,
> Montra sa souquenille immonde aux Pyrénées
> Et cria dans l'abîme et dans l'immensité

that the lice in the holes of his rags are like kings in their lairs. In "Ratbert," it is the "vieux podestat" Onfroy who delivers a rebuke to the exploiters. He is "ce héros d'un autre âge," a phrase that introduces the theme of the degeneration of virtue, so prominent in *Les Burgraves*. This sense of moral disintegration is developed at length in "Les Quatre Jours d'Elciis." Elciis, "un vieillard très grand," like a Job, exclaims: "Les hommes de mon temps faisaient la guerre franche;" whereas

> Ce temps-ci me répugne et sent la bâtardise.
> Quand venaient les hiboux, jadis l'aigle émigrait;
> Je m'en vais comme lui. Barons, c'est à regret
> Qu'on voit se refléter jusque dans vos repaires
> Ce grand rayonnement des anciens et des pères.

To summarize briefly: the evil nobles, whose fortresses are in the mountains, swoop down and despoil the plain by treachery, making war on the innocent, killing the virtuous until their moral descent is converted into a physical one and they now become the established rulers of the lowlands, and paradoxically, only a few upright souls are left barricaded in the mountain fastnesses.

Two poems that reveal this reversal of role can be juxtaposed with profit. The first, "La Confiance du Marquis Fabrice," sets the stage clearly:

Tout au bord de la mer de Gênes, sur un mont

. . . .

Un enfant, un aïeul, seuls dans la citadelle. . . .

The old man is one of those "héros d'un autre âge."

Maintenant il est vieux; son donjon, c'est son cloître;
Il tombe, et déclinant, sent dans son âme croître
La confiance honnête et calme des grands cœurs;
. . . il est hors de ce siècle vil.

His castle is seized by treachery; he and the little girl die. Punishment descends upon the evil Ratbert magically in the form of an archangel who strikes off the villain's head, sending him to Hell while bearing the old man up to Heaven.[14] The virtue of Fabrice in his citadel was great, but it was nonetheless a passive virtue. More noble yet is the life of Welf, Castellan d'Osbor, whose tale immediately follows that of Ratbert. The form is dramatic and includes an *envoi* at the end entitled, "Le Poète, à Welf," a structure which imitates the ending of *Les Burgraves*. Here we find the same situation as in "La Confiance du Marquis Fabrice": the only man not a slave in Germany is surrounded by the troops of the evil rulers. Hugo exalts the solitary hero: "Welf dépasse tout. C'est un Dieu." Like a god on the mountaintop, he is tempted, offered a chance to leave his perch and to join the ruling clique, to be a captain in the army. He refuses to sell out, either to the army or later to the emperor or finally to the church. The real temptation comes in scene v when a homeless girl, ten years old, asks asylum. He resists the lure of selfish security, lowers the drawbridge to take her in, and is quickly overpowered by the lurking villains. By descending into death, he has fulfilled the dicta that "So as ye do unto the least of these, so do ye also unto Me," and "he who loses his life for my sake shall have eternal life." Curiously, he seems a kind of Han d'Islande transformed into a saint; like his ancestor, he is alone in his lair, and like him he gives himself up "unnecessarily." Even more

14. A monk "Vit, dans les profondeurs par les vents remuées/ Un archange essuyer son épée aux nuées" (p. 334). The image of the sword (*épée, glaive*) is associated with just revenge and is set in radiant skies that hearken back to "Soleils couchants." But the avenging angel is making one of his last appearances.

133

revealing is this fragment of dialogue that reaches back to one that we quoted in Chapter I.

Le Vieillard, *regardant Welf garotté*

Je le croyais plus grand qu'un autre

Le Bourgeois

Quelle erreur.

Il est petit.

Another example of the descent to truth appears in "La Paternité," where three generations show a progressive moral decline, more or less as in *Les Burgraves*. The father slaps the son's face, but "tous deux sont grands." Of the two the old man, Jayme, is superior to his son Ascagne, just as Job was to Magnus. Jayme's nature is:

Etre clément au faible, aux puissants incommode,
Vaincre, mais rester pur, c'était la vieille mode;
Jayme fut de son siècle, Ascagne est de son temps.

The son is not hopelessly base. Outraged by the insult, he leaves his father's house. As for Jayme, upon his son's departure,

Il regarde celui qui partait disparaître;
Puis, quand son fils se fut effacé, le vieux maître
Descendit dans la crypte où son père dormait.

There a bronze statue of Jayme's father Alonze reposes for all eternity, a metallic concretization of Barberousse in his cave. Thus the trio, Statue-Jayme-Ascagne, resembles the group Barberousse-Job-Magnus. The action repeats the descent of Charles V into Charlemagne's tomb for guidance in *Hernani*. Jayme, too, prays before the statue for comfort and justification, and like Charles V, he receives a blessing. In the darkness the bronze hand caresses him.

The Western feudal barons are not the only group through which the poet explores his vision. Various sections deal with Eastern rulers and the same patterns emerge here as well. "Zim-Zizimi" tells of a wicked potentate who is exalted in human terms, but who is morally base:

Je dédaigne et je hais les hommes; et mon pied
Sent le mou de la fange en marchant sur leurs nuques.

134

At the end he falls victim to the "écroulement" of a "Soleil couchant," as man and castle are transformed into a disappearing bit of smoke at sunset:

> Zim se dressa terrible, . . .
> . . . Alors la Nuit entra;
> Et Zim se trouva seul avec elle; la salle,
> Comme en une fumée obscure et colossale,
> S'effaça; Zim tremblait, sans gardes, sans soutiens:
> La Nuit lui prit la main dans l'ombre, et lui dit: Viens.

"Sultan Mourad," which follows "Zim-Zizimi," suggests the theme of salvation by descent. The "hero" is evil incarnate and has the usual lofty perch of the powerful:

> Il fut sublime; il prit, mêlant la force aux ruses,
> Le Caucase aux Kirghis et le Liban aux Druses.

As he has slaughtered women and children in great numbers, Heaven's judgment awaits. He is told: "Tu sombrais parmi ceux que le mal submergea," but fortunately he is saved. One day he had turned away from grandeur downward to help a dying pig being tortured by flies. This insignificant act is in reality totally significant. In Heaven, the pig's testimony saves the sultan's soul.

A curious variation of the pattern occurs in "Avertissements et Châtiments," I, "Le Travail des captifs." Some slaves propose to an evil king that he construct his temple underground.

> Une caverne? dit le roi.—Roi qui gouvernes,
> Dieu ne refuse point d'entrer dans les cavernes,
> Dit l'homme, et ce n'est pas une rébellion
> Que faire un temple à Dieu dans l'antre du lion.
> —Faites,—dit le roi.

It is a trap, and the king is entombed alive forever in this underground temple. Now the king had been bothered by this idea of descent:

> Quand ils furent en bas, le prince s'étonna.
> —C'est de cette façon qu'on entra dans l'Etna. . . .
> C'est ainsi qu'on aborde à l'Hadès immobile,
> Mais ce n'est pas ainsi qu'on arrive au saint lieu.

135

—Qu'on monte ou qu'on descende, on va toujours à Dieu,
Dit l'architecte.

The slave's final remark here is both true and ironic in its context, for it
leads to God's judgment and Hell as well as to beatitude. The king had
not really made a choice in favor of good; rather, he was lured protesting
to his destruction. Salvation is not for him.

There is in this poem and in "Sultan Mourad" another feature of
interest: those in an inferior position (the pig, the slave) and by exten-
sion the masses, bring judgment on the mighty. This problem was raised
in an early section of *La Légende*, where in a part of "Asie" Hugo clearly
hesitated, as he showed both fear and sympathy for mass man, continuing
the uncertainty that he had manifested over the words "peuple" and
"populace" in the earlier years (see Chapter III). On the one hand, the
"Asiatic hordes" are Chaos itself:

L'Asie est monstrueuse et fauve; elle regarde
Toute la terre avec une face hagarde,
Et la terre lui plaît, car partout il fait nuit.

Against this darkness is Western civilization:

Mais la Grèce est un point lumineux qui l'ennuie;
Il se pourrait qu'un jour cette clarté perçât
Et rendît l'espérance à l'univers forçat;
L'Asie obscure et vaste en frémit sous son voile;

Et l'énorme noirceur cherche à tuer l'étoile.

As the mass of two million soldiers attacking the West is associated with
evil matter, Themistocles urges the Greeks to fight:

Et tout sera perdu, peuple, si tu n'opposes
La fermeté de l'homme à la trahison des choses.

Does not Hugo's use of "peuple" suggest his desire once more to define
man in the aggregate as something more than faceless mobs or "populace"? Yet the poet remains uneasy and a few pages later presents the
other side of the coin. In "Aide offerte à Majorien," we encounter hordes
of the Dark Ages, whose image is a "mer des hommes," driven by hunger
and thirst. They are faceless, called "Les Sans nombre," and their only
purpose in life seems to be to wander. They have been defeated in battle

by Caesar, Denatus, Spryx, Cimber, yet all these Roman generals are dead, while they endure. But in a curious conclusion, Majorien, a Roman officer, asks their leader Attila:

> Mais où donc allez-vous?
>   L'homme
>   La terre est le chemin,
> Le but est l'infini, nous allons à la vie.
> Là-bas une lueur immense nous convie.
> Nous nous arrêterons lorsque nous serons là.

In this mass quest we see a new dimension that goes beyond the private quest of an Ordener or an Otbert and even beyond the messiah, like Barberousse, who redeems his tribe. It suggests the uprising of an entire humanity eager to leave darkness and to claim its rightful place in the sun, under God's benevolent eye:

> Nul n'est plus grand que nous sur la terre où nous sommes.
> Nous fuyons devant Dieu, mais non devant les hommes.

Thus, *La Légende des siècles* during its first part (I–XXI) shows the fall from Eden, and if there is a cause, it is Cain's slaying of Abel rather than eating of forbidden fruit. After the fall, we witness the struggle of good against evil which reaches a nadir of pessimism with the decadent years of the Roman Empire. During the Dark Ages and medieval period, there were many attempts by heroic figures to overcome evil. The essence of this part, and of much of Hugo's earlier imagery of judgment from *Les Orientales* to *Les Burgraves*, is concentrated in the beautiful lines from "Les Chevaliers errants":

> La terre a vu jadis errer des paladins;
> Ils flamboyaient ainsi que des éclairs soudains,
> Puis s'évanouissaient, laissant sur les visages
> La crainte, et la lueur de leurs brusques passages;
> Ils étaient, dans des temps d'oppression, de deuil,
> De honte, où l'infamie étalait son orgueil,
> Les spectres de l'honneur, du droit, de la justice;
> Ils foudroyaient le crime, ils souffletaient le vice;
> On voyait le vol fuir, l'imposture hésiter,
> Blêmir la trahison, et se déconcerter

137

Toute puissance injuste, inhumaine, usurpée,
Devant ces magistrats sinistres de l'épée. . . .
Prêts à toute besogne, à toute heure, en tout lieu,
Farouches, ils étaient les chevaliers de Dieu.

Ils erraient dans la nuit ainsi que des lumières.

These lines suggest the skies of "Soleils couchants" and, when considered together with the lines from "Ratbert" where a monk saw "dans les profondeurs par les vents remuées,/ Un archange essuyer son épée aux nuées," they combine the earlier imagery of a celestial warrior with the theme of the avenging sword (*éclair, nuées, épée, flamboyaient*). Despite the strength and dedication of these avengers, their solitary power can do little to change this corrupt world and eliminate the forces of evil. More than they will be needed to make a better existence for man, and Hugo reflects this un-Romantic belief as he causes the paladins to disappear and to yield to the power of collective action by mankind. This new spirit invades *La Légende* in the period of the Renaissance, with "Le Satyre" representing man's combined efforts to continue the assault on the Heaven of injustice which had been begun by the Titan.

As the Renaissance begins, mankind is still a prisoner of fatality, in the same position as the fallen and buried Phtos:

Sous la difformité de la loi colossale;
L'homme se tait, plongé sous cet entassement.

André Vial, trying to synthesize the various interpretations given to the famous episode of the Satyr, approaches this section, properly we think, by a study of its form. His conclusion is simple yet profound: "Tous les thèmes du *Satyre* . . . sont envisagés sous [un] certain aspect: *c'est la forme commune sous laquelle ils ont été conçus qui importe*. Or, cette forme existe, évidente. . . . celle de la sédition, de l'insurrection." Vial goes on to conclude from this first observation:

Ce devenir, lorsqu'on l'envisage du côté de l'homme collectif, est animé par un esprit d'insurrection, dont chaque effort successif aboutit en même temps à une intelligence plus rationnelle des lois de l'univers, à une action plus efficace sur la nature, à une liberté nouvelle dans la vie de l'individu et des sociétés, à des rapports plus harmonieux entre les groupes, à une notion plus approchée, encore qu'irrévocablement inadéquate, du divin.[15]

One might even add to Vial's list Hugo's own desire for liberation as a poetic creator. Certainly, the sense of liberation is stressed both in the real world of social change (microcosm) and in the celestial sphere (macrocosm). The Satyr asks man:

Misérable homme, fait pour la révolte sainte,
Ramperas-tu toujours parce que tu rampas?

He calls man to rebel against the gods and kings: "Les rois, après l'avoir fait taire, l'abrutissent," and

Donc, les dieux et les rois sur le faîte,
L'homme en bas; pour valets aux tyrans, les fléaux.

The revolt is not only political but goes so far as to become a rebellion against matter itself. The Satyr dreams:

Qui sait si quelque jour, brisant l'antique affront. . . .
S'il n'arrachera pas de son corps brusquement
La pesanteur, peau vile, immonde vêtement. . . .
De sorte qu'on verra tout à coup, ô prodige,
Ce ver de terre ouvrir ses ailes dans les cieux!

As if urging mankind to take action, he himself, a symbol of all matter, swells in size and is transfigured into a cosmic presence, dethroning the Olympian gods who had at first laughed at him. Thus, the march of history began with a descent from the early Edenic state of man until it reached the cesspools of Rome, and then, after the Dark Ages, the thrust of history turned upward with the voyage of mankind finally completed in the Heavens. But the poem does not end here, for in our world, the microcosm, political or social liberation must wait a little longer. Evil is still strong, present both in the Roman Catholic church according to the poem on the Inquisition (XXVII), and even in Switzerland, famed for its democratic heritage and idealism. To the popular mind the country of William Tell is a snow-capped land of beauty and purity and freedom. In one of the poems from the section on the seventeenth century, "Le

15. "Un Beau Mythe de *La Légende des siècles: Le Satyre*," *Revue des Sciences humaines*, LXXXVII (July–Sept., 1957), 316.

Régiment du baron Madruce (Garde impériale suisse)," the contemporary Swiss troops seem as lofty and as noble as the mountains:

> Voilà le régiment
> De mes hallebardiers qui va superbement.
> Leurs plumets font venir les filles aux fenêtres;
> Ils marchent droits, tendant la pointe de leurs guêtres. . . .

They are so lofty that the poet exclaims:

> Le vertige me prend moi-même dans les airs
> En regardant marcher cette forêt d'éclairs.

But all this grandeur is false. "O chute! o ignominie! inexprimable honte!" Real nobility and loftiness are but a memory of the past.

> Et dire que la Suisse eut jadis l'envergure
> D'un peuple qui se lève et qui se transfigure!

Whereas once the Swiss had risen against the Austrian usurper, these troops are nothing but mercenaries in the pay of this feudal empire: "Ils soutiennent le vaste empire féodal." The poet is charitable enough to remind us that Switzerland will always symbolize liberty by the pure heights of her Alps: "Sa blanche liberté s'adosse au firmament." But it is not given to this nation to lead mankind to freedom. The culmination is prefigured in the earlier poem "1453." A giant (significantly enough) speaks out in prophecy:

> Mon nom sous le soleil est France.
> Je reviendrai dans la clarté,
> J'apporterai la délivrance,
> J'amènerai la liberté.

We look ahead confidently to the coming of the French Revolution, which will dethrone the Olympian gods of the *ancien régime*. Then comes the surprise that is so baffling for the critic. The poet skips over the French Revolution in order to excoriate Napoleon III. Hugo's preoccupation with the government that was responsible for his exile is understandable in human terms, but it weakens the unity and structure of *La Légende*[16]

16. Albert Py, *Les Mythes grecs dans la poésie de Victor Hugo* (Genève, 1963), p. 231, uses the terms "appauvri" and "trahi."

when Olympus is reduced to Saint-Cloud. As a result the tone of the section, "Les Temps présents" resembles more that of *Les Châtiments*[17] than any panorama of history. For instance, "Le Prisonnier" is a direct attack on Marshal Bazaine, who is hardly a towering figure of world history. The scale of myth is further reduced not only to satire but to family anecdote, as in a tasteless poem like "La sœur de charité," or to a more respectable anthology-piece like "Après la bataille." To the extent that Hugo deals with his private hatreds or family biography, Phtos the Titan shrinks to the size of a man named Victor Hugo, and the epic disintegrates. Many of these pieces seem to have only the most remote connection with the over-all structure. Many avoid modern history entirely, either through personal lyricism typical of *Les Contemplations* (e.g., "Après les Fourches Caudines" or in recollections of the ancient past "Dénoncé à celui qui chassa les vendeurs du temple"). The poet's effort to link his generation with that of the Titans is unconvincing because of this reduction in scale:

> Les titans, les lutteurs aux gigantesques tailles,
> Les fauves promeneurs rôdant dans les batailles!
> Nous sommes les petits de ces grands lions-là.

Yet despite the inadequacy of the treatment, some of Hugo's basic pattern emerges. In poem VII of this section, "1851—Choix entre deux passants," Hugo succeeds in capturing a certain grandiose quality through capitalized abstractions. The narrator must choose between the upward or the downward way:

> Et la Honte me dit:—Je m'appelle la Joie.
> Je vais au bonheur. Viens. L'or, la pourpre, la soie,
> Les festins, les palais, les prêtres, les bouffons,

whereas La Mort says:

> Mon nom est Devoir: et je vais
> Au sépulcre, à travers l'angoisse et le prodige.

17. Berret has already observed that *"La Légende des siècles* est inséparable de l'exil de Victor Hugo: elle est pour une large part la continuation des *Châtiments;* elle constitue en maint endroit le cahier de doléances et de confidences du proscrit" (*La Légende,* I, iii). We can only agree for many details, but surely Berret has overstated the case in calling this work a continuation of *Les Châtiments.*

141

The poet chooses the latter way, for it leads "vers l'ombre où Dieu paraît." Thus Hugo—this poem is indeed personal by its very dating—repeats Phtos' way to salvation.

Another important poem of this contemporary period is "Les Pauvres Gens." Here man has left the heights, and the opening line, "Il est nuit," suggests man trapped in darkness. On the realistic plane, it is merely a humble fisherman getting up before dawn to take to the sea. Outside, "le sinistre Océan jette son noir sanglot." But this family seems blessed, for though "le logis est plein d'ombre," one can sense something "qui rayonne à travers ce crépuscule obscur." The husband and father has left to go "down to the sea." The direction is not only Masefield's but Hugo's:

> Il s'en va dans l'abîme et s'en va dans la nuit.
> Dur labeur! tout est noir, tout est froid; rien ne luit.

The risk of going down and never coming up again is great. But this humble Titan is not alone. His wife and he have five children already and, in a gesture of human solidarity, take in two more when a poor widow dies. This act, like Welf's, is redemptive, one of many such acts in Hugo that create a basis for what contemporary critics have called a "mythologie du peuple,"[18] which finds a culmination in "Plein Ciel."

We referred in the chapter on *Notre-Dame* to the fact that the sun, an ideal, could be attained if only the bars of feudal restrictions could be broken. Unlike the individual man in the cage in the Bastille, but like the French of 1789, Phtos bursts his fetters, escapes from the mountain, and turns to the light. Metamorphosed into the Satyr, he reconquers Olympus. Within a context of pure mythology there is no problem. But in the final statement of *La Légende*, "Plein Ciel," it is liberated, finite man who rises into the air. By the very images that Hugo had been elaborating for years, man must reach the sun, having descended into the depths of poverty, suffering, danger, or death first. Yet human finitude makes this achievement impossible and the poem equivocates. In *Dieu*, Hugo rejected a first version that proclaimed "Je vis Dieu" for the more human "[Dieu]me toucha du doigt le front, et je mourus." In *La Fin de Satan* Nimrod's evil assault on God is in a first version described as at least partially successful: "il avait blessé Dieu," only to be changed to the interrogative "Avait-il blessé Dieu?" How much more awkward the prob-

18. E.g., René Journet et Guy Robert, *Le Mythe du peuple dans les Misérables* (Paris, 1964); Albouy uses the term "mythologie de l'humanité" (p. 304).

lem in "Plein Ciel," which starts with a technological invention, the airship! In the poem, Man climbs ("il monta aux étoiles") and casts off his fetters: "il abolit la loi de fer, la loi de sang,/ Les glaives, les carcans, l'esclavage." Like the Satyr, he rises "Hors de la pesanteur."

> Ce navire là-haut conclut le grand hymen.
> Il mêle presque à Dieu l'âme du genre humain.
> Il voit l'insondable, il y touche.

But an ambiguity remains: "hymen" and "presque" are mutually exclusive. "Il y touche" summarizes very well that process of arriving and being about to touch (Michelangelo had the same problem in the Sistine Chapel). Hugo cannot quite deify man, nor can he quite keep from so doing. But lest we consider the poet overly arrogant, it is well to recall not only those pages in *Dieu* where man's prowess is mocked, but also the very last line of *La Légende* where Hugo makes clear that Man may rise but God is beyond all gods, and He says in the closing words: "Je n'aurais qu'à souffler, et tout serait de l'ombre."[19] This then is the structure of Hugo's epic. It is not merely a rise, as Berret and Hugo, among others, have claimed. It is descent and rise,[20] and in its pattern it does not stand alone. In the preface of 1859, the poet wrote: "Plus tard . . . on apercevra la ligne qui, dans la conception de l'auteur, rattache *La Légende des siècles* à deux autres poëmes, presque terminés à cette heure, et qui en sont, l'un le dénoûment, l'autre le couronnement: *La Fin de Satan et Dieu.*" We remarked earlier that the latter work is outside the scope of this study, for it lacks genuine narrative action and plot. The coronation of which Hugo writes is more intellectual abstraction than ritual drama. But the term "dénoûment" is by definition a part of the process of narration. We have already alluded in an earlier chapter to a few details from *La Fin de Satan*, but a more systematic study is needed, all the more so because it was the first of the three to have come to the poet's mind.[21]

*   *   *

19. To the extent that Hugo the poet is a creator of universes, the same applies. The poet has only to blow out his lamp and his poetic universe becomes non-existent.

20. Zumthor, pp. 100–1, 117 has sensed this pattern but does not study it systematically.

21. *Ibid.*, p. 131.

As Hugo had included the poet's own descent in *Les Contempla-tions* and *La Légende*, so he revealed his poetic role in *La Fin de Satan:*

> Le penseur qui, pareil aux pauvres, va pieds nus
> Par respect pour Celui qu'on ne voit pas, le mage,[22]
> Fouille la profondeur et l'origine et l'âge,
> Creuse et cherche au delà des colosses, plus loin
> Que les faits dont le ciel d'à présent est témoin,
> Arrive en pâlissant aux choses soupçonnées,
> Et trouve, en soulevant des ténèbres d'années
> Et des couches de jours, de mondes, de néants,
> Les siècles monstres morts sous les siècles géants.

Hugo is once again Phtos groping his way through the darkness. Taking the book of Genesis as a point of departure, he opens up for us a primitive, antediluvian world in which evil has become commonplace. But again Hugo avoids the story of man's fall located in Eden. The poet concentrates on the fall of Lucifer from Heaven, who then finds himself in the ultimate vast cave of Hell where, like the black spider with its legs, there lurks in the depths of Evil (to use the language of *La Bouche d'Ombre*) "Un affreux soleil noir d'où rayonne la nuit." This evil had come into being through idolatry, represented by Isis-Lilith. Thus man is caught between Idolatry "en bas" and Fatality "en haut." As a result,

> Depuis longtemps l'azur perdait ses purs rayons,
> Et par instants semblait plein de hideuses toiles
> Où l'araignée humaine avait pris les étoiles.[23]

To destroy evil, God sent the Deluge from which the world was reborn. But alas, Isis, "l'âme du monde mort," still lives and with her, three instruments of bronze, wood, and stone with which Cain slew Abel. These become respectively the Sword, the Cross, and the Prison. Again, there is a parallel with *La Légende*, where the crime of Cain, so obsessive to Hugo, seems somehow at the origin of all evil. These three objects, Sword, Cross, and Prison, become titles for the major divisions of the work.

22. The idea of Hugo as *"mage"* (*Les Contemplations*, Book VI) is too well known to need discussion here.
23. Albouy, p. 169, comments on the frequency of this rhyme. We would add that "toile" and "étoile" suggest the barrier and ideal that we have been studying.

144

Nimrod, who with the sword of war stands as an incarnation of armed conflict, is pictured as having conquered the whole world. He has reached in his demonic nature, "L'altier sommet où l'homme en Dieu se transfigure" (p. 31). This sense of self-deification is given concrete elaboration by Nimrod's attempt to assault Heaven directly. The story, which goes far beyond Nimrod's mere appearance in the legend of Pécopin, is familiar to any student of Hugo's work but bears brief retelling. Accompanied by his eunuch Zaïm, whose condition suggests the ultimate impotence of war, Nimrod constructs a cage that is lifted by eagles so high that it rises out of sight of earth. The hunter's last gesture of loosing an arrow toward God before falling back to earth is perhaps the most dramatic example in the poet's work of the failure of direct ascent. After this failure of the upward thrust, Hugo next turned to Jesus of Nazareth, who was to try a different route, the route of humility and of descent.

The role of Jesus in the work of Victor Hugo is of great importance because of the manner in which it diverges from the Biblical narrative. At first the account seems orthodox enough. The world into which He makes His appearance is a somber one indeed. Under Roman domination (we remember what Hugo thought of the Roman Empire in "Au lion d'Androclès"):

> l'homme ne voyait rien
> Qu'une noirceur croissante au-dessus de sa tête;
>
> .   .   .   .
>
> L'ombre se résolvait en haine autour de l'âme.

Judea was dominated not only by the wicked Herod but by Caiaphas the High Priest, "l'homme sombre," a pederast (and therefore in Hugo's eyes wicked), head of the Sanhedrin (p. 69). The temple in which the latter meets recalls the earlier demonic caves, for it is described with the words "chaînes," "gonds," and "verrous," prison imagery suitable to the Bastille or to Lucrèce Borgia's room of execution. Within this *antre* there is a *grand autel* where Caiaphas lurks. Another *antre* belongs to a sibyl who dwells in a *caverne*. Her lineage is easily traced back through Guanhumara of *Les Burgraves* to Gudule of *Notre-Dame* and—as a crone—to the ghoul Isis-Lilith of *La Fin de Satan* itself. In her cave we find all the familiar vocabulary: *antre, caverne, vol de démons, ombre, gouffre, nuit, spectre, rit* (p. 86). She warns against any attempt to break out of the circle of fatality that holds man in bondage, saying that the fly cannot break through the barrier: "La mouche humaine allant heurter aux cieux son aile," and that the upward thrust will not succeed:

O sages, pour gravir les cieux où sont les Tables,
Vous hantez les hauts lieux, ces cimes redoutables
Que visite l'horreur et que la bise mord;
Vous y cherchez le jour, vous y trouvez la mort;
Certains sommets fatals ont d'âpres calvities
Où les hideuses croix, par le meurtre noircies,
Se dressent, attendant les pâles rédempteurs;
Et vous êtes, hélas! trahis par les hauteurs. (p. 89)

Hugo's vision is not so facilely optimistic that he condemns as ridiculous this sense of human impotence. When the Sibyl remarks that "L'infini ne se peut prendre dans un filet" (p. 91) and warns the poet that "Sonder/ C'est blesser" and that man is but ashes (p. 91), Hugo is engaging in a genuine debate with himself. Nonetheless, the vision of despair must be overcome, and Jesus is the One who will make the heroic attempt. As in orthodox tradition, He comes as light into darkness, "un homme radieux." The theme of descent is clearly marked:

Cet homme, qu'entourait la rumeur grossissante,
Semblait un dieu faisant sur terre une descente.

His humility is suggested by the word "pasteur" and later on, his riding on a donkey is recalled. Despite the hesitation of the word "semblait," his power is not feigned:

Calme, il forçait l'essaim invisible et hideux
Des noirs esprits du mal, rois des ténébreux mondes,
A se précipiter dans les bêtes immondes. . . .
Il lavait les péchés ainsi que des limons. . . .
Il calmait l'ouragan, haranguait l'animal.

And on a vaster scale, "Satan fuyait devant l'éclair de sa prunelle." Now, the role of a god is to be redemptive, if we may judge from world religions. Hugo sets the power of redemption against the backdrop of Judaism, which leads merely to Sheol, the final unredeemed darkness. The priest Sadoch explains the doctrine:

146

> La mort, c'est l'ombre. Il n'est pour l'homme
> Rien d'éternel après cette vie; il ne peut
> Rien retenir de lui quand Dieu brise ce nœud.

Not only the Jews, Sadoch claims, but their enemies find oblivion after death:

> Moïse commença par creuser une fosse,
> O juifs, pour y coucher la religion fausse.

But such a limited vision of life after death is surely the exception to the normal pattern of world religion. In discussing the Orpheus story, Mircea Eliade has shown the different visions of divine redemptive power in world religion, but he has also shown its deep unity:

> Avons-nous le droit de considérer Orphée comme un "chaman" et de comparer la descente de Christ aux Enfers aux descentes similaires des chamans en extase? Tout s'y oppose . . . ces descentes sont valorisées de manières très différentes. . . . Mais un élément de-meure immuable, qu'il ne faut pas perdre de vue: c'est la persistance du motif de la descente aux Enfers *entreprise pour le salut d'une âme;* l'âme d'un malade quelconque (chamanisme, *stricto sensu*), de l'épouse (mythes grecs, nordaméricains, polynésiens, central-asiatiques), de l'humanité tout entière (le Christ), peu nous importe pour l'instant. La descente, cette fois, n'est plus seulement initia-tique et entreprise pour un avantage personnel, elle a un but "salvi-fique": l'on "meurt" et l'on "ressuscite" non plus pour achever une initiation déjà acquise, mais pour sauver une âme. . . . la mort symbolique ne sert pas uniquement à sa propre perfection spirituelle . . . mais elle se réalise pour le salut des *autres*.[24]

To return to Hugo's Jesus, we must admit there is a difference between Christ's descent into Hell and his descent into earthly life, but Christian-ity ascribes to both a redemptive quality, and, as any student of religion knows, death and resurrection are necessary elements in this act of salvation. In fact, this is the supreme test: can Jesus, with His divine power, save others in Hugo's cosmos? To set the stage, the poet reaches

24. *Images et symboles* (Paris, 1952), p. 218.

back into Jewish legend and places under Golgotha still another cave that fits in with the others in his work:

> Au fond de l'horizon est le Golgotha fauve;
> Mort sans arbre, sans herbe et sans fleurs; sommet chauve
> Et propre à la croissance des gibets;
>
> . . . .
>
> Le vaste Adam est là, sous la terre dormant.
> Si bien que le Calvaire est le noir renflement
> De ce grand corps gisant sous la morne campagne,
> Et qu'un air de cadavre en reste à la montagne.

This vision is a demonic parody of what the historians of religion call the Axis Mundi, with the sacred tree, which links earth and heaven, transformed into the cross on a hill that should be a sacred mountain but is in truth a bitter wasteland. Hugo has a sure instinct for mythological truth. To the question "Can Jesus of Nazareth, the New Adam, save the Old Adam?" Christianity answers yes; *La Fin de Satan* says no.

For a time the reader is deceived. In the section "Le Triomphe," as Jesus rides in lowly splendor on the donkey, His success is predicted:

> Il vient ôter la nuit de dessus l'âme humaine;
> Il fera reculer l'hydre qui triomphait;

and in an open antithesis to His negative counterpart in the poem, "Il est plus radieux que Nemrod n'était sombre" (p. 112). This "corps de lumière" (p. 116) is expected to descend into death in accord with the exigencies of mythological patterns of religion, and does:

> Mais le sauveur va droit au peuple et s'y meurtrit.
> Dieu livre le messie aux multitudes viles.

His path is "funeste" to be sure, but it is also "triomphant" (p. 114).[25] The hopeful vision, reasonably orthodox up to this point, disintegrates by means of the images that are by now familiar. First, Jesus has his hands tied (p. 131) and is led into the "antre" of the Sanhedrin. Like Esmer-

---

25. An entire study is needed on the totality of Hugo's view of Jesus, for his attitude is not always clear. In a letter to Michelet (June 9, 1856) published by J.-M. Carré in the *Revue de France*, I (1924), 729, Jesus "a été une incarnation saignante du progès," but in *Toute la lyre*, I, 15–17, Jesus cries "Je suis Dieu" and Prometheus says "Je suis l'Homme."

alda in her lightless dungeon, visited only by the wicked priest Frollo, Jesus finds himself in the presence of the evil[26] Caiaphas in the court. The parallel between these two Hugolian texts is made explicit when Hugo comments: "Montfaucon à côté du Golgotha s'élève" (p. 165). The setting would fit either text:

> Dans une sorte d'ombre inquiète et sacrée;
>
> . . . .
>
> La nuit ne sort jamais de ce lieu sans fenêtres. (pp. 133–34)

Like Esmeralda, who is the one light in the courtroom, the Christ by His presence judges His accusers more strongly than can any gypsy girl.

> Christ est debout devant ces hommes ténébreux;
> Son œil inépuisable en rayons luit sur eux.

After the crucifixion,

> Jésus,
> S'en alla, comme Abel, comme Job, comme Elie;
> Quand il eut disparu, l'œuvre étant accomplie. . . .
> Le serpent releva son front dans les décombres.

We must not be misled by the phrase "l'œuvre étant accomplie." Hugo suggests that His effort was a failure:

> Après le Golgotha, Jésus, ouvrant son aile,
> A beau s'être envolé dans l'aurore éternelle;
> Il a beau resplendir, superbe et gracieux,
> Dans la tranquillité sidérale des cieux. . . . (pp. 163–64)

His message is betrayed constantly, and He is helpless to prevent it.

> Dans l'azur qu'aucun souffle orageux ne corrompt,
> Christ frémissant essuie un crachat sur son front.

Thus although there is grandeur, there is also finality in Hugo's concluding words to this section: "Ainsi mourut Jésus" and on Golgotha "la religion, sinistre, tua Dieu." Jesus' efforts, Hugo suggests, ended in failure, not a moral one but one of power.[27] His departure left a serious vacuum that Hugo hastened to fill in accord with his typical patterns of

26. Caiaphas is described as "pareil à Satan plus encor qu'à Moïse" (p. 138).
27. "Je suis la force, enfants; Jésus fut la douceur," says Mohammed in "Islam" (*Légende des siècles,* II, 163).

narrative creation. The freed criminal, Barabbas, comes to the cross and realizes what has happened:

> Alors, sur cette âpre colline,
> On ne sait quel esprit entra dans les ténèbres
> De cet homme, et le fit devenir effrayant.
> Un feu profond jaillit de son œil foudroyant;

and then the poet makes use of the idea of Adam buried under Golgotha:

> L'âme immense d'Adam, couché sous le Calvaire,
> Sembla soudain monter dans ce voleur sévère.
> Et Barabbas debout, transfiguré, tremblant,
> Terrible, cria:
> > "Peuple, affreux peuple sanglant,
> Qu'as-tu fait?"

He goes on to condemn the people who have killed the Christ. The pattern is clear: Barabbas is another incarnation of the Titan or Prometheus, of the Satyr and of the various heroes who excoriate the tyrants in *La Légende des siècles;* he can be traced back through Barberousse and Ruy Blas, even to Han d'Islande, in that he arises to confront and condemn the wicked. Like all the others (including Jesus), he is an outcast from the dominant society—the "Proscrit." This motif reaches so pervasively back into Hugo's younger period that we should not limit this myth, as does Paul Zumthor, to "le mythe du proscrit de Jersey" (p. 65). Barabbas, then, is the man of energy who possesses the power that Jesus lacked.[28] He possesses it, we remember, by means of the buried Adam (a symbol of man) welling up in him. Even Isis-Lilith, the cosmic spirit of evil, recognizes this power lurking in the anthill ("fourmilière obscure") of the world. This spirit explains that man's potential for revolution— announced by Barabbas—may perhaps be realized one day in France. At the moment, France, like the Titan, is in bondage (p. 215), symbolized as we have seen before by the Bastille. Hugo explains his symbols carefully:

> Ce peuple étrange est plus qu'un peuple, c'est une âme;
> Ce peuple est l'Homme même. . . .

28. Albouy draws attention to Jesus' limitations in a passage of the *Reliquat* where Jesus is "plus qu'homme, presque Dieu" (p. 268).

The French, not Jesus, are the "New Adam": "Ce peuple, c'est Adam, mais Adam qui se venge"; a Promethean Adam: "Adam ayant volé le glaive ardent de l'ange"; a Titanic Adam: "Et chassant devant lui la Nuit et le Trépas" (p. 214). France, not the Christ, is to bring deliverance to mankind. So we should not be surprised when in *Dieu* Hugo puts the Angel of Rationalism(!) above the griffin of Christianity (France, we must remember, is after all the country of Descartes). The Christ seemed too weak to bring about the ultimate good. The title "Puissance égale bonté" from *La Légende* is not an idle concept to Hugo.

The idea that power comes from Adam, buried under the earth, not only provides an echo of the buried Titan but anticipates the part of the poem that deals with the salvation of Satan, the ultimate outcast buried in Hell. As Hugo develops the section on the fallen archangel, he again supplies the image of the chained prisoner:

> Ne sens-tu pas qu'il faut que toute chaîne
> Se rompe, et que le mal finisse?

And if fifty years of imagery mean anything, some final act of irruption that will receive the poet's approval should be expected. But for the first time, Hugo faced a radically new problem. The jailer is not the "false" god Jupiter, or any corrupt social institution or class. He is the God of the universe and therefore a revolt against Him cannot be holy. Satan is blocked. Flying upward or going down, he realizes that all directions are closed to him:

> Oh! je monte et descends et remonte sans cesse,
> De la création fouillant le souterrain;
> Le bas est de l'acier, le haut est de l'airain. (p. 203)

Here there is no final stone that the Titan can remove. This time the outcast is prisoner of the Absolute, trapped like the fly in Claude Frollo's cell:

> Frappant des pieds, des mains et du front l'infini,
> Ainsi qu'un moucheron heurte une vitre sombre. (p. 204)

A deft compromise resolves the tension. The Angel of Liberty, daughter of God *and* Satan, is the instrument of the latter's redemption. The

151

outcast is resurrected as Lucifer. The poem ends here with the equivalent portion of man's deliverance in the "real" world left unfinished. There are only a few lines on the French Revolution.

It is quite possible that the characters of *La Fin de Satan* can be viewed in terms of the poet's biography. Baudouin suggests, "Il est une région de son âme où sa fille bien-aimée Léopoldine se confond avec l'ange liberté" (p. 249). Zumthor is even more categorical: "Le voile des symboles se déchire, toute affabulation épique est alors interrompue: Satan, c'est Hugo lui-même" (p. 252). Although we have already suggested that Hugo found substance for his literary characters from his own person, to call Satan Hugo is an arbitrary act of the critic who chooses to ignore artistic transformation and reduce the creative act to autobiographical projection. If the myth is "impoverished" here, it is the critics who have stripped it of its riches.

The drama of the resurrection and resanctification of Hugo's Satan needs to be viewed in the sequence of imagery that the poet had developed. What is Satan in Hell but a demonic religious figure in a cave? Are we not dealing with a cosmic version of the ominous altars and crosses of *Han d'Islande, Bug-Jargal, Notre-Dame?* Whereas the necessity of verisimilitude in the earlier texts required the use of imagery, in *La Fin de Satan* imagery could be replaced by open myth.

The mechanism of Satan's conversion is as interesting as the fact of his rebirth. As Zumthor has observed, evil is dissociated from Satan and attributed to Isis-Lilith. She announces proudly: "Tremble! Ananké, c'est moi. Tremble! Le voile, c'est moi" (p. 221). As Ananké, she brings with her the old image of the fly and the spider, albeit somewhat disguised. "Quoi!", she says to Angel Liberty, "la mouche entre où n'ose entrer Léviathan!" and:

> Si je poussais un cri, tu te sentirais prendre
> Par ce qu'on ne voit pas, l'invisible forêt
> Lâcherait son hibou, la nuit se lèverait
> Et t'envelopperait dans la grande aile onglée.

The spider is now an owl, but "envelopperait" suggests its origin. Now rays of light emanate from the undismayed angel who swells to the size of a sun, and Isis-Lilith is obliterated. The parallel with the poem from *La Légende*, "Puissance égale bonté," is clear. In the latter, God took a spider offered to him by the spirit of evil and set it in the firmament:

Une aube étrange erra sur cette forme vile;
L'affreux ventre devint un globe lumineux;
Et les pattes, changeaient en sphères d'or leurs nœuds,
S'allongèrent dans l'ombre en grands rayons de flamme, . . .
Car Dieu, de l'araignée, avait fait le soleil.

The conclusion is surprising but inescapable. God (light, goodness) and Evil (black, ugliness) are united in a profound oneness of form, where each has a radiant center and projections (rays of the sun, legs of the spider) that envelop man. One is the *revers de la médaille* of the other. A flip of the coin, a moment's sleight of hand, and we pass from God to Satan, from Satan to God, and ultimately, it can even be argued that, being one coin, Satan and God are not separate entities. The myth formed in this fashion even suggests that one may be a Satan and descend into Hell and gain salvation and climb again to the heights of Heaven. Even Jesus is forgotten in the apotheosis. Beyond this point, one may explain the sources of Hugo's thought, one may approve or disapprove of Hugo's position. He may be Manichean ("Le Mal, c'est la Matière"), or he may not be (Manicheism is low on the ladder of values in *Dieu*); he is certainly blaspheming by orthodox standards if the savior Christ is replaced by Adam. Zumthor summarizes it well: "cet ouvrage est à sa place au centre de l'œuvre immense de Hugo. C'est Babel en effet. L'ouvrage impossible d'une divinisation de l'homme" (p. 320).

Our purpose has not been to judge but to show the structure of these epico-mythic works and to discover the direction that Hugo's earlier imagery was taking. The basic form of *La Légende* and *La Fin de Satan* is akin to that of the other works in its pattern of descent and rise, but here the hero—at least the hero operating in the "real" world—is mankind itself which undertakes the quest. Following a descent into the abyss, mankind finally emerges transformed (as is typical of myth), a new creation that can then construct a perfect world. But our task is not yet complete, anticlimactic as it may at first seem. While writing this epic poetry, Hugo was also continuing his prose fiction, in which he would try to readapt myth to the exigencies of verisimilitude. In novels where no avenging angels can appear to decapitate a villain, myth must appear as imagery. *Les Misérables* and the novels that follow will be gigantic attempts at creating first mythic and then apocalyptic syntheses of the human and the cosmic.

153

MYTH AND SOCIETY

LES MISÉRABLES

V ICTOR HUGO declared shortly before the publication of *Les Misérables:* "Ma conviction est que ce livre sera un des principaux sommets sinon le principal de mon œuvre,"[1] and indeed since its appearance it has received world-wide popular acclaim. It has also received equally wide critical scorn, partly because of its stylized characters and partly because of its inadequate sociology, which fails to capture a sense of lived reality, so necessary for a true novel. These differing judgments suggest the need for a close critical look at this famous text.

Its supposed genesis is well known. Some facts are well established: It was begun in 1845 under the title of *Les Misères,* continued until 1848, interrupted until Hugo went into exile, and finally published under its definitive title in 1862. Its original inspiration goes back much farther, probably to *Le Dernier Jour d'un condamné* (1829), which dramatized the stark plight of prisoners on their way to the Toulon galleys and told about a prisoner sent to jail for stealing a loaf of bread. In 1834, Hugo protested vehemently against the death penalty in his short story, *Claude Gueux.*[2] But recently, Professor Jean Pommier has shown that the first notes on Monseigneur Miollis (the historical prototype for Monseigneur Myriel) date, not from 1828–1830, as has been widely repeated, but from 1834.[3] A well-established academic tradition has claimed that the central character of the novel, known ultimately under the name of Jean Valjean, was based on the life of a real person, one Pierre Maurin.[4] Again, it is the indefatigable Jean Pommier who has proved that this attribution of source is unsound, and that more than likely the origins of the character

1. Letter to Albert Lacroix, March 23, 1862, *Correspondance,* II, 383.
2. For all this side of Hugo's thought see Paul Savey-Casard, *Le Crime et la peine dans l'œuvre de Victor Hugo* (Paris, 1956), and René Journet et Guy Robert, *Le Mythe du peuple dans les Misérables* (Paris, 1964).
3. "Premiers pas dans l'étude des 'Misérables'" in *Centenaire des Misérables (1862–1962). Hommage à Victor Hugo* (Strasbourg, 1962), p. 33.
4. Gustave Simon, editor of the edition of *Les Misères* (Paris, 1927) was the main perpetrator of this legend, now discredited.

come not from history but from literature, to be specific, from Paul de Kock's *La Laitière de Montfermeil,* which was certainly the inspiration for the locale of Jean Valjean's first encounter with Cosette.[5] This rectification supports the idea that literary inspiration is as important as historical source in the genesis of the work and bears out our assertion that we are dealing only partially with a true novel. Indeed, if we recognize that Hugo's text is a blending of novel and theological epic, which owes its existence not only to contemporary history but also in part to a Dantean vision, the stylized characters and inadequate sociology are then only partly valid objections, and the work can be judged on its own particular qualities.

As a matter of fact, because the opening section of *La Fin de Satan, Et Nox Facta est,* dates from 1854, and the more mythic parts of *Les Misérables* from 1860, scholars have already pointed out parallels between the two and have even viewed the novel as "l'épanouissement du poème."[6] Gaudon observes that both have the same structure, fall and redemption, and that only eleven days after abandoning *La Fin de Satan,* Hugo went back to work on his novel. But as we shall show, the themes, structure, and images remind one equally of those of *La Légende.* The principal theme is announced within the text of the work when Hugo intrudes to comment in terms that recall his preface to *La Légende:*

> Le livre . . . est . . . la marche du mal au bien, de l'injuste au juste, du faux au vrai, de la nuit au jour, de l'appétit à la conscience, de la pourriture à la vie, de la bestialité au devoir, de l'enfer au ciel, du néant à Dieu. Point de départ: la matière, point d'arrivée: l'âme. L'hydre au commencement, l'ange à la fin.[7]

This passage emphasizes the voyage toward a distant ideal, a theme central to both *La Fin de Satan* and *La Légende* and in a wider context, one which is at the heart of the entire body of nineteenth-century French literature. Hugo's problem for the novel—and it is a novel as well as a romance—was to reduce the epic scope to a more human one in order to

5. Pommier, pp. 33–35.
6. Jean Gaudon, "Je ne sais quel jour de soupirail," in *Centenaire des Misérables,* p. 149.
7. The four volumes composing *Les Misérables* in the E.I.N. are numbers III–VI of the series of tomes called *Romans.* We are keeping this numbering, with the result that Vol. III is actually the first of the four, etc. The reference is to VI, 78.

make the reader believe in its reality. Here, roughly, was Hugo's announced method:

> Faire le poëme de la conscience humaine, ne fût-ce qu'à propos d'un seul homme. . . . ce serait fondre toutes les épopées dans une épopée supérieure et définitive. La conscience, c'est le chaos des chimères, des convoitises et des tentatives, la fournaise des rêves, l'antre des idées dont on a honte. (III, 228)

Personal moral conscience will be blended with cosmic imagery whose transcendent purpose is reflected in the age-old idea of a universe constructed of macrocosm and microcosm:

> En même temps qu'il y a un infini hors de nous, n'y a-t-il pas un infini en nous? Ces deux infinis (quel pluriel effrayant!) ne se superposent-ils pas l'un à l'autre? Le second infini n'est-il pas pour ainsi dire sous-jacent au premier? . . . Ce moi d'en bas, c'est l'âme; ce moi d'en haut, c'est Dieu. (III, 225)

But although the inspiration and vision are both moral and mythic, as *Les Misérables* is set in "reality," this presence of reality adds ballast, or an anchor, which is the world of things, or of objects.[8] In another of Hugo's many generalizing intrusions into the fabric of the narration,[9] he explains that "tous les aspects des choses sont des pensées de Dieu" (IV, 292), thus linking our world of objects with the transcendent one. Man makes the connection between the real and divine worlds by prayer, Hugo claims; the artist, or at least the author of *Les Misérables*, starts with objects which he transforms into symbols and then, going beyond the symbolism of *Notre-Dame de Paris*, creates a world of myth that points to God. But Hugo is not content with a dual universe, and he goes on to create another world beneath our "real" world. For instance, he makes clear that the sewer system under Paris parallels the city streets above, and in a social dimension the criminal world of Paris lies underneath that

---

8. In the preface to *Les Travailleurs de la mer*, Hugo will refer to *Les Misérables* as stressing "l'anankè des lois," with the "anankè des choses" reserved for his maritime work. But objects have an important role to play here as well.

9. Michel Butor, "Victor Hugo, romancier," *Tel Quel*, XVI (Hiver, 1964), rightly stresses the importance of the digressions but tends to overlook the importance of the action, scorning it as "les aventures de Jean Valjean" (p. 60). Both are needed to keep the equilibrium between the real and the abstract.

of accepted middle-class society. Hugo explains: "Tous les linéaments que la providence trace à la surface d'une nation ont leurs parallèles sombres, mais distincts dans le fond" (V, 161). He calls the underworld a "troisième dessous" (IV, 433). He has thus set up a very traditional universe of Heaven, Earth, and Underworld or Hell.

The unifying center of the action of the novel in this vast setting is the hero himself, Jean Valjean, whose story is familiar to any student of French literature. Upon the death of his parents when he was young, he was brought up by his married sister. When her husband died leaving her with seven children, the twenty-five-year-old Jean stepped in to support her family. "Cela se fit simplement, comme un devoir" (III, 89). When faced with starvation of the children one winter because of unemployment, he stole the famous loaf of bread that brought about his arrest. Hugo makes it clear that Jean was not to be blamed for his crime, nor is he at all vicious: "Jean n'était pas, on l'a vu, d'une nature mauvaise. Il était bon lorsqu'il arriva au bagne" (III, 96). So Hugo puts the blame squarely on society in general and on the penal system in particular. After years in prison, his sentence increased because of his futile attempts to escape, the admirable young man has become transformed into a Satan. The language in which his soul is described has obvious analogies to the section of *La Fin de Satan, Et Nox Facta est.*

> Jean Valjean . . . haïssait dans les ténèbres. . . . Il vivait habituellement dans cette ombre, tâtonnant comme un aveugle et comme un rêveur. Seulement par intervalles, il lui venait tout à coup . . . un pâle et rapide éclair qui illuminait toute son âme, et faisait brusquement apparaître partout autour de lui . . . aux lueurs d'une lumière affreuse, les hideux précipices et les sombres perspectives de sa destinée. (III, 97)

In this transformation, Hugo makes a serious error that flaws the otherwise fine achievement of his novel. Jean Valjean's "Satanism" is not impressive. He is not a guilty rebel cast from Heaven because of his pride. Even in *La Fin de Satan* this point is glossed over with one brief reference to Lucifer's envy. Here Jean is rather a persecuted victim. So why should he feel a sense of guilt as he does? Even if we accept him as a "Satan malgré lui," his crimes are barely petty larceny. He steals the silverware and Petit Gervais' coin. The whole Satanic nature of the hero

157

is built upon the most insignificant of crimes. The reader cannot be impressed, particularly as Jean's virtue shines through his rough exterior even when he is supposedly least admirable. The whole basis of the work is weakened from its inception.

But if one can put aside this serious defect, the story shows great strength and consistency. We first pick up the hero's trail at Digne, where Jean is desperately trying to reintegrate himself into society. An outcast from the world of bourgeois respectability, as Lucifer was an outcast from Heaven, he makes a great effort to be accepted once again but fails, as did Lucifer when he flew toward the distant stars in *Et Nox Facta est*. As he leaves Digne in despair, Jean says: "Je m'en suis allé dans les champs pour coucher à la belle étoile. Il n'y avait pas d'étoile" (III, 79). This is a good example of Hugo's technique of placing real suns or (stars) in the universe of true myth, and in the world of human reality transforming them into imagery. Jean Valjean, like Satan, finds himself alone, and the book makes it abundantly clear that the world of social injustice is a modern form of Hell. The occasional references to Dante are no accident. There is no hope in prison as there was none at the gate of Dante's inferno, to which Hugo explicitly refers (III, 96). Later, when the criminals are being taken to the galleys, "Dante eût cru voir les sept cercles de l'enfer en marche" (V, 89), etc.[10] But this Satan in Hell seems much more like some form of a god, as we shall develop in the following pages,[11] and we may well suspect that this uncertainty concerning his nature is similar to the confusion in other works where spiders become suns, where Satan becomes Lucifer, and where evil is good if the Creator makes it so. The first obvious reference to the Christian tradition, a description of a hill resembling Golgotha, suggests a parallel between Jean Valjean and that other criminal Barabbas of *La Fin de Satan*. We

10. See Pierre Albouy, *La Création mythologique chez Victor Hugo* (Paris, 1963), pp. 208–304. One should remember also the importance of the section on Dante in *William Shakespeare*, and in their *Journal; Mémoires de la vie littéraire* (ed. R. Ricatte [Monaco, 1956]) the Goncourts quote Hugo as saying, "Dante a fait un enfer avec de la poésie; moi j'ai essayé de faire un enfer avec de la réalité" (11 juillet, 1861). But it is curious that Hugo should say that there are seven circles of Hell, when there are really nine in Dante. Also (*vide infra*, p. 161) when Hugo imagines that there are battles between dragons and hydras in the *Inferno*, we may deduce that the poet did not check the source but superimposed his own vision of Dante on his vague memory of the original.

11. We claim no originality here. See Georges Piroué, *Victor Hugo romancier: ou les dessous de l'inconnu* (Paris, 1964), p. 46; Albouy, p. 302.

remember that the latter approached the sinister hill in a state of trance as Jean Valjean does outside Digne:

> La terre était donc plus éclairée que le ciel, ce qui est un effet particulièrement sinistre, et la colline, d'un pauvre et chétif contour, se dessinait vague et blafarde sur l'horizon ténébreux. Tout cet ensemble était hideux, petit, lugubre et borné. Rien dans le champ ni sur la colline qu'un arbre difforme qui se tordait en frissonnant à quelques pas du voyageur. (III, 73)

The image is clear to an alert reader, but the hero's destiny as a new savior (or like Barabbas, the herald of a new spirit of salvation) is to be postponed for a time. Jean flees from this hill and retraces his steps, as yet unwilling to assume the tremendous responsibility as savior of others, when others have persecuted him so mercilessly.

The famous episode of the bishop's candlesticks takes on its clearest meaning in the light of this background. Refusing to follow a divine call, Jean Valjean has it thrust upon him. Thus, the evil act of stealing the silver service turns out to be the first step on the road to salvation. At this point in the narrative Jean is not saved, for he shortly afterward steals Petit Gervais' coin and then suddenly disappears from sight, only to reappear in Montreuil-sur-mer as M. Madeleine, without any explanation. Upon his reappearance, the reader observes that he has undergone a change, for now he is ready to help others, as when he acts to save old Fauchelevent, pinned under his heavy cart. Jean has to get down on his hands and knees and lift the weight upward, a pattern of action that strongly reminds one of the necessity of descent to achieve salvation. This new man is now (against all realism) embarked on a new career first as mayor of the town and also as its leading industrialist. In these roles, he is able to create material prosperity through technological innovations and appears to have become the savior of the region. But this success, while real in the material sense, is illusory in a more profound one. By adopting the name of M. Madeleine, he has left his true identity and as mayor of *Mont*reuil-*sur*-mer, there may be a word play on place names (as there certainly was with Digne). He is now on top of a mountain.[12]

12. As mayor and industrialist, he is too far above the common people to realize that Fantine's expulsion from her job and her subsequent fall into prostitution is a miscarriage of justice.

Improbable as it may at first seem, he has like Christ been taken up on a mountaintop and tempted. But the hero's deep desire to regain his true name indicates what will happen. It is well-known of course that in Hugo's sequence of composition, his name was first Jean Tréjean, and then Vlajean (= Voilà Jean, *Ecce Homo*) or Valjean (III, 89), the Jean who must go down into the valley to become Jean once again. Jean–Val–Jean.

In this context, the otherwise implausible tale of old Champmathieu takes on its proper meaning and is an episode of great importance in the salvation of the hero. Champmathieu, one remembers, was mistakenly identified as Jean Valjean and was on trial at Arras for a minor theft. If convicted as a parole-breaker, he would be sentenced to life imprisonment. Hugo first presents the reader with the human moral dilemma which the real Jean debates in the chapter "Une tempête sous un crâne." If he saves the useless vagabond, he must expose himself, be arrested, and the prosperity of Montreuil-sur-mer will fade away. If he remains silent, an innocent man will be condemned. But there is more to this debate than human issues. There is the first overt association of Christological imagery with the hero. Just prior to this section, in a chapter entitled *"Christus nos liberavit,"* Hugo writes: "La sainte loi de Jésus-Christ gouverne notre civilisation, mais elle ne la pénètre pas encore" (III, 197), for slavery still exists in Europe under the guise of prostitution. There is here a suggestion of the idea seen in *La Fin de Satan* that Jesus is somehow above humanity, too weak through his absence to renew it from within. This task of salvation must fall to others. But although Hugo did not always understand Jesus or Christianity very well, his respect for the Nazarene was immense. He likens Jean Valjean to him, as a voice says to the hero: "Pense! comme elle disait il y a deux mille ans à un autre condamné: Marche!" (III, 233) and "Dix huit cents ans avant cet homme infortuné, l'être mystérieux, en qui se résument toutes les saintetés et toutes les souffrances de l'humanité, avait, lui aussi, pendant que les oliviers frémissaient au vent farouche de l'infini, longtemps écarté de la main l'effrayant calice qui apparaissait ruisselant d'ombre et débordant de ténèbres dans les profondeurs pleines d'étoiles" (III, 243). The moment is as critical for Jean as it had been for Jesus. He had tried desperately to bury his real name, and for the most noble of reasons, for should his real identity become known, "le jour où ce nom reparaîtrait, il

160

ferait évanouir autour de lui sa vie nouvelle, et qui sait même peut-être? au dedans de lui sa nouvelle âme" (III, 231). The dilemma he faces challenges his conscience, which, through the magic of Hugo's pen, becomes a universe of its own where moral drama takes on concrete form. Just as the Caveau Perdu of *Les Burgraves* concretizes Job's remorse, here Hugo looks into "les profondeurs de cette conscience" and finds a real inner universe: "Il y a un spectacle plus grand que la mer, c'est le ciel; il y a un spectacle plus grand que le ciel, c'est l'intérieur de l'âme" (III, 228). Although to the casual observer, the outside is calm, if one looks inside one finds "sous le silence extérieur, des combats de géants comme dans Homère, des mêlées de dragons et d'hydres comme chez Dante. Chose sombre que cet infini que tout homme porte en soi" (III, 228).

This somber world is given concrete expression by Jean's remarkable dream which populates a surrealistic wasteland with dull gray forms of corpses standing in judgment on him. This inner world of horrible dream finds an equivalent in the outer world. As Jean passes by nocturnal landscapes on the way to Arras, Hugo muses: "Peut-être, dans la région la plus vague de son esprit, faisait-il des rapprochements entre ces horizons changeants et l'existence humaine" (III, 254). This world of nature is as frightening as the nightmare: "Tout ce qu'on entrevoyait avait des attitudes de terreur. Que de choses frissonnent sous les vastes souffles de la nuit" (III, 256). Despite the terror of nightmare and landscape, the hero does not turn back, as he had at Digne some eight years earlier. He accepts in the physical world the difficulty of making his way through the "brouillards bas, courts et noirs [qui] rampaient sur les collines" (III, 256), to the end of his trip, as in the inner world of his conscience he accepts the presence of various fears to complete a voyage to truth and duty. He is now emotionally aware that to stay mayor at the expense of Champmathieu is to "rester dans le paradis, et y devenir démon," whereas "rentrer dans l'enfer" will mean that he can "devenir ange" (III, 242). Arriving at the courthouse, he is still "en proie à une sorte d'hallucination," but finally because he has worked through his moral problem, he is freed from nightmare, the formless shapes become solidified, "il rentra pleinement dans le sentiment du réel" (III, 271). He saves the vagabond, reclaims his real name, evades the police, and disappears into the *bas fonds* of society. His first major step on the road to salvation was achieved because he dared to abandon the heights and humble himself for others. Georges Piroué, though occasionally assuming that salvation lies in an upward direction (pp. 29–30), does see in this case that "il faut descendre aussi. . . . Jean Valjean n'est jamais mieux inspiré, en dépit des apparences, que lorsqu'il renonce à sa position privilégiée de bourgeois pour plonger en plein enfer" (p. 30). But before he can achieve true atonement, he must first save some others. Criminals like Thénardier are beyond any salvation apparently, but he can succeed with Javert, Cosette, and Marius.

Javert, that symbol of the law, that incarnation of inflexible rectitude who spends his life tracking down the fugitive Jean Valjean, is none other than a personification of fatality which, like the spider, pounces upon the hero as he struggles toward the light of day. The spider image is made explicit in Part II of Book V, where Jean Valjean drags Cosette through the labyrinthine streets of Paris, hotly pursued by the detective. When the victim is trapped at the center of the web:

[Javert] heureux de le sentir pris et de le voir libre, le couvait du regard avec cette volupté de l'araignée qui laisse voleter la mouche et du chat qui laisse courir la souris. La griffe et la serre ont une sensualité monstrueuse, c'est le mouvement obscur de la bête emprisonnée dans leur tenaille. . . . Les mailles de son filet étaient solidement attachées . . . [mais] quand il arriva au centre de sa toile, il n'y trouva plus la mouche. (IV, 181)

But the outcome of the struggle between spider and fly is a surprise. The fly not only escapes but will later try to save the spider's soul,[13] and in this effort Jean Valjean succeeds, despite the policeman's suicide. By freeing Javert against all conceivable self-interest at the barricade of the insurrectionists, he opens up a new vision of the universe, one that transcends the Law and leads the policeman in his turn to free the prisoner. Javert has become "une conscience brusquement opérée de la cataracte" (VI, 160), and before his new vision of truth he is frightened: "Tout un monde nouveau apparaissait à son âme. . . . Il apercevait dans les ténèbres l'effrayant lever d'un soleil moral inconnu" (VI, 158–59).

13. An actual image of a beneficent spider saving the fly (cf. Quasimodo and Esmeralda) occurs when Jean saves a man while escaping from the galleys: "On eût dit une araignée venant saisir une mouche; seulement ici l'araignée apportait la vie et non la mort" (IV, 75).

He had had a superior, one M. Gisquet; "il n'avait guère songé jusqu'à ce jour à cet autre supérieur, Dieu" (VI, 160). Javert, unable to understand what has happened to him, is finally "vaincu et terrassé" (VI, 162). The spider has been vanquished by the fly, which has become transformed as well. Suddenly, Jean is "un homme debout . . . l'auréole sur le front" (VI, 160). Despite Javert's conversion to a more divine vision that shows the power of love over the negative restrictions of the law (a reference to the road to Damascus makes this change clear; VI, 161), the suicide cannot but leave the outcome ambiguous. For Hugo, self-destruction is a "mystérieuse voie de fait sur l'inconnu, laquelle peut contenir dans une certaine mesure la mort de l'âme" (VI, 147). But as Javert wanted to "donner sa démission à Dieu" (VI, 160), death was the only way for him to meet his new superior, and we are led to feel that Javert will not be damned.

The relationship between Jean Valjean and Cosette is more complex than that between Jean and Javert. Cosette first encounters her savior on Christmas Eve, appropriately enough, in the dark forest of Montfermeil[14] where the evil Thénardiers have sent her for water. As the experience will be soul-shattering, the scene is appropriately set: "Plus elle cheminait, plus les ténèbres devenaient épaisses" (IV, 91). She is a fly in the grip of the spider who appears disguised as Nature: "Les ronces se tordaient comme de longs bras armés de griffes cherchant à prendre des proies," and "Cosette se sentait saisir par cette énormité noire" (IV, 94). In her despair she calls out, "O mon Dieu," and Jean Valjean appears. Hugo proves the juxtaposition no accident: "Depuis qu'elle avait rencontré ce bonhomme dans le bois, tout était comme changé pour elle" (IV, 142); "elle sentait quelque chose comme si elle était près du bon Dieu" (IV, 124). Again: "L'entrée de cet homme dans la destinée de cet enfant avait été l'arrivée de Dieu" (IV, 142). Jean Valjean is clearly operating as a savior of others, even though not yet fully saved himself.

Obliged to flee the region, Jean and Cosette go off to Paris where he must once again save the girl. Of course, his role as savior is complicated by his role as victim, and soon he and his ward are fleeing through the streets of Paris chased by the spider Javert. We recall that in escaping,

14. The erotic nature of the forest in Hugo's psychology is made clear by Henri Guillemin, *Hugo et la sexualité* (Paris, 1954), p. 97, and in Hugo's poetry it is often a symbol of rutting matter or nature. But the text of the novel permits the critic to view it only as the fear of the unknown in a child. For a discussion of the forest as the terror inspired by nature, see Albouy, p. 338.

Jean climbed a wall with Cosette on his back and found himself on the grounds of a convent, where Cosette hides for many years. At first glance, this pattern of action might seem to contradict our hypothesis that to go up is the way to destruction, for are they not saved by climbing a wall? Technically, perhaps, but the descent imagery quickly reasserts itself. Old Fauchelevent (now working there as a gardener) says to him: "Vous tombez donc du ciel!" (IV, 172), a phrase repeated later (IV, 233). And once in the convent, the fugitives are not yet in safety. Jean Valjean and Cosette must get out secretly in order to be able to return "legally" as kin to Fauchelevent. There is no problem for the girl, who can be hidden in a basket, but Jean must go out in a coffin.

The episode of the convent of the Petit-Picpus provides Hugo with the opportunity for a long digression on monastic orders. Although charitable in tone, it formally condemns their existence in the nineteenth century. "Le cloître catholique proprement dit est tout rempli du rayonnement noir de la mort" (IV, 218). It is a tomb, it is death because it is sterile: "Claustration, castration" (IV, 221). Yet the very presence of thick walls, grill, and gleaming crosses warns us to pay attention. We have seen too many such places in Hugo's work not to realize their importance. It is a place of sacred horror,[15] a gate that gives passage from one world to another. Hugo says: "Cette existence claustrale si austère et si morne . . . n'est pas la vie, ce n'est pas la liberté; ce n'est pas la tombe, car ce n'est pas la plénitude . . . c'est une frontière étroite et brumeuse séparant deux mondes . . . c'est la pénombre du tombeau" (IV, 231.) Jean Valjean, to find salvation, must go through this "détroit" (IV, 255) and pass from one world to another, must descend from life to death by permitting himself to be buried alive. Of his earlier experience on the road to Arras to save Champmathieu, Hugo had written: "Quel homme n'est entré, au moins une fois dans sa vie, dans cette obscure caverne de l'inconnu?" and "Il s'enfonçait dans cette nuit comme dans un gouffre" (III, 247).[16] That descent, formerly taking place in his conscience, will be in the coffin absolutely physical.

15. Victor Brombert, "Victor Hugo, la prison et l'espace," *Revue des Sciences Humaines,* CXVII (Jan.–Mars., 1965), notes that "l'image du couvent est associée aux images de la mère" (p. 72), in the sense that Baudouin gives to it: the sacred horror of the womb, a place that attracts and repels.
16. "Dans une caverne," reads a variant, cited by Allem in the Pléiade edition, p. 1568.

The sun is setting as the coffin is buried,[17] a traditional death image, and indeed Jean Valjean must come as close to death and resurrection as is possible within a framework of novelistic verisimilitude. In the coffin he faints and nearly does die from suffocation, while above the earth the rites of the dead have been spoken over him. Upon his emergence, "Jean Valjean eut quelque peine à se remuer et à marcher. Dans cette bière il s'était roidi et était devenu un peu cadavre. L'ankylose de la mort l'avait saisi entre ces quatre planches. Il fallut, en quelque sorte, qu'il se dégageât du sépulcre" (IV, 271). Even the word "résurrection" appears in the text (IV, 270). The result of this death and rebirth—despite the seeming ultimate quality of the act—is not the final, definitive one for the hero. By it, however, he and Cosette are provided with years of peace and education, but greater tests are yet to come.

With the passage of time Cosette has grown up, but puberty and physical maturity do not give her any greater emotional awareness of her relationship with her adopted father. She seems quite unaware, when Jean idolizes her and conceives of her as his Paradise (V, 330) or star (VI, 258), that this love is in large measure suppressed eroticism. As she grows up Jean becomes increasingly jealous of any young man, and thus when she falls in love with Marius, the central episode of the novel can begin. Under Jean's saintly exterior, there lurks some of the Hugolian *faune*. If he can overcome his suppressed erotic love, he will indeed be worthy of salvation, even of sanctification. His final and most difficult task will be to descend into Hell to save Marius because Cosette loves him, and then later to step aside and permit the young couple to be happy.

Marius is not merely a foil for Jean. An important character in his own right, he introduces us into the world of politics, whereas in the apolitical world of Jean Valjean, our attention has been centered chiefly on the wider problem of social injustice. Marius' political evolution, critics are unanimous in claiming, is not unlike Hugo's own. Brought up by his royalist grandfather Gillenormand, the young man is unaware that his ostracized father is an authentic military hero of the Napoleonic wars. When he learns the truth of his father's career, he resembles Javert who

17. The setting sun or end of day accompanies other moments of anguish through the novel: e.g., Jean's arrival in Digne, in Arras, at Montfermeil, his robbing of Petit-Gervais, etc.

had been operated on for a spiritual cataract: "le voile qui couvrait Napoléon aux yeux de Marius se déchira peu à peu" (IV, 346). The imagery captures the voyage toward a luminous ideal: "Il se mit à graver lentement, pas à pas . . . d'abord les degrés sombres, puis les degrés vaguement éclairés, enfin les degrés lumineux et splendides de l'enthousiasme" (IV, 371). But by now we should know that direct ascent does not lead to true light. The Sun of Austerlitz is a false gleam and Marius must learn, as the ABC (= abaissé) group of real Republicans informs him, that there is something greater than glory. Combeferre puts it simply, "Etre libre" (IV, 386). These two words destroy Marius' enthusiasm for the dazzling Napoleonic heights,[18] and he decides consciously to set out on his own, on a kind of self-created *via dolorosa*. He descends into poverty, "admirable et terrible épreuve dont les faibles sortent infâmes, dont les forts sortent sublimes" (IV, 391). Poverty's darkness can be fecund: "la misère, presque toujours marâtre, est quelquefois mère; . . . la détresse est nourrice de la fierté; le malheur est un bon lait pour le magnanime" (IV, 392). The mother imagery is obvious. Marius succeeds in passing into this underworld of poverty: "Il était sorti du plus étroit; le défilé s'élargissait un peu devant lui" (IV, 394). We recognize here the language of mythic descent. In this state of poverty (Hell for a typical bourgeois) he finds the real pearl of great price, Cosette, and falls in love with her. The truth that Marius finds in love is, as always in Hugo, a dangerous discovery, for love reveals to the young man a further abyss, "un gouffre mystérieux qui s'était entr'ouvert, puis brusquement refermé" (IV, 416). At this moment Jean Valjean suddenly changes dwellings and Marius loses track of Cosette. The hope of happiness seems crushed and the descent threatens to become death in permanent darkness rather than a prelude to a joyous return: "Marius descendait lentement ces degrés lugubres qu'on pourrait nommer l'escalier des caves et qui mènent dans des lieux sans lumière" (V, 48). Even when his eyes are fixed on his star Cosette, "Marius descendait cette pente à pas lents." Commenting on the difference between the two lovers, Hugo observes: "Marius était de ces tempéraments qui s'enfoncent dans le chagrin et qui s'y séjournent; Cosette était de ceux qui s'y plongent et en

18. "Marius baissa la tête" (IV, 386); "Cette soirée laissa à Marius un ébranlement profond, et une obscurité dans l'âme. . . . Marius fut sombre" (IV, 388).

sortent" (V, 104). Marius is not an authentic hero because, unable to struggle back to the light himself, he must be brought back. Therein lies the key difference between him and Jean Valjean. Otherwise, they have much in common: their basic rectitude, their love for Cosette, and both are even lured by false summits. When Marius finds Cosette again in the house in the Rue Plumet, he is in Heaven as is the girl. "Ces deux êtres vivaient . . . très haut" (V, 186). But fatality wills otherwise. The combination of Marius' poverty and Jean Valjean's perpetual flight from justice separates them again. Convinced of the impossibility of happiness, he turns back down to the darkness in the book entitled "Marius entre dans l'ombre." Choosing permanent self-immolation, he heads for the barricade of the 1832 insurrection. This is an honorable way of committing suicide, and while motivated in part by republican sympathies, Marius wishes to die because he has lost Cosette:

> Cette voix qui à travers le crépuscule avait appelé Marius à la barricade . . . lui avait fait l'effet de la voix de la destinée. Il voulait mourir, l'occasion s'offrait; il frappait à la porte du tombeau, une main dans l'ombre lui en tendait la clef. Ces lugubres ouvertures qui se font dans les ténèbres devant le désespoir sont tentantes. (V, 293)

There is no point in analyzing in these pages the history of the insurrection nor in discussing Hugo's political ideas. This task has been well done by other scholars. However, we wish to point out briefly what this upheaval meant to Hugo. The novelist distinguishes carefully between *émeute* and *insurrection* (V, 229–30) and considers the former improper even if taking place on a large scale ("La Vendée est une grande émeute catholique," V, 230), because it is only a fractional group which sets itself against the whole. On the other hand, in an insurrection the great majority attacks with intent to overthrow a usurping minority. Thus, the Satyr on Olympus became Pan or All Nature before overthrowing the usurping Olympians. Despite the popular name *émeute* given to this event of 1832, Hugo interprets it as part of the general republican trend of the century and therefore as a noble insurrection. In this instance it failed and the insurgents were slaughtered. So once again Hugo can create for his literary purposes a cave or tomb of trapped victims in the center of a twisting labyrinth of streets (the web again). It becomes not only a place of death, however, but also a source of light, for Truth stands with those at the barricade. Hugo unites death and apotheosis in the simple phrase: "Parfois, insurrection, c'est résurrection" (V, 230). The imagery also has a political side. The insurgents' *quartier* is not only the mythical "monstrueuse caverne" (V, 296) but a volcano where one can hear "la sombre voix du peuple" (V, 278) in the vast conflagration. Even the earth itself is equated with "le peuple" (V, 21). Linking *Les Misérables* to *La Fin de Satan,* Hugo evokes the French Revolution, referring to "les cabarets du faubourg Antoine [qui] ressemblent à ces cavernes du Mont Arentin bâties sur l'antre de la sibylle et communiquant avec les profonds souffles sacrés" (V, 33), and centuries later France in 1789 played out in history the episode of Barabbas' receiving Adam's strength in order to become the New Adam. It is in the name of the French Revolution that the insurgents have raised their barricade to which Marius goes:

> Après avoir franchi la zone de la foule, il avait dépassé la lisière des troupes; il se trouvait dans quelque chose d'effrayant. Plus un passant, plus un soldat, plus une lumière; personne. . . . Entrer dans une rue, c'était entrer dans une cave.
>
> Il continua d'avancer. Il fit quelques pas. Quelqu'un passa près de lui en courant. Etait-ce un homme? une femme? étaient-ils plusieurs? Il n'eût pu le dire. Cela avait passé et s'était évanoui. (V, 294)

It would be difficult not to recognize the similarity between this passage and the one in *Notre-Dame de Paris* when Pierre Gringoire makes his way toward the Cour des Miracles. But thirty years has made a difference: Clopin Trouillefou has become Enjolras, the "populace" is now the "peuple." What was evil is now good and as in *La Fin de Satan* there has been a reversal of values.

The barricade of *Les Misérables* is more than a realistic detail of Parisian political history. It is also a concretization of political and class differences. Marius' passage from the complacent, money-grubbing, triumphant bourgeoisie across the "no-man's land" to a desperate, noble, dying group of revolutionaries is social comment but it is also as mythic in its way, as was Jean Valjean's passage from life to death when he was buried alive. In the traditions of world mythology as well as in Hugo, reality itself becomes fluid and unstable at these moments of awful passage. In legend, dragons or clashing rocks (the *symplegades*) appear as symbols of this instability. Hugo attempts to achieve the same effects with more reasonable imagery. In *Notre-Dame* Pierre Gringoire enters the Cour des Miracles, sees "legless" men running, and has a sense of hallucination. This hallucinatory quality is not possible to convey on the stage, and therefore it is not until the prologue to *Les Burgraves,* based on the legend of Pécopin, that we find it again, this time in the fog that swirls around, blurring the contours of objects and making reality fluid. This distortion of reality at moments of crisis is normal in *Les Miséra-bles.* When Jean Valjean is about to steal the silverware in the semi-darkness of the bishop's room, "dans les grossissements fantastiques de la première minute, il se figura que ce gond venait de s'animer et de prendre tout à coup une vie terrible, et qu'il aboyait comme un chien pour avertir tout le monde" (III, 106). After the episode of stealing the coin from the boy, "une bise glaciale . . . donnait aux choses . . . une vie lugubre. Des arbrisseaux secouaient leurs petits bras maigres avec . . . furie" (III, 117). These transformations of nature are of course projections of the character's troubled mind, and Hugo does try to link the phenomenon to psychology when he defines hallucination as a state where "on ne voit plus les objets qu'on a autour de soi, et l'on voit comme en dehors de soi les figures que l'on a dans l'esprit" (III, 120). We recall that M. Made-leine had a similar experience on the way to Arras, and Cosette alone in the forest of Montfermeil saw all nature turn into a living nightmare with "d'effrayantes torses d'arbres, de longues poignées d'herbes frémissantes" (IV, 93). As the author says: "on est sans défense contre tout cela."[19] Only by counting aloud can Cosette restore a sense of the real (IV, 94).

In the earlier convent scene, Hugo had created a distortion of reality at that "frontière étroite et brumeuse séparant deux mondes." Here at the barricade, this dissolution of forms is suggested by the very real smoke from gunfire, which is analogous to the fog. It seems to the insurgents as if the houses themselves are abandoning them, an hallucinatory and animistic way of saying that the bourgeois are locking their doors: "Ce

19. A delicate touch, rare in *Les Misérables,* is an ironic reprise of Cosette in the forest by Eponine Thénardier in the Parisian jungle. Eponine confesses to Marius: "Savez-vous, la nuit, quand je marche sur le boulevard, je vois les arbres comme des fourches, je vois des maisons toutes noires grosses comme des tours de Notre-Dame . . . je me dis: 'Tiens, il y a de l'eau là!' " (IV, 454). Her fear provides an example of poetic justice, for it was the Thénardiers who had persecuted Cosette; now it is their turn to suffer, even if through the likeable and innocent Eponine.

169

mur voit, entend, et ne veut pas" (VI, 71). The barricade does separate two worlds, but Marius seems not to be aware of what he is doing because he is in a kind of trance that leaves him unable to think clearly. He is fortunate that Jean Valjean arrives to save him, seizing him like a beneficent spider (VI, 89) and plunging with the unconscious youth into the sewers of Paris.[20]

It is no coincidence that the entrance to the sewers is a small aperture blocked by a grill that has been torn loose. Without involving ourselves in Freudian analysis, we may remark that the parallel with the broken grill of the Caveau Perdu of *Les Burgraves* is an obvious one which forecasts an optimistic ending, as the web of fatality is broken. The hero carries the wounded and unconscious Marius into the intestine of Leviathan, to use Hugo's phrase. The mythic descent into Hell is suggested by the word "Leviathan" and the repeating pattern is made explicit by the author: "L'impression qu'il avait autrefois éprouvée en tombant de la rue dans le couvent,[21] lui revint. Seulement ce qu'il emportait aujourd'hui, ce n'était plus Cosette, c'était Marius" (VI, 91).

The episode of Jean Valjean in the sewers of Paris is so well known that it often makes sophisticates smile charitably, if condescendingly, at "le père Hugo." Yet ironically enough, it is the culminating point of the action of the novel and is probably the center which gives meaning to the lesser images that have prepared it. The sewers are an image of death. In a theoretical digression Hugo explains that the ancient Roman sewer system "a engouffré le monde" (VI, 95) and in the Orient, sewers were "monstrueux berceaux de la Mort" (VI, 97). Yet they are for Hugo also the repository of truth, for when all the masks drop in death, the reality is visible in the "égout." Hugo admires this "sincérité de l'immondice" (VI, 98), and he then associates himself with the hero, defining the role of the socially conscious writer as one who "doit entrer dans ces ombres" (VI, 99). In this descent into Hell he likens himself not only to his own hero, Jean Valjean, but also to those non-military heroes of history, Bruneseau and Nargaud (of symbolic name!) who had explored the sewers under the militarist Napoleon Bonaparte. Hugo's admiration for these two unsung heroes, who scorned military glory for social usefulness,

20. Marius later thinks that his recollection of Jean Valjean's act of saving him was only an hallucination (VI, 193).

21. By now, Hugo himself sees the climbing the wall into the convent as a descent.

is greater than his love for any Napoleon and parallels Marius' political evolution beyond Bonapartism to republicanism. After all, the sewers are dangerous because men have died in them. Hugo depicts them as a *fosse* in the sense of tomb (VI, 111), as a labyrinth of the underworld that parallels the streets above (VI, 115), and as an ocean (VI, 113). Hugo once again links his double universe to Dante's Inferno by saying that "Jean Valjean était tombé d'un cercle de l'enfer dans l'autre" (VI, 114). And, as with Dante, who had to descend into and through Hell in order to reach Heaven after having been lost in a dense wood, so does Hugo recognize that for his hero at this moment, "Descendre, c'était en effet le salut possible" (VI, 126). Here in the sewers Jean, who was carrying Marius as a cross (VI, 125), could see farther than ordinary reality. He had passed into an "état visionnaire" (VI, 119) where "la pupille se dilate dans la nuit et finit par y trouver le jour, de même que l'âme se dilate dans le malheur et finit par y trouver Dieu." The high point of the underground trip is of course the lowest spacial point: the descent into the *fontis*, a possibly bottomless hole where in faith the hero walks out into deeper filth, hoping that he will not drown. He goes into this filth up to his nose but finds solid footing at the last moment and emerges "tout ruisselant de fange, l'âme pleine d'une étrange clarté" (VI, 133). Can we not see in this language a reflection of the earlier passage in which Hugo evokes the Christ on the Mount of Olives, facing the cup which appeared to Him "ruisselant d'ombre et débordant de ténèbres dans des profondeurs pleines d'étoiles"? And yet despite the descent into death in the sewers, Jean Valjean has still not finished his task. Emerging to the light, he finds his way blocked once more by a locked grill. Despairing, he feels that fatality-death has finally caught him, that even descent was vain: "Ils étaient pris l'un et l'autre dans la sombre et immense toile de la mort, et Jean Valjean sentait courir sur ces fils noirs tressaillant dans les ténèbres l'épouvantable araignée" (VI, 135). But descent is still the way to salvation, for he is saved by the evil Thénardier,[22] who opens the grill with a key. All seems serene finally, for Javert is dead, Marius recovers to marry Cosette, and Jean Valjean under the name of Ultime Fauchelevent can live happily with them. But we have already seen that for Jean to betray his name is to fail to achieve

22. Who is himself described as a spider at Montfermeil and in the "masure Gorbeau."

atonement. He is now caught in the spider's thread of his own honesty, to use Hugo's image (VI, 227). Book VII of Part V is entitled "La Dernière Gorgée du Calice" and here is his ultimate test. He reveals to Marius his true identity, dissociates himself from Cosette, and begins to die by degrees. Marius accepts this inhuman solution largely because he is convinced, wrongly, that Jean had killed M. Madeleine and Javert. The happy ending is achieved only by another intervention of the evil Thénardier who (with evil motives) reveals the truth.[23] At the last moment, realizing that he was a saint, Marius and Cosette fly to his bedside for a final scene of reconciliation before, as the title of the last book puts it, the "suprême ombre" becomes the "suprême aurore." His radiant soul is received into Heaven, its transformation completed. Not only is Cosette saved for a virtuous life, as her mother had not been, but even Marius, who for so long had not "accompli tous les progrès" even less than one hundred pages from the end of the novel, is exalted. In the final scene, after having learned the entire truth, he is "rayonnant" (VI, 281). Indeed, his salvation was the most difficult of all to achieve, but Jean Valjean has lived out his earlier decision, made at the time of the Champmathieu affair: "Se livrer, sauver cet homme . . . redevenir . . . le forçat Jean Valjean, c'était là vraiment achever sa résurrection, et fermer à jamais l'enfer d'où il sortait! Y retomber en apparence, c'était sortir en réalité!" (III, 234).

This apotheosis can lead us finally to the one responsible for it all, to the character to whom we have not as yet referred: Monseigneur Myriel. What role does this other Christ-figure play in the totality of the novel's vision? There is no doubt as to his Christ-like nature: "Il y avait presque de la divinité dans cet homme ainsi auguste à son insu" (III, 109). He even arrives in town riding on a donkey, and in the early *Les Misères*, there is an explicit parallel to Jesus riding on an ass.[24] Before Jean Valjean, he had learned the truth according to the Hugolian universe: he had tried the heights and had rejected them. He had been a "grand seigneur" before becoming a humble priest. Although rising to the rank of bishop, he refuses to act according to his wordly station. Jean Valjean's earlier experience with another (arch)bishop, while a prisoner of

23. In the necessity for evil to help in salvation, can one not see a parallel with *La Fin de Satan*, where Liberty is the daughter of Satan as well as of God?
24. Pléiade edition, p. 1515 (ed. Maurice Allem [Paris, 1951]).

the galleys, shows why the clergy should not rise too high above the common people. The sun of their truth is too distant. Hugo recreates the image of the fly in a dark recess blocked from reaching the sun. The barriers are the prison guards and the social laws that they protect:

> Dans cette pénombre obscure et blafarde où il rampait . . . il voyait . . . s'échaffauder . . . une sorte d'entassement effrayant de choses, de lois, de préjugés . . . qui n'était autre chose que cette prodigieuse pyramide que nous appelons la civilisation. Il distinguait . . . ici l'argousin et son bâton, ici le gendarme et son sabre, là-bas l'archevêque mitré, tout en haut, dans une sorte de soleil. (III, 98)

He felt in this situation that "une chose monstrueuse était sur lui," a suggestion of the lurking spider of Fate, with the sun behind it.

But Myriel, conscious of the fact that the humble cannot approach the mighty, turns downward to meet them. He removes the locks from his doors so that anyone may enter, he has no rich carriage, he gives most of his budget to the poor. He even sleeps downstairs in his house, which he has taken in exchange for the lofty episcopal palace. But despite his virtue, he is limited in power. In the important Chapter XIV that ends Part I, Book I, "Ce qu'il pensait," Hugo makes explicit that "l'évêque doit être timide" (III, 62). He can go only so far because of the administrative nature of his job and its semi-social aspects, whereas an "apôtre" can be bold. Myriel loves and prays "jusqu'à une aspiration surhumaine" (III, 63), but harrowing Hell is beyond him. "Il n'avait rien du prophète et rien du mage," and "Mgr Bienvenu [i.e., Myriel] n'était point de ces hommes-là. Mgr Bienvenu n'était pas un génie" (III, 62). He declares with Jesus: "Aimez-vous les uns les autres" (III, 63) and stops there. Hugo concludes: "Mgr Bienvenu était simplement un homme qui constatait du dehors les questions mystérieuses sans les scruter, sans les agiter, et sans en troubler son propre esprit, et qui avait dans l'âme le grave respect de l'ombre" (III, 64). He resembles the Jesus of *La Fin de Satan* in that he proclaims the gospel of love and yet lacks the power to bring a new world into being. As the horror of Jesus' crucifixion penetrated Barabbas, he gained power from below and proclaimed himself the New Adam. Likewise in *Les Misérables*, Bienvenu-Myriel inspires Jean Valjean—as much a Barabbas-figure as a Christ-figure—to save the humble people individually, and he blesses the "Conventionnel G." who

173

had tried to do it on a wide socio-political scale at the time of the French Revolution. G. unwittingly evokes *La Fin de Satan* when he states: "la révolution française est le plus puissant pas du genre humain depuis l'avènement du Christ. . . . la révolution française, c'est le sacre de l'humanité" (III, 45). Hugo is indirectly suggesting that in the modern world the church, if it is to be true to Christ, should support secular forces of liberalism rather than tie itself to the outdated monarchy.

There is infinitely more that can be said about *Les Misérables*, but much of it—particularly that which concerns Hugo's vision of the *peuple*—has been said elsewhere. However, one aspect of the work merits brief mention. We remarked earlier in this study that Hugo began, albeit in fragmented and partial form, to provide the characters of *Notre-Dame de Paris* with a mythological dimension. In *Les Misérables* the mythology is more important, as one would expect from a novel with a mythic hero written during Hugo's exile. Of course, some of the traditional imagery of mythology is routine, decorative, and at times trivial and does not concern us here. Some is even comic. For example, Marius' talkative grandfather, whose values are frivolities of the eighteenth century, likens himself to the garrulous Nestor and Cosette to Venus. There are also, however, more serious analogies. Gavroche is an "étrange gamin fée" (VI, 54), Enjolras is described as Apollo and like the hero-god, he is invulnerable throughout the battle at the barricade (VI, 86), but the image is not worked out systematically into the total creation of the novel. Beyond these routine comparisons one finds (not surprisingly) that the imagery is that of *La Légende des siècles*. The characters become Titans chained under mountains; they erupt as did the Satyr and are at times compared to Prometheus. Each represents in some way the *peuple* and gains strength from the masses. This lower class can be openly violent as in 1789 or more hidden in their activity, but they are an agency for transformation: "Les utopies cheminent [like Phtos] sous terre . . . ces énergies [qui vont] vers le but, et la vaste activité simultanée, qui monte, descend et remonte dans ces obscurités et qui transforme lentement le dessus et le dehors par le dedans" (IV, 431). Time and time again we witness the transformation of ordinary people into Titans. Of course we expect it in the military context of the battle of Waterloo with its "hommes géants sur des chevaux colosses" (IV, 31). Hugo comments:

"Ces récits semblent d'un autre âge. Quelque chose de pareil à cette vision apparaissait sans doute dans les vieilles épopées orphiques racontant . . . ces titans à face humaine . . . dont le galop escalada l'Olympe, horribles, invulnérables, sublimes; dieux et bêtes" (VI, 32). We recognize the Satyr without difficulty. Hugo also converts Cambronne of Waterloo into a Titan beleaguered amid "les Jupiters tonnants," "sous l'accablement du nombre, de la force, de la matière," hurling "cette parole du dédain titanique" which he uttered to the past in the name of the Revolution (IV, 46).[25]

But in less epic times in the middle of the nineteenth century, less openly epic techniques are needed. The Champmathieu case provides a good example of Hugo's technique. At the trial, the prisoner at first sat mute and bewildered. When he finally understood that he was to speak in his own defense, "Cette fois l'homme entendit. Il parut comprendre, il fit le mouvement de quelqu'un qui se réveille . . . regarda le public, . . . posa son poing monstrueux sur le rebord de la boiserie . . . et tout à coup . . . il se mit à parler. Ce fut comme une irruption" (III, 276). After speaking,

> l'homme se tut, et resta debout. Il avait dit ces choses d'une voix haute, rapide, rauque, dure et enrouée, avec une sorte de naïveté irritée et sauvage. Quand il eut fini, l'auditoire éclata de rire. Il regarda le public, et voyant qu'on riait, et ne comprenant pas, il se mit à rire lui-même.
>
> Cela était sinistre. (III, 277)

Champmathieu is midway between Le Satyre and Gwynplaine.

On the sociological plane, it is the Parisian people who are the new Satyr, about to overthrow the forces of injustice. "Si l'heure sonne," the cat is changed into a lion (the idea of swelling in size again) and the mild "faubourien va grandir, ce petit homme va se lever, et il regardera d'une façon terrible, et son souffle deviendra tempête et il sortira de cette pauvre poitrine grêle assez de vent pour déranger les plis des Alpes. C'est grâce au faubourien de Paris que la Révolution . . . conquiert l'Europe.

25. An interesting parallel: Cambronne at Waterloo shouting "Merde!" is portrayed as the great French hero there. The similarity between him and Bruneseau and Nargaud in the excrement-filled sewers is inescapable and is another example of the tight construction of the work.

Il chante, c'est sa joie . . . il délivrera le monde" (III, 138).[26] Gavroche is a symbol of Paris (IV, 301) and like the Satyr is "misérable" and yet "tout-puissant" (V, 139), and, like him, he sings before his enemies. Through him Hugo warns society:

> Qui que vous soyez qui vous nommez Préjugé, Abus, Ignorance,
> Oppression, Iniquité, Despotisme, Injustice, Fanatisme,
> Tyrannie, prenez garde au gamin béant.
>   Ce petit grandira.
>   De quelle argile est-il fait? De la première fange venue. Une
> poignée de boue, un souffle, et voilà Adam. (IV, 291)

Not only the idea but the vocabulary is similar: "argile," "fange," "boue" are the first state of the boy as they were of the Satyr. The idea that Gavroche is the New Adam links *Les Misérables* also to *La Fin de Satan*. In fact all these characters, Barabbas and Satan, the Titan and the Satyr, Champmathieu, Gavroche and Jean Valjean, are various forms of the same protean figure who appears for a while to be an evil outcast but who is an instrument for good. With the exception of Satan, who is prisoner of God Himself, they all rise at some moment, after descending into the depths, to bring judgment on the wicked. As Victor Brombert concluded of Jean Valjean:

> pour que la libération et la vision acquièrent leur pleine beauté et
> leur haute signification, il fallait d'abord passer, comme Jean Val-
> jean, par la prison et par l'obscurité. Il fallait d'abord passer par le
> rétrécissement vicieux de l'égout. Là était la lumière, et là était
> l'issue.[27]

26. What is true of a downtrodden class is equally true of Truth itself. Jean Valjean realizes, as he ponders his fate, that his ideas "avaient grandi devant l'œil de son esprit; elles avaient maintenant des statures colossales" (III, 235).
    27. P. 79

THE MYTH
CONCENTRATED

LES TRAVAILLEURS
DE LA MER

LES MISÉRABLES, like the rest of Hugo's earlier work, is a story whose primary element is the land. The action takes place on land, Jean Valjean is buried alive in the earth, his treasure is buried in the earth, and even the imagery reflects this terrestrial orientation. For example, when Marius heard the truth of the message of republicanism, it was like "la terre au moment où on l'ouvre avec le fer pour y déposer le grain de blé; elle ne sent que la blessure; le tressaillement du germe et la joie du fruit n'arrivent que plus tard" (IV, 388).[1] But partway through the composition of this work, Hugo found himself in exile, first in Belgium and then on the Channel Islands. Here on these islands his work was profoundly affected by the constant presence of the ocean. E. de Saint-Denis summarizes it well: "on ne peut pas comprendre les œuvres écrites à Jersey et à Guernesey, si l'on oublie cette présence continuelle, obsédante et impérieuse d'une mer,"[2] and he quotes pertinently from *William Shakespeare* the passage on *hommes-océans*, which we reproduce here because it shows so well the impact of the sea on Hugo's imagination:

Ces ondes, ce flux et ce reflux, ce va-et-vient terrible, ce bruit de tous les souffles, ces noirceurs et ces transparences, ces végétations propres au gouffre, cette démagogie des nuées en plein ouragan, ces aigles dans l'écume, ces merveilleux levers d'astres répercutés dans on ne sait quel mystérieux tumulte par des millions de cimes lumineuses, têtes confuses de l'innombrable, ces grandes foudres errantes, ces nuits de ténèbres coupées de rugissements, ces furies, ces

1. See n. 7, chap. VII.
2. "Victor Hugo et la mer anglo-normande," *Etudes classiques*, XXXI (July, 1963), 293.

177

frénésies, ces tourmentes, ces roches, ces naufrages, ces flottes qui se heurtent, ces tonnerres humains mêlés aux tonnerres divins, ce sang dans l'abîme, puis ces grâces, ces douceurs, ces fêtes, ces gaies voiles blanches, ces bateaux de pêche, ces chants dans le fracas, ces ports splendides, ces fumées de la terre, ces villes à l'horizon, ce bleu profond de l'eau et du ciel, cette âcreté utile, cette amertume qui fait l'assainissement de l'univers, cet âpre sel sans lequel tout pourrirait, ces colères et ces apaisements, ce tout en un, cet inattendu dans l'immuable, ce vaste prodige de la monotonie inépuisable variée, ce niveau après ce bouleversement, ces enfers et ces paradis de l'immensité éternellement émue, cet insondable, tout cela peut être dans un esprit, et alors cet esprit s'appelle génie, et vous avez Eschyle, vous avez Isaïe, vous avez Shakespeare, et c'est la même chose de regarder ces âmes ou de regarder l'océan. (Ire partie, II)

But it would be an error to oversimplify and state that prior to exile, marine imagery is non-existent in Hugo's work. Saint-Denis, and before him, J. K. Ditchy, have shown that Hugo's first serious experience with the ocean dated from the middle 1830's.[3] And even before 1834, the lines from "La Pente de la rêverie,"

> Mon esprit plongea donc sous ce flot inconnu,
> Au fond de l'abîme il nagea seul et nu,

show the mythic use to which he will put the vastness of the sea. As the imagery of the above quotation is not yet the result of direct observation, this fact should remind critics not to rely excessively on establishing biographical details to explain Hugo's art. But even so, a progressive shift in marine imagery is definitely perceptible after 1834—we saw an example in *Le Rhin* in a preceding chapter—and it becomes particularly marked after 1852 and in all Hugo's remaining novels. This shift is already visible in *Les Misérables,* where those pages written well after the completion of *Les Misères* have more marine imagery than the rest. For example, in the chapter "L'Onde et l'ombre,"[4] of late composition, Hugo compares poverty to an ocean in which the "damnés" of society are

3. "Il n'a rien écrit qui indique une observation directe jusqu'en 1834," concludes Ditchy, *La Mer dans l'œuvre littéraire de Victor Hugo* (Paris, 1925), p. 26.
4. Pt. I, Bk. II, chap. VIII.

drowning, having fallen overboard from a ship far from land. Here, not the earth but "l'océan . . . est une tombe." All the swimmer's efforts are in vain. "Il sent au-dessous de lui les vagues monstres de l'invisible" (III, 100–1). When we move from the figurative language of *Les Misérables* to the real marine world of *Les Travailleurs*, the inchoate monsters will not be long in making their appearance.

Two episodes in *Les Misérables* show the transition of this imagery from it to *Les Travailleurs*. The first is the world of the sewers of Paris, where under the apparent solidity of the pavement lies the watery filth of the "égout." Hugo establishes a direct parallel with the seashore by means of the famous metaphor of the Breton coast and of the man who thinks that he is walking on firm ground only to be sucked down through the quicksands into a watery grave (VI, 128–31). "Ressemblance de plus de Paris avec la mer," Hugo writes, "Comme dans l'Océan, le plongeur peut y disparaître" (VI, 113). Translated into social terms, the entire sinister underworld beneath official society becomes "une sorte de polype ténébreux aux mille antennes" (VI, 108). Elsewhere, four thieves are referred to as "le polype monstrueux du mal habitant la crypte de la société" (IV, 438). Even in a military context, at Waterloo, we find that "chaque escadron ondulait et se gonflait comme un anneau de polype" (IV, 32). This polyp is called a hydra in marine language and is a small, tentacled creature. In earlier years, when Hugo used the word "hydre," he gave to it the sense of the classical monster, but little by little it became associated with the ocean and evolved into a giant sea creature akin to the octopus (except that Hugo often uses it as an abstraction). The menacing creature with its predatory arms lurking in the *crypte* makes one confident that it is another form of the spider.

The second episode from *Les Misérables* which prefigures certain image patterns in *Les Travailleurs* is Cosette's dream, after she found a love letter under a stone. She is both attracted and repelled by this declaration, and in her dream she saw the stone "grosse comme une montagne et pleine de cavernes" (V, 109). The soaring mountain of love is located on top of fearsome caves, imagery which probably explains more about Hugo, the male, than about Cosette. One may recall that the grotto of Walderhog and Habibrah's cave were both located in mountainous terrain. Hugo even intervenes in his novel to comment on the imagery, and although his remarks refer ostensibly to the underworld of

179

crime, they apply to love as well: "Connaît-on bien la montagne," he asks, "quand on ne connaît pas la caverne?" (V, 161). In love, both Cosette and Marius are unaware of the dangers of the "abyss," of this cavern that Marius had briefly glimpsed when he first fell under Cosette's spell. Marius, as will Gilliatt later, has his encounter with the octopus:

> Le regard des femmes ressemble à de certains rouages tranquilles en apparence et formidables. On passe à côté tous les jours paisiblement et impunément sans se douter de rien. Il vient un moment où l'on oublie que cette chose[5] est là. . . . Tout à coup on se sent saisi. C'est fini. Le rouage vous tient, le regard vous a pris.[6] . . . Vous êtes perdu. Vous y passerez tout entier. (IV, 423)

In *Les Misérables,* this experience with love is not necessarily deadly, despite its tone of horror: "selon que vous serez au pouvoir d'une créature méchante ou d'un noble cœur, vous ne sortirez de cette effrayante machine que défigurée par la honte ou transfigurée par la passion" (IV, 424). Cosette transforms Marius. Good, not evil, was lurking the cave, as befitting a novel whose dominant note is optimism. In *Les Travailleurs* the encounter will be yet more formidable.

Upon approaching this extraordinary work, one of Hugo's greatest, critics are faced with the same problem that bothered Hugo's editor. The novel, written on Guernsey between June, 1864, and April, 1865, included a semi-separate section entitled "L'Archipel de la Manche," which Hugo put at the head of his narrative. But Lacroix, his Brussels' editor, rejected this proposal and, as a result, the prologue was not published until 1883. From a financial viewpoint Lacroix may have been correct; from a literary one, he most certainly was not. This preamble to the work is important to critics for two reasons: first, it provides clues to an understanding of the main text and second, it reveals Hugo's desire to separate what in *Les Misérables* had been more or less united, myth and sociology. Whereas Stendhal, Balzac, Flaubert, and Zola had no difficulty in fusing them by various devices of image, symbol, and structure, it seems almost as if Hugo had been unhappy with the combination in *Les Misérables.* In any case, for *Les Travailleurs* he frankly isolated most of the genuine

---

5. The word not only anticipates "l'anankè des choses" of *Les Travailleurs* but also suggests Hugo's reduction of nubile women to their sexual organs.
6. "Voir, c'est dévorer," p. 223.

sociology of the Channel Islands in this prologue, where he deals very interestingly with geology, races, customs, language, etc. It is this section which merits the often-criticized title "Les Travailleurs de la mer" rather than the larger part which tells of Gilliatt's solitary quest. Here too, Hugo articulates his doctrine of progress, which fits in better with sociology than with pure fiction. He even associates geology and climate with politics because—Hugo believes—thanks to the mysterious workings of wind and sea, the inhabitants have found liberty and developed "une incorruptible attitude au progrès." Hugo admires them: "ces espèces de petites nations font preuve de civilisation. Aimons-les et vénérons-les" (p. 49). They even export their civilization to other lands. Mess Lethierry in the main novel is their representative. Yet even in this sociological section, Hugo's symbolic vision is at work. The Channel Islands represent all mankind: "ces microcosmes reflètent en petit, dans toutes ses phases, la grande formation humaine" (p. 49). The islanders' audacity, proclaims Hugo, "va à la lumière." These theoretical considerations in the preface permit Hugo to condense or concentrate the purely descriptive and narrative elements into the main text.

Whatever political or sociological overtones can be found in this work, the author himself points out the lack of any immediate political purpose in a letter to Paul Meurice: "Ce n'est pas un livre de combat, il est écrit, non pour la minute, mais pour la postérité."[7] If he speaks in a letter to Pierre Véron of his avowed intention to "glorifier le travail, la volonté, le dévouement, tout ce qui fait l'homme grand,"[8] it is less for man in the aggregate than in an individual sense, for he intended to deal with the personal encounter with love and to show that "le plus implacable des abîmes, c'est le cœur, et ce qui échappe à la mer, n'échappe pas à la femme." This remark helps to clarify the epigrammatic phrase from the book's preface in which Hugo stated that he wanted to show "l'anankè des choses" after having examined "l'anankè des dogmes" in Notre-Dame de Paris and "l'anankè des lois" in Les Misérables. It was at this point that Hugo added the phrase that we have examined in earlier chapters: "A ces trois fatalités qui enveloppent l'homme, se mêle la fatalité intérieure, l'anankè suprême, le cœur humain." But nowhere does Hugo discuss the form that his exploration will take, nowhere does he give a clue to the

7. Correspondance, II, 523 (Jan. 23, 1866).
8. Ibid., pp. 536–37.

mythic nature of the work, yet it is on this basis that it must be approached. In *La Fin de Satan* and in *La Légende des siècles,* Hugo's tendency was to take traditional figures of mythology and to give them his own interpretation. In *Les Misérables* he tended to start with human characters and then to associate them with traditional mythological figures. But in *Les Travailleurs de la mer* he was to create his own mythic figure in Gilliatt, an original creation who would nonetheless conform closely to the general pattern of myth.

Myths are symbolic expressions of the effort of the human psyche "to conduct people across those difficult thresholds of transformation that demand a change in the patterns not only of conscious but also of unconscious life."[9] Baudouin has shown this truism to apply to Hugo in that these artistic creations served to help their author through his own psychic crises, but as literary critics must concentrate on the actual work created, our focus must not be on Hugo but on Gilliatt and his quest, whether or not it parallels in any way the life of his creator. We can do no better in showing the general outline of mythic narrative than to quote from Joseph Campbell's admirable synthesis of mythology, from which emerges a "monomyth:"[10] "A hero ventures forth from the world of common day into a region of supernatural wonder: fabulous forces are there encountered and a decisive victory is won: the hero comes back from this mysterious adventure with the power to bestow boons on his fellow man."[11]

Les Travailleurs de la mer fits this pattern to an astonishing degree and with a clearer outline than was the case in *Les Misérables.* The "world of common day" is described at great length in the prefatory *Archipel de la Manche,* with its emphasis on the reality of the islands. Even when we move to the fictional part of the story, we are at first still located in a reasonable world that is recognizable as our own. The opening sentence "La Christmas de 182 . . . fut remarquable à Guernesey" (p. 55) is reassuring, for it fixes us in time and space and leads us to believe that we are dealing with a true novel. In the following pages Hugo presents characters as normal human beings whom we recognize well enough. It is

9. Joseph Campbell, *The Hero with a Thousand Faces* (New York, 1956), p. 10.
10. Whether all myths are reducible to a monomyth is perhaps open to debate. But the prevalence of the basic form is so great in Western culture that even if Campbell overstates the case, his findings are of value to the literary critic.
11. Campbell, p. 30.

true that the first of these, Gilliatt, is a solitary figure who inhabits a haunted house, for Hugo informs us that "le diable y vient la nuit" (p. 57). But we soon realize that this is not to be taken seriously, that these are merely old wives' tales of no reliability. We are reassured by Hugo's mockery of local superstitions and are convinced that we are operating in a universe governed by natural law. Thus, despite the hero's isolation, he is after all only a simple fisherman, "ce n'était qu'un pauvre homme, sachant lire et écrire" (p. 76). He lives with his elderly mother from whom he will one day inherit a trunk full of wedding clothes, put away for the day when he will take a wife. Lest we be tempted to think of the hidden treasures of romance or myth, Hugo is careful to call this locked trunk "une malle pas du tout mystérieuse" (p. 62). Further, Hugo presents the "haunted" house in a description that is solidly real: "Vous pouvez y étudier les vieilles modes de papier peint, les griffons de l'empire, les draperies en croissant du directoire, les balustres et les cippes de Louis XVI." For the moment we are not so far from Balzac. Yet the very next sentence should be significant to any reader of Victor Hugo: "L'épaississement des toiles pleines de mouches indique la paix profonde des araignées" (p. 57).

The other characters seem even more ordinary. Mess Lethierry, despite Hugo's statement that he had had in earlier years a "Herculean" career, is not a mythic figure, but a fine example of realistic characterization, one of the very best in Hugo. His title is carefully explained to show his position in the hierarchy of the island, and his ambitions are rooted in the time and place where he lives. His invention of a steamboat and his subsequent fortune in commerce are proof of his practical talents, and his doting on a pretty niece reveals normal human emotions. Those who cluster about him are not at first glance extraordinary. Déruchette is a very unexceptional heroine, an empty-headed flirt who is spoiled by her uncle. The appearance of her future husband, Joë Ebenezer Caudray, results from no magic—the administrative machinery of the Protestant church has simply assigned him to a parish on the island. As for the evil Rantaine, his theft of money is somehow almost reassuring by its very human quality. Only Clubin seems set apart from normal humanity.

But the solid reality of life on this island is actually a thin veneer covering a vaster world whose power is felt in the ocean waves that break against the coast. Hugo suggests the mythic quality of this weird universe when he explores legends like that of "Le Roi des Auxcriniers," a fantastic and sinister marine figure ("un poisson qui est un spectre, et qui a une figure d'homme," p. 68). But even before confronting the ocean and its denizens, we discover that on the land itself there are ominous openings into the unknown. Hugo warns his reader: "L'erreur commune, c'est de prendre l'être extérieur pour l'être réel" (p. 91). Behind the realistic façade there is a deeper reality. A good example is to be found in the house on the hill at Plainmont. After informing his reader that this is a haunted house, Hugo takes pains to explain away any supernatural element. He states flatly that the mysterious lights seen occasionally in the house have a very un-supernatural source: smugglers use the dwelling from time to time. And there is certainly a comic aspect to the scene where some children ("les déniquoiseaux") dare approach the haunted house. But as if whistling past a graveyard, Hugo allows his matter-of-fact tone to give way to uneasiness: "Hantée ou non, l'aspect en est étrange" (p. 149). He adds the following details: "La nuit, la lune lugubre entre là. Toute la mer est autour de cette maison" (pp. 149–50). These facts are not merely intended to increase suspense as in a typical gothic novel. This house seems so disturbing to Hugo because it may be a point of passage from the world of our reality to a transcendent one. Like a sacred tree or mountain, it is a "center," to use a term borrowed from primitive religions. Indeed, Hugo now adds religious language as he describes the house as "quelque chose de semblable à un énorme autel des ténèbres" (p. 155). The transition from one world to another is openly discussed: "L'immense dispersion de la vie extra-humaine a-t-elle sur ce sommet désert un nœud où elle s'arrête et qui la force à devenir visible et à descendre?" (p. 150). Whatever the answer, "l'horreur sacrée est dans ces pierres," and this holy horror sets the house apart in the presence of the cosmic forces of the universe, sea and sky. In spite of Hugo's rational explanations for the phenomena observed there, his conclusion shows thoughtful doubt: "Les crédules ont tort, sans doute, mais à coup sûr les positifs n'ont pas raison. Le problème persiste" (p. 151).

Another such place, described immediately after the house at Plainmont, is a house in St. Malo, called the Jacressarde, where Clubin comes to buy a revolver. On a small scale this dwelling provides a social commentary of the underworld of crime; its courtyard is a distant reminder of the Cour des Miracles of *Notre-Dame*. There is even an alchemist in residence, although he is a comic, not a demonic figure, for the Middle Ages have had their day, and the Satanism of Claude Frollo's alchemy is no longer believable. The house also reminds one of the underworld of *Les Misérables*, for as Hugo puts it, "Il y a dans toutes les villes . . . au-dessous de la population, un résidu" (p. 165). But the really important part of this house is its well: "La Jacressarde était plutôt une cour qu'une maison et plutôt un puits qu'une cour" (p. 166). The well is a kind of shaft or passage that leads from our world to one beneath, at whose entrance the dregs of society sleep at night, forming a "chapelet circulaire" (p. 166). "Chapelet" means not only string but rosary, and we notice that religious imagery again reappears *au seuil du gouffre*, to use Hugo's expression in *Dieu*.[12] The abyss is an opening over Hell; the "misérables" are formless beings only vaguely visible in the darkness (Hugo calls thems "larves," p. 167). The wretches huddled at this spot can even find death by drowning in the well.

Because both houses are situated on the edge of the Unknown, we may expect to find that blurring of reality that is characteristic of such places of passage. The house at Plainmont expands in a kind of hallucination: "La maison visionnée leur faisait l'effet de grandir démesurément. Dans cette illusion d'optique de la peur il y avait de la réalité" (p. 158). Although Hugo "explains" this impossibility by the fact that as the boys approached the house it seemed bigger to them, Hugo's language actually suggests that the changing size is independent of the boys' point of view. Did not the Satyr grow in like manner? At La Jacressarde also it is night when we arrive on the scene, those hours when forms dissolve and become blurred, a "rendez-vous funèbre où remuaient et s'amalgamaient dans le même miasme, les défaillances . . . des visages qui ont le regard de la mort, peut-être des baisers de bouche de ténèbres" (p. 167). This living nightmare is closer to Dante than to the world of common day.

Now that doubt has been cast upon the comfortable solidity of reality, the heroic quest is prepared. We have already mentioned that the hero of such a quest is solitary and in some way superior. Hugo intensifies this difference between Gilliatt and the ordinary man with this extraordinary statement: "Gilliatt était l'homme du songe" (p. 79), and "Peut-être y

12. "Je suis le regardeur formidable du Puits," says the Hibou in *Dieu*.

avait-il en Gilliatt de l'halluciné et de l'illuminé."[13] The hero is not a genius but rather a "pensif." He opens himself to "rêverie," and in his simplicity, without even knowing it, he can be invaded by "horreur sacrée." It is into this inner "aquarium de la nuit" that "l'Inconnu apparaît" (p. 80). Gilliatt is obviously the man to penetrate into the unknown, and his trip to the ocean will also be a voyage into his own unconscious psyche.

Conforming to the pattern of mythic action, Gilliatt must be summoned to the quest. As Campbell puts it: "A blunder—apparently the merest chance—reveals an unsuspected world, and the individual is drawn into a relationship with forces that are not rightly understood" (p. 51). It may be that as Freud suggested, accidents are not really accidents at all, but in the universe of this tale, the "blunder" or rather the mere chance that occurs in the first chapter remains unexplained, for the excellent reason that there is no explanation: Déruchette writes Gilliatt's name in the snow; Gilliatt reads it and falls in love with her. In the world of legend, these chance encounters often take place near some sacred spot that unites microcosm and macrocosm: an Omphalos, a sacred tree, a secret spring, etc. These sites are absent from this story, but the ocean is nearby, and Gilliatt can and will descend into it. Of course he cannot refuse the call to adventure, for there will be no quest and no story if he does. Furthermore, he has already passed the test necessary for his election as hero: in open competition with other young men he had won a *panse,* a broad-beamed boat, which like a magic sword will permit him to succeed in his quest.

The plot is made possible by Clubin's treachery. For years he had posed as the most virtuous man in the region, a model of rectitude. During this time, however, he was hiding his true Satanic nature behind a mask of hypocrisy. As we remarked in the opening chapter, Hugo was not a good creator of characters, and it is typical of his lack of understanding of human complexity that he does not seem to realize that one cannot live a role fully and yet remain unchanged by it. At any rate, Clubin makes plans to wreck Mess Lethierry's steamer and make off with the money that he had extorted from Rantaine. Everyone will think that he has died heroically, while he makes a new life in the New World. But Clubin's

13. Because this study is formal rather than biographical or ideological, we omit any discussion of the knotty problem of Hugo's debt to Illuminism.

method is dangerous from any point of view, and to wreck a boat in the fog is an heroic, if heroically evil, undertaking. The ship sets out loaded with cattle, the quintessence of the world of "common day" and of material solidity. Passengers on board discuss the quality of livestock and American politics (pp. 195–96). But then the ship plunges into fog, that symbol which we encountered before in *Les Burgraves* and as smoke in *Les Misérables*. The "upper" world is blotted out, save for an occasional rift in the fog that gives a quick moment's vision. Michael Riffaterre has summarized Hugo's technique admirably, showing how in a state of hallucination, solids seem to become fluids under the impact of "effroi" and "mouvement."[14] When motion ceases, "l'hallucination durcit, la réalité se recompose" (p. 232). This occurs when the ship suddenly founders on the rocks and is held fast. Then with the cessation of motion, the fog lifts and reality becomes "recomposed." Hugo intrudes to comment on this experience of passage into the Unknown:

> Une brusque déchirure de l'ombre laisse tout à coup voir l'invisible, puis se referme. Ces visions sont quelquefois transfiguratrices. . . .
> La solitude dégage une certaine quantité d'égarement sublime. C'est la fumée du buisson ardent. Il en résulte un mystérieux tremblement d'idées qui dilate le docteur en voyant et le poète en prophète."
> (p. 79)

It is all there: the smoke or fog, the tear in the veil, the trembling which accompanies the change of state.

The passengers take to the lifeboats, leaving the villain alone. When the fog lifts, Clubin discovers that he is not where he expected to be, but he still hopes to survive because he is a good swimmer. Sighting a ship nearby, he dives down into the water to swim to it. But descent to salvation operates only for the virtuous, and retribution for Clubin's evil life comes swiftly as he is drowned in the tentacles of the octopus. The stranded ship, once more seen as a solid material object, becomes the goal of Gilliatt's quest.

As a consequence of Clubin's treachery, Lethierry is financially ruined. His entire fortune was sunk in the craft and his profits had been stolen by Rantaine. Therefore, Lethierry makes an offer: the man who can bring

14. "La Vision hallucinatoire chez Victor Hugo," *Modern Language Notes,* LXXVIII (1963), 229.

back the engine of the ship can have Déruchette in marriage. Here it is appropriate to recall the close identification that Hugo, as well as Lethierry, makes: that Durande and Déruchette are two forms of the same name (p. 107). In going after the ship Gilliatt is going after the girl. Both are tied in with cosmic forces: "Qui sait mener une barque sait mener une femme. Ce sont les deux sujettes de la lune et du vent" (p. 116). With the king's (i.e., Lethierry's) ritual promise of marriage to his daughter, the hero can set out. But he must expect to overcome unusual obstacles before obtaining his greatest desire.

The hero of myth or legend who sets out upon the quest normally receives a warning or some form of assistance.[15] We remember the birds whose warning Pécopin ignored in Hugo's "own" legend. The result of this *hubris* was disaster. Even in *Han d'Islande,* Ordener picks up a guide early in his voyage, Benignus Spiagudry. That the hero has to dragoon his helper into aiding him is a comic parody of the usual situation, but even so, Hugo knew enough of mythic patterns to make Ordener invulnerable, for the aiding figure is "the benign, protecting power of providence,"[16] which description may help explain Spiagudry's first name. But in *Les Travailleurs de la mer,* the reader notes with apprehension that no such figure comes to Gilliatt's aid. All his tools, the *panse* included, are his own. This implicit assumption that he needs no divine aid is a dangerous one indeed, but he sets out nonetheless and disappears from human view. He is thought to have died in his attempt at salvage, assuming that anyone thinks of him at all.

As Gilliatt leaves the land for the sea, he crosses a boundary that Hugo associates with the phenomenon of decomposition of reality. The prefatory Archipel de la Manche opens with this statement: "L'Atlantique ronge nos côtes." Even stone is not as solid as one would think: "de vastes blocs s'écroulent." As a matter of fact, even the stone island is disappearing, for the stone is being hewed out and sold in England (p. 27). The coastline is unstable not only in fact, but also in visual mirages:

> Qui longe cette côte passe par une série de mirages. A chaque instant le rocher essaie de vous faire sa dupe. Où les illusions vont-elles se nicher? Dans le granit. Rien de plus étrange. D'énormes crapauds de pierre sont là, sortis de l'eau sans doute pour respirer;

15. Campbell, pp. 69–77.   16. *Ibid.*, p. 71.

des nonnes géantes se hâtent, penchées sur l'horizon; les plis pétri-
fiés de leur voile ont la forme de la fuite du vent; . . . on voit les
doigts des mains ouvertes. Tout cela c'est la côte informe. Approchez,
il n'y a plus rien. La pierre a de ces évanouissements. . . . A mesure
qu'on s'avance ou qu'on s'éloigne ou qu'on dérive ou qu'on tourne,
la rive se défait . . . les aspects se désagrègent pour se recom-
poser. . . . Rien ne change de forme comme les nuages, si ce n'est les
rochers. (p. 12)

Reading these lines, one recalls "Soleils couchants" of 1828.

The rocks lead to the sea, that "symbol for the primordial undifferenti-
ated flux, the substance which became created nature by having form
imposed upon or wedded to it," wrote W. H. Auden.[17] The poet added:
"The sea, in fact, is that state of barbaric vagueness and disorder out of
which civilization has emerged." In short, it is chaos. On the psychological plane, Campbell (among others) has remarked pertinently that "the
regions of the unknown (desert, jungle, deep sea, alien land, etc.) are
free fields for the projection of unconscious content. Incestuous *libido*
and patricidal *destrudo* are thence reflected back against the individual
and his society in forms suggesting threats of violence and fancied
dangerous delight—not only as ogres but also as sirens of mysteriously
seductive, nostaglic beauty" (p. 79). Gilliatt will encounter these forces
in his quest for love and sex. Déruchette is a symbol of the Unknown
which appears before him in all its frightening attractiveness and is the
more compelling because of the hero's virginity and solitude. Gilliatt even
discovers as he watches girls bathing in the sea that "une femme nue lui
faisait horreur" (p. 126). But he must fulfil his destiny.

As Gilliatt leaves the shore alone in his boat, he completes the process
of human isolation toward which the story has been pointing, for the hero
must confront the cosmos and the Unknown completely alone. As he
enters into the world of natural forces, where social considerations are
stripped away, a nearly pure mythic adventure emerges. First the hero
must pass, like Jason, through the *symplegades*, the clashing rocks. In
this case, they are the two upright stones that hold the wreck of the
Durande in their grasp.[18] Léon Emery compares the Durande to a cap-

---

17. *The Enchafèd Flood* (New York, 1950), p. 7.
18. Thus forming a typical Hugolian H, as has often been pointed out.

tured princess guarded by two hideous dragons, the rocks,[19] and we agree up to a point. The Durande (= Déruchette) is indeed held fast by these ugly guardians who appear to spread death about them,[20] and Gilliatt is coming to the rescue. But this place is really only a threshold to the underworld. After saving the ship's engine, he must go beyond and under to face the greater and more terrible combat of the octopus. Of course even his first task is Herculean, and to succeed, Gilliatt must become a Hercules or in Hugo's more familiar terminology, a Titan. It is true that prior to his departure, he was already a "sauvage" (p. 85) with a profile "d'un barbare antique" (p. 75). He could already lift "des fardeaux de géant" (p. 75). But these early attributes do not prepare the hero adequately for the task that he must face. As Gilliatt arrives on the rocks, alone and completely cut off from land, the birds steal the food that he has brought with him and he has to subsist on marine life. Like Vulcan he must make a forge from little but the natural substances around him. Because he succeeds, "Gilliatt sentit une fierté de cyclope, maître de l'air, de l'eau, et du feu" (p. 273). In order that he may seem equal to his task, Hugo uses certain stylistic devices to make the reader feel that his hero, like the Satyr, has grown in size: "Il lui semblait par moments donner des coups de marteau dans les nuages" (p. 274). Later, in his fight to protect the ship from the fury of a hurricane, Gilliatt not only succeeds, but he also manages to convince the reader of the possibility of what he has done. In his total effort and in his suffering, he is a "Job Prométhée," a titanic figure. The word "titan" or "titanic" appears several times in the text.

Now that the story has its hero, we need to look more closely at his quest, whose feminine nature we have already suggested. In fact, all of Gilliatt's important dealings are with women. First, like many characters in Hugo ranging from Gennaro to Jean Valjean, he has no real father. As a young man, he lives with his mother in an isolated house, and in this house there is a secret chest, even if it *is* "pas du tout mystérieuse," with its contents of a bridal trousseau. After his mother dies, he falls in love with Déruchette and sets forth on his quest for her. Out on the reef, the worlds of sea and sky have a special meaning for him: "à de certaines heures, regarder la mer est un poison. C'est comme, quelquefois, regarder

19. *Vision et pensée chez Victor Hugo* (Lyon, n.d. [1939]), p. 107.
20. ". . . on eût dit que des ventres de géants avaient été vidés là" (p. 253).

une femme" (p. 82). Later, the sea is described as a cat, a normally feminine image (p. 249). Then sea and woman are explicitly associated: "ce chaos . . . est le récipient universel, réservoir pour les fécondations" (p. 255). The wind plays a masculine role[21] with the result that the encounter of winds and waves is copulative. Hugo speaks of the "équilibre des forces génésiaques" during some storms: "Le vent maltraite la mer. . . . L'écume ruisselle à mille plis sur les reins de l'écueil comme la robe de lin sur les hanches de Vénus Anadyomène. . . . On entend le sanglot de la création" (pp. 326–27). Sea and sky find their sexual union through the image of the waterspout:

> Des souffles froids surviennent, puis des souffles chauds. La trépidation de la mer annonce une épouvante qui s'attend à tout. Inquiétude. Angoisse. Terreur profonde des eaux. Subitement l'ouragan, comme une bête, vient boire à l'océan; succion inouïe; l'eau monte vers la bouche invisible, une ventouse se forme, la tumeur s'enfle; c'est la trombe . . . effrayant coït de l'onde et de l'ombre. (p. 324)

And as Gilliatt is fearful before the feminine presence of Déruchette, the heavens themselves are silent before the aggressive sexuality of the sea: the thunder stops its crashing. Hugo comments: "Il semble qu'il ait peur" (p. 324). The religious imagery that usually appears at moments of crisis and of overt or covert sexual activity is again present. The waterspout is likened to "la colonne de la bible" (p. 324), another of many forms of the sacred tree or ladder linking the two universes.[22] By this union order is created. Alone, the sea was chaos, but now: "Accouplement est le premier terme, enfantement est le second. L'ordre universel est un hyménée magnifique. Point de fécondation par le désordre. Le chaos est un célibat" (p. 328). Hugo then reduces the scale of his vast image, likening the wind and sea to the lion and lioness in heat (p. 344) and later gives it some human quality by comparing it to Adam and Eve, thus forming a link with the human Gilliatt and providing an echo with "Le Sacre de la femme" of *La Légende des siècles*.

21. In primitive myth, the wind was thought to fecundate females. See Robert Graves, *The Greek Myths* (Baltimore, 1955), I, p. 27.
22. Hugo's rational explanation of the Axis Mundi is slanted more to the eighteenth-century idea of the Great Chain of Being (p. 330), the one portrayed in *Ce que dit la bouche d'ombre*.

Since the elements themselves are described in blatant sexual terms, we may well ask whether Gilliatt's encounter with the Durande is another, disguised, sexual encounter. The machinery within the wooden hull is the only precious part, somehow reminding one of the precious bridal trousseau in the old chest. As we saw Hugo equate the power of love with the "rouage d'une machine" above, possibly the engine, with its parts intact, can be associated with Déruchette's sex, particularly as the boat "is" the girl. Speculation on this point must remain a bit hazardous, for the text is not entirely clear, but the hero's subsequent encounters will leave no doubt.

Earlier in this chapter we mentioned Cosette's dream of the rock under which Marius places his love letter. She saw it as a "pierre grosse comme une montagne et pleine de cavernes." What was sublimated sexual dream in *Les Misérables* is here converted into literal reality, although we must remember that the reality lies still in a nightmare world of fog and water and night, as if the subconscious now had its own physical universe. Under the Douvres rocks, the sea "se fait, dans cette montagne secrète, qui est à elle, des antres, des sanctuaires, des palais" (p. 276). The caves have a "végétation hideuse et splendide." Here there are "monstres qui prennent racine." In a "magnificence affreuse," in which the female sea "y développe à l'aise son côté mystérieux inaccessible à l'homme,"[23] "elle y dépose ses sécrétions vivantes et horribles" (p. 276). What could be clearer?

This underwater cave is described in terms that collect the various themes and images that we have been exploring up to this point:

> Ces constructions . . . ont l'enchevêtrement du polypier [the hydra and the spider], la sublimité de la Cathédrale [Notre-Dame de Paris], l'extravagance de la pagode [a further example of the religious temple], l'amplitude du mont [the hills above the grotto of Walderhog, Habibrah's cave, Cosette's stone, the *mons veneris* of the swelling sea, etc.], la délicatesse du bijou [pearls have long been a feminine symbol], l'horreur du sépulcre [*Lucrèce Borgia, Les Misérables*]. (pp. 276–77)

Gilliatt had passed by this grotto for weeks without any awareness of the lurking danger, even though he had once glimpsed the octopus

23. In the sense of the male as well as in the sense of mankind.

vaguely through the water, just as Marius had passed by Cosette "tous les jours paisiblement et impunément sans se douter de rien." Like Marius, Gilliatt had forgotten that the cave was even there, and so when he makes his perilous descent in the underworld and enters into this bloody[24] grotto, Hugo must intervene to warn that it is "à ses risques et périls." As the hero moves farther in, he finds that "la fissure était resserrée et le passage presque impossible" (p. 278). He finally squeezes his way through the rocks (again the suggestion of the *symplegades*) into "une caverne extraordinaire." Gilliatt saw before him "sous la vague une sorte d'arche noyée. Cette arche, ogive naturelle façonnée par le flot, était éclatante entre ses deux jambages profonds et noirs" (p. 279). The legs are not the only suggestion of a living person, obviously a woman: "on croyait deviner une âme mystérieuse dans ce grand diaphragme vert s'élançant et s'abaissant en silence" (p. 281). Here in this place of ultimate encounter for Gilliatt, there is light, "un jour inconnu." "Il n'y avait plus dans cette clarté rien de notre lumière" (p. 280). On the one hand it is a dark cave, on the other it glows with light. If we recall that in "Puissance égale bonté" sun and spider, light and dark are really one, we may understand the function of the interplay of light and dark here: sex is both good and evil. Hugo makes a more direct comparison when he intervenes to remind the reader: "Nous avons indiqué ailleurs l'identité de forme entre le soleil et l'araignée" (p. 133) and he is careful also to make the link, obvious though it be, by saying that the octopus is "arachnide par la forme" (p. 372). Thus, seemingly incidental descriptions in earlier pages reveal their true meaning in the light of this central image. We are told about spiders in Paraguay, "velues, grosses commes des têtes d'enfants . . . [qui] attaquent l'homme auquel elles lancent leurs poils qui s'enfoncent comme des flèches dans la chair et y soulèvent des pustules" (pp. 113–14). When the storm breaks, the first drops of rain hitting the rock are described as "trois ou quatre larges araignées de pluie" (p. 352). The sea itself, as the storm closes in on the hero, becomes a "pléiade noire," a "centre d'irradiation de courants [qui] . . . se fermaient en quelque sorte sur lui" (p. 297). So too the octopus, normally grayish (p. 372), becomes luminous in the mating season (can Hugo *never* escape his patterns of imagery?),

24. ". . . cet aspect d'abattoir et de boucherie étrangement empreint dans l'entre-deux des Douvres" (p. 277).

shedding a wan light, "épanouie en une irradiation blême, soleil spectre" (p. 374) resembling the storm itself, with its wan light emanating from a pale sun (p. 351). Like the sun, the octopus has "rayons"[25] and these have "du flamboiement dans leur ondoiement" (p. 372). And when Gilliatt is seized by the beast, he is "la mouche de cette araignée" (p. 327), and like other Hugolian characters seized by a spider he is "lié, englué, impuissant" (p. 374). And just as a fly is drained of his life's fluid by the spider, Gilliatt will be "vidé dans cet épouvantable sac."

That the octopus is the central image in Hugo' text is indicated not only by the importance of the spider in *Notre-Dame* but by many details in *Les Travailleurs*. For instance, the *ventouse* is not only the suction cup of the octopus' tentacle, but it is Hugo's word for the waterspout that united sky and sea in sexual combat. We recall his reference to the Paraguayan spiders which raise pustules on the flesh, suggestive of those raised by the octopus on Gilliatt's body. The locale of the action is important as well. At the end of the cave there is the inevitable "antre," a "tabernacle" in a "sanctuaire" (p. 284). Above the waves at low tide, one can see "une pierre . . . ayant une ressemblance d'autel." The Druid altar in *Han d'Islande* was not an incidental detail. But whereas Han, the monster in the cave, was masculine, here and indeed ever since *Lucrèce Borgia*, the dangerous figure has more often been feminine. In the cave the altar is enlarged into an entire temple: "Il semblait qu'une déesse vînt d'en descendre." And the goddess is naked: "une femme toute nue . . . était probablement sur cet autel tout à l'heure" (p. 284). Hugo likens the absent divinity to a "Diane pouvant aimer" (p. 284), a peculiar comparison indeed, until one remembers that this terrible goddess had Acteon destroyed for his voyeurism. Campbell comments that this goddess of mythology can be seen as the "bad" mother, "against whom aggressive fantasies are directed, and from whom a counter-aggression is feared."[26] Small wonder then, that the battle in the cave is so desperate. When Gilliatt kills the monster by cutting out its staring eyes[27] with his knife, he has somehow overcome the terrors of sexuality and freed himself from its

25. "Tout s'explique par le mot Rayonner" (p. 331).
26. P. 111.
27. The eyes of the octopus, amid the "haillons" and "chiffons" of its tentacles, somehow parallel the eye of the hurricane and its wisps of clouds, also called rags, "guenilles livides" (p. 351).

grip on him. Henceforth, he will have more freedom in his acts, a freedom that can be used to serve others.

What did Hugo, who often intervened to interpret his text, think of the octopus? Was he consciously aware of the sexual implications of his imagery? One might think so, particularly as he had earlier remarked concerning the metamorphosis of girl to woman: "Quand la femme se fait, l'ange s'en va" (p. 91). A woman is redeemed only when she becomes a mother: between puberty and maternity she is a fearsome creature who leaves Hugo more than uneasy. Yet, when talking specifically about the octopus, Hugo lifts the discussion to a more abstract level and sees it rather as a symbol of the frontier between matter and the unknown spirit world. After the zoologist, firmly fixed in our world, catalogues and classifies the beast rationally, Hugo explains that then the philosopher must reveal its abstract meaning: "Ces créatures l'inquiètent presque sur la création." They are "les formes voulues du mal." "Ces animaux sont fantômes autant que monstres. . . . Ils touchent la frontière humaine et peuplent la limite chimérique. Vous niez le vampire, la pieuvre apparaît. . . . l'optimisme, qui est le vrai pourtant, perd presque contenance devant eux. Ils sont l'extrémité visible des cercles noirs. Ils marquent la transition de notre réalité à une autre" (p. 375). The octopus proves the existence of Satan, and then Hugo adds the curious comment that seers like John of Patmos and Dante were capable of sensing the presence of these "bêtes fauves" of the soul and of denouncing them, which shows Hugo's desire to have his universe considered as one of mind as well as of the Channel Islands. Through the octopus the finest minds are tempted into becoming Manicheans, Hugo believes. Do we not have here a personal confession, in which he has admitted that the octopus is the evil beast in his own soul? But after this dangerous excursion into self-analysis, Hugo returns to the safer world of physical reality and decides not to condemn the octopus because it is one of the scavengers who are needed to keep the world clean. After all, he comments, "toute la nature que nous avons sous les yeux est mangeante et mangée" (p. 376). This direction of thought, however, serves only to show that Hugo's attempt at explaining the meaning of these forms is of little value in understanding Gilliatt's quest, to which we now return.

The reader will recall that the hero set off on his journey without any assistance from a divine messenger who might have given him the necessary protection from harm. This *hubris,* even if unintentional, does not go unpunished. At the last moment, with the ship's engine rescued and lowered into his boat, the *panse* begins to leak. To stop it from sinking, he plugs the hole with a tarpaulin and starts to bail, but he is so weak from exhaustion that he can do little. Night falls, enveloping Gilliatt in total blackness. As the water pressure increases, the tarpaulin begins to balloon inward. More stuffing is needed. Gilliatt removes all his clothing and uses it to plug the leak. Will it hold? The hero, alone in darkness, is finally at the end of even his Herculean strength, naked as when he came into the world. Against the leak, he can do no more: "Ce magnanime effort de deux mois[28] titaniques aboutissait à un anéantissement" (p. 391). At this supreme moment:

> dans l'accablement de toute cette énormité inconnue, ne sachant plus ce qu'on lui voulait . . . il renonça, il se coucha tout de son long le dos sur la roche, la face aux étoiles, vaincu, et joignant les mains devant la profondeur terrible, il cria dans l'infini: Grâce!
> Terrassé par l'immensité, il la pria. (p. 391)

Alone before God, Gilliatt is forced to admit what Hugo was always reluctant to confess but always did: Man is not God. While God is ultimately beneficent, even in the form of the infinite presence of the Night, He is terrifying. Hugo even uses the imagery of the spider and octopus to describe Heaven's hold on one: "on se sent pris. On est à la discrétion de cette ombre. Pas d'évasion possible. On se voit dans l'engrenage" (p. 304). But by an act of prayer, in which the hero humbles himself before the divine, he may be granted some mercy. Hugo is no longer the believer in a grim fatality when he writes: "La prière s'adresse à la magnanimité des ténèbres; la prière regarde le mystère avec les yeux mêmes de l'ombre, et, devant la fixité puissante de ce regard suppliant, on sent un désarmement possible de l'Inconnu" (p. 399).[29]

By his virtue and by his prayer, Gilliatt has enlisted God on his side.

---

28. So blurred is the sense of reality that the reader is surprised to learn that he had been there for only this period of time.

29. In a letter to Franz Stevens, *Correspondance*, 1836–1882, Hugo wrote from exile: "J'habite dans cet immense rêve de l'océan, je deviens peu à peu un somnambule de la mer et devant toute cette énorme pensée vivante où je m'abîme, je finis par ne plus être qu'une espèce de témoin de Dieu." Ditchy, p. 46.

Saved, he sleeps. When he awakens he is refreshed. The sea is calm and beautiful: "L'apaisement de la mer était inexprimable. Elle avait un murmure de nourrice près de son enfant. Les vagues paraissaient bercer l'écueil" (p. 393). Piroué, among others, puns on the situation: "Une mer qui est aussi une mère," a coherent image within the universe of this work.[30] He has achieved atonement. Now he is in a position to return to land, not only with the engine, but also with Lethierry's money which he had found in a box attached to the belt of Clubin's skeleton at the rear of the cave, and to bestow boons on mankind. All seems calm and assured.

The tension is still present, however, for Gilliatt does not understand his new role as savior. He still thinks of himself as the simple fisherman eager to win Déruchette's hand. In other words, a hero of a humble romance. But he returns just in time to overhear Caudray propose to Déruchette and be accepted. Lethierry seems to understand better than he what has happened: "Tu es donc allé jusqu'en enfer?" (p. 419). Indeed, the hero's appearance justifies the question. Gilliatt, "l'homme qui faisait ces choses était devenu effrayant," wrote Hugo early in his hero's stay on the reef.[31] Weeks later, he is a monster in rags, brutish, bleeding, hairy. When Déruchette sees him, she faints in terror, unable to cope with this Titan (p. 424). Transformed into a mythic figure by his experience, he is too great for any accomodation to this world. One can hardly imagine Gilliatt with his pipe and slippers married to Déruchette, living *L'Art d'être grand'père*. A god must save others and then leave them.

His task of bestowing boons is one of sacrificial immolation, not one of bourgeois self-gratification. Like Christ who reappeared briefly among His disciples in order to promise them eternal life and save them from despair, Gilliatt, after harrowing Hell, reappears to save Lethierry from despair by giving him the engine and the 75,000 francs recovered from Clubin's skeleton. Realizing the impossibility of marrying Déruchette, and freed from his own sexual obsessions, he assumes willingly his role as savior, almost magically overcomes all the obstacles to her marriage with Caudray, and even gives her his chest with the trousseau as a gift. Leaving joy behind him, he returns to the sea in death and leaves this

30. In other works, Hugo sometimes varies. In *Autrefois* of *Les Contemplations*, he states: "La mer, c'est le Seigneur."

31. Hugo's ink sketch of *Gilliatt sortant de l'écume* is a superb capturing of the sublime yet terrifying hero. For a reproduction, see the Edition du Seuil edition of his novels, III, 135.

world with his task accomplished. Like other mythic heroes, he has been in the world but not of it, and with his disappearance into the ocean ("il n'y eut plus rien que la mer," p. 453), he has returned to the maternal sea, which is now the very embodiment of infinity.

Such is *Les Travailleurs de la mer,* one of the finest creations of Hugo's long career. Only on rare occasions does his pen falter: his essay on electricity intercalated into the text might have been better left unwritten, and occasionally his concretization of the abstract gets out of hand (e.g., "La vie est le prodigieux serpent de l'infini," p. 337) and his hypotheses strained (e.g., "le réel est l'asymptote du possible," p. 338). The great power of the work is achieved by reducing what is sometimes prolixity in *Les Misérables* to a concentration on one solitary figure facing the infinite forces of the cosmos. Viewed from this perspective, the oddity of the dialogues, the simplicity of the characterizations are more strengths than weaknesses. But despite this triumph, Hugo was demiurge, a creator who could not stop creating. He still had not given up his political vision which for him was symbolized by the French Revolution. As a result, since his last two fictional works were to deal with history once again, the mythic qualities would be subordinated to open prophecy or Revelation as Hugo tried to bring his work to its conclusion.

FROM MYTH
TO APOCALYPSE

L'HOMME QUI RIT

WHAT MORE could Hugo have to say in prose fiction? After his early romances he had tried his hand at an historical novel elaborated in complex imagery (*Notre-Dame de Paris*), a "contemporary" novel based on image and myth with political and social overtones (*Les Misérables*), and had finally condensed—if this word can ever be applied to Hugo—his mythic vision into its purest form in *Les Travailleurs de la mer*. Yet no sooner did this last-named work appear in March, 1866, than its indefatigable creator started on a plan for another "historical novel," *L'Homme qui rit*. Hugo himself explained his purpose in attempting so soon still another work. In a note he remarked: "Sous ce titre: *Etudes sociales*, l'auteur commence une série . . . qui a aujourd'hui prélude pour première page *l'Homme qui rit* c'est-à-dire *l'Angleterre après 1688*, se continuera par *la France avant 1789* et s'achevera par *93*."[1] These three books would form a triptych based on three loci of power: aristocracy, monarchy, and democracy respectively. The middle work (*La Monarchie*) was never written, but *93* would follow in an attempt to proclaim, through the events of the French Revolution, Hugo's optimistic vision of a future society.

There was another reason that impelled Hugo to take up his pen at least one more time. He wrote:

> On a voulu voir dans Ananké toute une profession de foi, et l'on a déclaré que l'auteur de *Notre-Dame de Paris*, des *Misérables* et des *Travailleurs de la mer* était fataliste. Il est le contraire. Il pense, quant à lui, que la série de ses œuvres est une série d'affirmations de l'Ame. A cette série il ajoute aujourd'hui ce livre.
>
> Contre la fatalité l'homme a deux armes: la conscience et la

---

1. E.I.N., p. 577.

liberté; la conscience qui lui indique le devoir, la liberté qui lui signale le droit.[2]

We are today in a better position than the poet-novelist himself to judge the accuracy of this remark. We can agree that in *Les Misérables* fatality is not omnipotent, but in *Notre-Dame* it certainly is, and as for *Les Travailleurs* it could be argued either way, because one can claim either that fatality is at work in Gilliatt's destiny or that he succeeds in his quest. What is clear from the quotation is Hugo's desire to study "conscience" and "liberté" in a political context of free and therefore responsible choice.

This struggle of the individual against fatality will appear—as one would expect—as a journey to some ideal along whose path there lurks some form of the menacing spider. Thus images abound and myth is discernible, but to them will be added another element, one that was already visible briefly in *Notre-Dame* and was more developed in *Les Misérables*: prophecy or revelation. One will recall Jacques Coppenole's prophecy of the fall of the Bastille in the former work, and in the latter, Enjolras' sermon from the barricade is even more important. This harangue looks ahead to an ideal society of the future, which Georges Gusdorf has shown to be a humanitarian socialism reflecting Hugo's own views.[3] But although imagery and mythic patterns do not clash in *Les Misérables* with Enjolras' Revelation, the young man is not at the center of the novel; this place is occupied by Jean Valjean. More generally, the imagery of Enjolras' sermon is not worked out systematically in the entire work. Léon Cellier has called *L'Homme qui rit* "une reprise des *Misérables*,"[4] and indeed the two have much in common: both heroes are outcasts, both save an orphan girl, both die at the end in a state of rapture, etc., but there is an essential difference between the two works: Apocalyptic imagery is at the heart of *L'Homme qui rit*, whereas in *Les Misérables* it was merely important.

The setting that Hugo chose was England, in which he had been interested long before he went into exile,[5] as one may remember from

2. E.I.N., p. 581.
3. "Quel horizon on voit du haut de la barricade," *Centenaire des Misérables (1862–1962). Hommage à Victor Hugo* (Strasbourg, 1962), p. 190. See also Elliott M. Grant, *The Career of Victor Hugo* (Cambridge, Mass., 1945), 262–265, for an assessment of the precise nature of Hugo's "humanitarian socialism."
4. " 'Chaos vaincu'—Victor Hugo et le roman initiatique," *Centenaire des Misérables*, p. 215.
5. John H. Thomas, *L'Angleterre dans l'œuvre de Victor Hugo* (Paris, 1933).

Amy Robsart, Cromwell, and *Marie Tudor,* and his presence in the Channel Islands after 1852 increased this interest. Hugo was very eager to have the reader believe in the accuracy of his portrayal of this setting. *L'Homme qui rit* is studded with precise details of the clothing of various court officials and of the possessions of innumerable English noblemen. Various bills presented to Parliament are cited and the protocol of their introduction laboriously explained. Social conditions of unemployment, sickness, etc., are given with specific locales. Dates, historical personages, and places abound. But the genuine historicity of all this mass of material is slim, and many of Hugo's "facts" are inaccurate. For instance, Hugo invented the whole league of *comprachicos* who mutilated children,[6] as well as their medical manual by one Dr. Conquest, *De Denasatis,* and all the Latin citations taken therefrom. When he did not invent his sources and used, for example, Macaulay's *History of England,* a tendentious work at best and badly translated into French, he often read hastily and copied inexactly.[7] His historical figures are caricatures, his portrait of conditions in England one-sided. In the face of the evidence, Thomas' conclusions are quite mild, but the point emerges clearly:

> le romancier se travestit en historien et cite à propos de ses textes, latins, pour la plupart, des noms, des titres, des précédents historiques; mais c'est toujours le romancier qui parle et ce serait s'exposer à de grandes déceptions que de considérer ces digressions "historiques" comme des pièces justificatives. (p. 224)

Yet Hugo claimed—even in his own outline—that "ce livre est avant tout impartial."[8] We recall his desire, cited above, to make "études sociales" *à la* Balzac, and Hugo tried to implement his alleged history by a judicious conclusion on English history. He recognized that the peerage rendered great service to England in checking the unlimited power of the monarch. As he puts it in the body of the text: "remercions-la," an accolade that he follows with his own biased viewpoint, "enterrons-la" (p. 458). Thus,

6. *Ibid.,* p. 184. For a particularly astute explanation of the genesis of the mutilating comprachicos in Hugo's imagination, see P. Berret, "Les Comprachicos et la mutilation de Gwynplaine dans L'Homme qui rit," *Revue d'histoire littéraire de la France* XXI (juillet-déc. 1914), 503–518.

7. This carelessness reveals the lack of genuine historical interest and was visible as early as *Notre-Dame de Paris.* See Max Bach, "Le Vieux Paris dans *Notre-Dame:* Sources et ressources de Victor Hugo," *PMLA,* LXXX (1965), 321–24.

8. E.I.N., p. 583.

there is neither serious historical accuracy nor impartiality, a fact that suggests that the text is less of a novel than a piece of imaginative propaganda. In fact, if analyzed as literature, the text shows by its apocalyptic imagery an archetype of Hell which Hugo places in opposition to an archetype of Eden inhabited by the two young people in love.

Before going any farther, a *caveat* or two is in order. *L'Homme qui rit* is an extremely bad piece of writing, so bad in fact, that few critics have bothered to take it seriously on the grounds, no doubt, that it was not worth the effort.[9] The weaknesses are particularly annoying at times because they are so unnecessary. For instance, unfortunate bits of "humor" abound, of which the following is a prime example: "Un jour on apprit qu'il était arrivé au vieil absent, lord Linnaeus Clancharlie, diverses choses dont la principale était qu'il était trépassé" (p. 169). More serious is Hugo's logorrhea. Repetitions, long, drawn-out dialogues, accumulations of pointless details far exceed any of Hugo's previous efforts, which were hardly known for their concision. Nor can this excess be justified by any comparison to the verbal creativity of a Rabelais, or even by suggesting that we have, like Flaubert's *Bouvard et Pécuchet*, an example of Menippean satire (or "anatomy," to use the term of Northrop Frye), for the serious prophetic visions (and Hugo is *au fond* deadly serious) hardly permit the intrusion of this unassimilable genre.

Another weakness is unassimilated autobiography. In his portrait of the republican exile, Lord Clancharlie, Hugo has given us a self-portrait. Clancharlie is "ce vieillard vêtu des mêmes habits que le peuple, pâle, distrait, courbé, probablement du côté de la tombe, debout au bord du lac [read *de la mer*] à peine attentif à la tempête et à l'hiver, marchant comme au hasard, l'œil fixe, ses cheveux blancs secoués par le vent de l'ombre, silencieux, solitaire, pensif" (p. 158).[10] It is only too easy to see Hugo in exile, or at least the image of himself that he wished to project.

9. Criticism from Hugo's day is, as usual, based more on the critics' (or their newspapers') attitude toward republicanism than on the value of the works. Certainly the editor of the E.I.N. is prejudiced in the exile's favor (see pp. 591–96). In more recent times, Paul Claudel is nearly alone in championing this bizarre creation, which he calls "cet album de lithographies épiques et paniques qui à mon avis est le chef-d'œuvre du grand poète," in *Réflexions sur la poésie* (Paris, 1963), p. 46.

10. Cf.

J'étais le vieux rôdeur sauvage de la mer,
Une espèce de spectre au bord du gouffre amer. . . .

"Octobre," *L'Année terrible*, p. 39.

Further, the accusations against the poet made by partisans of Napoleon III, who accused him of vainglory in persisting in his "ridiculous" exile, are repeated here with little change. One detects immediately Hugo's own sarcastic attempts to justify himself against them.

We have already mentioned the inadequate history. Should this be viewed as a defect? After all, Revelation has no need for mundane historical accuracy. But Hugo not only made clear in his notes his desire to interpret the aristocracy as a politico-social phenomenon, he also claimed in the novel that his portrait represents the actual society of its day. This claim constitutes a real defect, for we are not convinced by it. Because of Hugo's difficulty in fusing reality and symbolism, there are some odd distortions. To give an extreme example of Hugo's inability to blend the two credibly, we are told that Duchess Josiane's eyes have one blue pupil and one black pupil. The genetics are more than doubtful, even if the symbolism is explicit: that the colors represent Heaven (blue) and Hell (black). There are still other defects that will become apparent in the course of our analysis, but even so this work, remarkably bad as it is, is a work that rewards the serious critic for his effort.

It opens with a "première partie" of four brief chapters called "La Mer et la Nuit," a title repeated at the conclusion of the text. In both places it is night, there is a boat with passengers fleeing the country, and there is death by drowning. Using the sea to suggest the wider vision of immensity, Hugo frames the main action of his story, which takes place on land. The two essential scenes of the prologue or first part announce the theme for the main work: on the land, the ten-year-old Gwynplaine wanders alone in a blizzard, finds the infant Déa, and is rescued by Ursus and his wolf, Homo, in the nick of time, while at sea, the evil band of *comprachicos* is escaping to Spain, leaving civilization behind. Here are individuals totally cut off from humanity, battling the elements alone, and, as each must go through the ultimate testing, let us follow each in turn.

According to the story, the late King James II had paid these *comprachicos* to disfigure a noble child, son of Lord Clancharlie. Driven from England by a later edict, they board their ship and leave the child behind on the coast. The boat slips off into the darkness and enters a blurred world of unstable forms, as is typical in Hugo's places of passage from one world to another. Portland Bay appears "blafarde dans son demi-cercle de collines; il y avait du rêve dans ce paysage nocturne" (p. 45). Soon even this reality will disintegrate: "Un chaos allait faire son entrée"

(p. 46). As the criminals were leaving, storm warnings were plentiful ("l'avertissement ne lui avait point manqué," p. 65), but the outcasts are so confident in their human powers that they dare to face the infinite after abandoning a child to certain death in a winter storm. They further tempt retribution by setting out for a paradise that is not God's. "Cocagne!" cries out one sailor, thinking of this fabled land of luxury and idleness. Although the sailors are the riff-raff of all nations, their leader, a Dutchman, is of a different kind. His name is Genardus Geestemunde, whose name means "Mouth of the Spirit" and perhaps also "Spirit of the World." He is steeped in crime but at least his god is God. He knows his guilt and accepts judgment on himself, and when he speaks, he speaks with the Mouth of the true Spirit. In him, Hugo is trying to show a man who knows himself to be responsible for his acts. Recognizing this responsibility (an attitude that marks a sharp change from the fatalism of *Notre-Dame*), the "songeur tragique," Geestemunde, raises his head and speaks to "un point de l'espace" and says solemnly: "C'est juste. Quant à moi, je consens" (p. 78), because, as he later explains to the others, "ce qui est fait contre un enfant est fait contre Dieu" (p. 116). From this moment on, only confession and repentance can be of any use as the ship is quickly dismasted, the rudder destroyed, and the captain swept away. The victims plunge blindly toward destruction. Here Hugo has recourse to various images, and it is perhaps a sign of his failing powers that they seem about the same as those in *Les Travailleurs de la mer*, untransformed by some new vision. For example, one finds this forced and unsuccessful bit of religious imagery: "La tempête ressemble à l'intérieur d'une cathédrale tendue de deuil. Mais aucun luminaire dans cette cathédrale" (p. 90). Furthermore, the cloud is "pareil au-dessous d'un hydre . . . et par endroits ce ventre livide adhérait aux vagues." Waterspouts appear, "succions [qui] soulevaient ça et là sur le flot des cônes d'écume" (p. 87). As night falls, the world becomes suddenly "une voûte de cave" (p. 90), and ships, like this one, are "des mouches dans la toile d'araignée de la mer" (p. 77). The familiar imagery continues unabated: the vessel is helpless, "saisi, garotté, paralysé" (p. 107). The language that so well described Esmeralda in the torture chambers has here lost its force, for it does not rise from the physical reality of objects in the novel (octopus, torture chamber, cathedrals, etc.) but is merely pulled in from Hugo's vast storehouse of images. One old image is, however, reworked with fresh ingenuity. We remember that Gilliatt's *panse* at one moment threatened to sink from a leak, and here too, after avoiding the perils of reefs and rocks, the *Matutina* springs a leak and begins to sink. But where Gilliatt's prayer is answered, for he is virtuous, in *L'Homme qui rit,* "aucune voix ne lui répondit" (p. 121). The victims are helpless before "l'effrayant refus céleste" (p. 120), and they all die when the boat sinks. The lesson is clear: God sits in judgment on man and destroys evil in either its personal or social form. We say social form because, although the *comprachicos* constitute but a small group of outcasts, this group was hired by the King of England to do his dirty work, and therefore the monarch and the society he represents must also undergo God's wrath.

As the reader leaves the ocean scene to follow Gwynplaine on the land, he finds the same concept of an individual lost in a cosmic void. Like the boat at sea, he is in a closed "voûte de cave," with snow and rocks beneath his feet and a "brume opaque" (p. 45) above him. But the boy, although unaware of it at first, is about to experience a transition to the world of human company. Hugo anticipates this change of world: "Les aventures de l'abîme ne sont limitées en aucun sens; tout y est possible, même le salut. L'issue est invisible, mais trouvable" (p. 126). The presence of the rest of mankind is prepared in generalized terms: "On l'avait amené là et laissé là. *On* et *là,* ces deux énigmes représentaient toute sa destinée; *on* était le genre humain; *là* était l'univers" (p. 50). *We,* as mankind, are responsible for setting the child in his situation, but he will have a free choice as to his manner of facing it. He will not have to wait long before coming upon the various manifestations of social Hell and Heaven between which he must choose.

As at this point the apocalyptic imagery becomes dominant, it is necessary to schematize the key images of this rather special literary form. We can do no better than to reproduce the chart given by Northrop Frye[11] to which we have added the final two columns:

			(demonic parody)	
World	*Group*	*Individual*	*Group*	*Individual*
divine	society of gods	one God	society of Satans	Satan
human	society of men	one man	society of evildoers	one evil man (e.g., tyrant)
animal	sheepfold	one lamb	pack of wolves	wolf
vegetable	garden or park	one tree (of life)	wasteland	gallows or cross
mineral	holy city	one building or temple	evil city	prison, cave, or dungeon

11. *Anatomy of Criticism* (Princeton, N.J., 1957), p. 141.

205

Gwynplaine's first encounter is with a gallows. Approaching a hill, he can see "sur cette éminence une configuration qui semblait dans la brume un arbre" (p. 50). The fog is marking the moment of passage from cosmic to social world. The "tree" is the demonic parody of the sacred tree of life, the Axis Mundi, whose Christian version is the cross of Christ, and for Hugo, who for years had opposed capital punishment, any gibbet or gallows. Gwynplaine stands before this apparition like Barabbas before Golgotha in *La Fin de Satan*. The young boy is at one of those centers which open onto an extra-terrestrial world as in the tradition of primitive myth: "Il existe des réalités ici-bas qui sont comme des issues sur l'inconnu" (p. 52) and "Il y a dans l'invisible d'obscures portes entrebâillées." The hill seems "dans les espaces un centre, ce qui est effrayant à dire" (p. 53). But this center is a demonic center created by an evil society; it is not the Way.

Gwynplaine, having stumbled upon the "vegetable" form of the demonic world, is about to have his first encounter with the mineral. After finding the infant Déa in the snow, he trudges on looking for human habitation. As demonic worlds, whatever their form, are sterile wastelands, we should not be surprised at the setting of a howling blizzard, totally devoid of life. In his search for salvation ("Croire à un gîte, c'est croire en Dieu," p. 60), Gwynplaine enters the town of Weymouth,[12] and the mythic overtones of the experience are suggested by the chapter title: "Toute voie douloureuse se complique d'un fardeau." The evocation of Christ's *via dolorosa* effectively reinforces the experience at the gallows. But salvation appears to be at hand. With the appearance of human dwellings, Edenic imagery replaces demonic imagery:

> Plus rien à craindre. Il avait en lui cette chaleur subite, la sécurité. Ce dont il sortait était fini. Il n'y aurait plus de nuits désormais, ni d'hiver, ni de tempête.[13] Il lui semblait que tout ce qu'il y a de possible dans le mal était derrière lui. La petite n'était plus un poids. (p. 133)

Alas, the Promised Land is but an illusion. No smoke, symbol of human warmth and of vertical contact with the divine world, reaches up to

---

12. What seems an ironic pun here on the Mouth (or opening) to the Way, is probably only a coincidence, but it does fit neatly into the pattern.
13. See Revelation, 21:4.

Heaven: "Aucune fumée n'en sortait" (p. 133). All is dark and cold; thistles, symbol of the wasteland, grow nearby. The boy knocks at the door of a large house: "La maison de gauche était large, haute, toute en pierre, avec toit d'ardoise" (p. 133). The stone of the building is emphasized, as if Hugo wished to insist on the hard mineral quality. This house belongs to a rich man, but the thatched house of the poor man is no more hospitable. In both dwellings there is "la même surdité aux misérables" (p. 134). These houses, bolted and locked, are "maisons spectres" and "l'enfant sentit le froid des hommes plus terrible que le froid de la nuit." This demonic hostility is not unthinking fate. Rich and poor alike are responsible for their indifference. As Hugo puts it bluntly: "C'est un froid qui veut" (p. 137).

Crossing a bridge, Gwynplaine passes through another hamlet equally unwilling to open its door, and we learn that "il y avait là moins de maisons de bois que de maisons de pierre" (p. 136). Finally, Gwynplaine leaves the evil town and in so doing saves himself. Out in nature again he comes upon what will prove to be the Heavenly City. Curiously, it is first presented as Hell. The boy hears a threat, a "grincement," "un rugissement," a "rictus féroce," of a wolf. In a kind of "vaste éclairage sépulcral" he sees a hut on wheels. As he approaches, "la menace devint furieuse." Now it is a "hurlement," and he hears chains grinding and becomes aware of "deux rangées de dents aigües." He is told to go away. But all this hostility is illusion and double parody: as the hoped-for town was not Heaven but Hell, this is not Hell but Heaven. We might guess the truth from the fact that "du toit sortait un tuyau, et du tuyau une fumée" (p. 139). The contrast with Weymouth is evident and this paradox is laboriously continued within the hut. We learn that the man is called Ursus, the wolf, Homo.[14] Ursus speaks hatred of mankind but practices total love. He speaks the literal truth when he looks at the world outside and calls it "damné pays" (p. 143) and refers to the youth as "boy de [from] l'enfer" (p. 142). But normally his conversation is ironic. He comments, with an air of seeming approval, that thanks to society's laws, "vagabonds sont punis, les honnêtes gens qui ont des maisons à eux sont gardés et protégés, les rois sont les pères du peuple" (p. 146). We soon realize that he means exactly the opposite, that he hates the society

14. Hugo first called him Lupus. See *Reliquat*, p. 544.

organized in this fashion. Hugo continues the irony as he develops the idea that this tiny world of the rolling hut, this island of poverty, is really true wealth. Although they are all social outcasts, disfigured, blind (Déa), misanthropic, accompanied by a wolf, "ils étaient dans un paradis" (p. 232). "Avec leur enfer, ils avaient fait du ciel" (p. 239).

This perfect world has its appropriate levels. The *charrette* itself is the sacred temple of paradise. It is later enlarged and becomes the Green-Box, green the color of an idyllic park or garden, as well as of hope. The wolf acts like a lamb, and the misanthropic Ursus is in reality a fine man. He, in turn, "maniaque de noms latins" (p. 231) had baptized the infant girl Déa, thus creating a "divine" figure by her very name, and her virtue and her ethereal qualities fit the role admirably. These people constitute a divine society from which evil is absent. Hugo was apparently conscious of the apocalyptic quality of his family, for Ursus explains to the wolf: "Tu représentes l'homme, je représente la bête; nous sommes le monde d'en bas, cette petite représente le monde d'en haut. . . . De cette façon l'univers complet, humanité, bestialité, divinité sera dans notre cahute" (p. 231).

The idea that the hut is the divine temple, although admittedly it is built out of wood rather than of stone for the exigencies of verisimilitude, needs more exploration. We see it first as a refuge from the world outside. When it later becomes the Green-Box, Hugo tries to give it the solidity of stone and to suggest its paradisiacal qualities at the same time: "la Green-Box redressait son panneau comme une forteresse son pont-levis. . . . D'un côté l'univers, et de l'autre cette baraque; et dans cette baraque il y avait la liberté, la bonne conscience, le courage, le dévouement, l'innocence, le bonheur, l'amour, toutes les constellations" (pp. 267–68). The temple also has its warning against the evils of the outside world. Inscribed on its walls is a series of statements concerning the power of the nobility and the monarchy. For instance: "un roturier qui frappe un lord a le poing coupé," a statement followed immediately by: "Le lord est à peu près roi. Le roi est à peu près Dieu." The lord or king is a false idol to those in true paradise.

Warning against false gods is not the only function of the temple, for we discover that religious rites take place there regularly, befitting its role as divine center. For once we are not viewing the demonic rites of evil, despite an ironic stage description that the scene resembles "une bouche d'enfer" (p. 250), like those of the *Obi* in *Bug-Jargal*, or the temple of the octopus in *Les Travailleurs,* or any of the others. Nightly the London *peuple* (the seats reserved for the gentry remain vacant, significantly enough) witness a creation drama entitled *Chaos vaincu.* J.-P. Weber has called this play a clumsy effort "d'une indigence et d'une sottise navrantes."[15] Because Hugo insisted that his whole work was valid on a "real" plane as well as on a prophetic one, Weber's objections have some validity. It is difficult to imagine throngs of poor Englishmen paying money to see such a brief drama—in Spanish!—despite all of Hugo's attempts to have us suspend our critical judgment. Léon Cellier has noted perceptively, however, that this play cannot be so easily dismissed, for it plays an important role in the total meaning of the work.[16]

The drama is a Manichean rite, as the text makes clear, where matter is evil and spirit is pure. Hugo describes the ritual: "Un effet de nuit. Au moment où la triveline s'écartait, la foule massée devant la Green-Box ne voyait que du noir. Dans ce noir se mouvaient, à l'état reptile, trois formes confuses, un loup, un ours et un homme" (p. 252). Wolf and bear, representing the "forces féroces de la nature" assault the man (Gwynplaine) who after a desperate struggle (representing man's struggle with chaos) is about to be defeated, when he cries out for help and a pure voice is heard in song. A white form (Déa) arrives and intones:[17]

Noche quitate de alli
El alba canta hallali.
Es menester a cielos ir,
Y tu que llorabas reir.
Gebra barzon!
Dexa, monstro,
A tu negro
Caparazon.

The man, inspired by this encouragement, overcomes his adversaries. Then Déa puts her hand on his forehead and proclaims salvation:

15. *La Genèse de l'œuvre poétique* (Paris, 1960), p. 159.
16. Pp. 217–23.
17. Hugo gives the following translation in footnotes: "Nuit! va-t'en!—l'aube chante hallali! Il faut aller au ciel,—et rire, toi qui pleurais. Brise le joug!—Quitte, monstre.—ta noire—carapace. Oh! viens! aime!—tu es âme,—je suis cœur."

O ven! ama!
Eres alma,
Soy corazon.

Then as a final act, Gwynplaine turns his disfigured face to the light, whereupon all the spectators burst into gales of laughter because of his grotesque ugliness (p. 254). For the English rabble the "play" has ended, but for the critic there is more to be said. Hugo comes to our assistance by explaining that this play shows "comment la divinité adhère à l'ébauche, de quelle façon s'accomplit la pénétration de l'âme dans la matière, comment le rayon solaire est un cordon ombilical, comment le défiguré se transfigure, comment l'informe devient paradisiaque" (p. 255). These, claims Hugo, are "mystères entrevus." The theme of the struggle between flesh and spirit, and the idea of finding paradise are also to be played out on the stage of England, as this ritual is enacted on the boards of the Green-Box.

The reaction of the spectators to the grotesque ugliness of Gwynplaine's face merits some commentary. The "soleil de rire" that greets his appearance in the light evokes the episode of La Fête des fous when the crowd roars "Noël" at the sight of Quasimodo. The scene also reminds one of the Homeric laughter on Olympus which greeted the Satyr. Cellier correctly judges this tempest of mirth, this "immense rire prométhéen" (p. 256), when he calls it "un soleil bienfaisant."[18] For we know by now that for Hugo, the *peuple*, not the aristocracy, is the repository of truth. The *peuple* understands *Chaos vaincu,* "cette victoire de l'esprit sur la matière, aboutissant à la joie de l'homme" (p. 256). The common people are participants in this religious ritual which thereby becomes a form of communion in which the elect are comforted and refreshed. The limited Eden of the little family of ambulatory actors is enlarged to include the suffering humble masses of the nation.

One day the evil Duchess Josiane comes to see the play and, in her perverted taste, desires Gwynplaine *because* he is grotesque. She plays the role of the serpent in the Garden tempting the chosen from the true faith. And Gwynplaine, a virgin at twenty-five, is tempted. As Josiane is prominent at court as well as sexually attractive, her appearance also serves as the link with the aristocratic society of early eighteenth-century

18. P. 219.

210

England, that is, the demonic social world. Ursus had already had some contact with this dangerous community through his brushes with the law. One day he was picked up and haled before a three-man tribunal on charges of blasphemy and malpractice of medicine, these accusations culled from remarks he had made during monologues to his audience prior to the main theatrical performance, in which he recommended simples and touched on philosophical matters. Ursus had defended himself ably and was released. The point of the episode is that his three judges are named Minos, Rhadamanthe, and Eaque, the French spellings of the three judges of the Infernal Regions. Hugo did not even attempt to make their names English and the presence of these three mythical names in a British court seems particularly unfortunate. But at least Ursus knows what he is up against, and as he leaves,[19] he tells his wolf: "J'ai vaincu les trois têtes de Cerbère" p. (296).

Yet Gwynplaine will leave his paradise and accept a life in the Hell of noble society because of the temptation of the woman and also because he had been robbed of his birthright. This change of state raises the question of the hero's responsibility and freedom in his decision, a matter that Hugo explores with some care. If we see the plot in its simplest terms, Gwynplaine at the beginning is alone, miserable, hungry, cold, disfigured. By the greatest of good fortune, saved by Ursus, he is soon with a family, happy, fed, warm, and considered beautiful by Déa (whom he adores) because she is blind. The boy's responsibility in this change was partial. That Ursus was in his path was an accident, or fate, but that the boy did not give up and kept seeking shelter was a free choice. Similarly, his finding Déa in the snow was fate; his saving her was an exercise of freedom. It is this same combination of fate and freedom that he finds before him in his more adult crisis. It is fate that Josiane sees him and then writes him an amorous note just when he is feeling the temptations of the flesh. After an anguished night, he chooses to reject the temptation only to have fate step in again. Up to this point he has been Gwynplaine, the traveling buffoon. But now he finds himself seized by "Justice" and taken through the entrance of the Southwark jail where he descends into the Hell of its dungeon. Here he learns the truth of his real identity as Lord Clancharlie, and "sous cette transfiguration croulant sur lui à coups

19. Leaving, he bows before the judges. "Ployé en deux, il salua tout" (p. 296). Thus has the spider-victim image been given social meaning of servility.

211

de tonnerre" (p. 361) he faints. When he comes to and remembers who he now is, he exults: "Ah! C'était donc cela! j'étais lord. Tout se découvre. Ah! l'on m'a volé, trahi, perdu, déshérité, abandonné, assassiné! le cadavre de ma destinée a flotté quinze ans sur la mer, et tout à coup il a touché la terre, et il s'est dressé debout et vivant! Je renais. Je nais!" (p. 379). By his descent he is indeed reborn to a new life, but it was not a voluntary descent. The new life, he thinks, is "lumière" rather than the "ténèbres" he had previously known. Like Jean Valjean in the sewers, he was "à l'endroit où le chaos devient cloaque" and "c'est de là que je sors!" (p. 379), he exults. But what a difference! Jean Valjean emerges saving his enemy, Marius; Gwynplaine cries out at the end of his tirade: "Revanche!" Revenge is hate, not love, and leads the hero—by his own choice, one must keep in mind—on a false, even a demonic, path. Like a René (= je renais) who fails to find the "sainte montagne"[20] that was the salvation of his sister Amélie and who can only climb the sterile slopes of the volcano of passion, Gwynplaine-René will turn away from the true path to begin the ascent of the mountain of social caste and sexual attraction, an effort as futile for him as it was for Chateaubriand's hero. We already know that in Hugo's work the way to salvation is not by climbing, and true to form, the author intervenes here to make the warning again: "A la cour, ce qui élève abaisse," (p. 219) and "on croit monter à l'Olympe, et l'on arrive à Bedlam" (p. 304). The temptation of St. Gwynplaine, to use Hugo's own chapter title, is like that of Christ:

> Gwynplaine avait été en même temps enlevé sur un sommet et précipité dans un abîme. . . . Il était sur la montagne d'où l'on voit les royaumes de la terre. . . . La tentation y est gouffre, et si puissante que l'enfer sur ce sommet espère corrompre le paradis. . . . Là où Satan tente Jésus, comment un homme lutterait-il?
>
> Des palais, des châteaux, la puissance, l'opulence, toutes les félicités humaines à perte de vue autour de soi, une mappemonde de jouissances étalées à l'horizon, une sorte de géographie radieuse dont on est le centre, mirage périlleux. (p. 378)

The warning becomes even more urgent. Hugo intervenes to speak directly to his character: "L'ascension t'élèvera et t'amoindrira. L'apothéose a une sinistre puissance d'abattre" (p. 381).

20. François-René de Chateaubriand, *Atala, René, Les Aventures du Dernier Abencérage* (Paris, 1962), p. 237.

At this point, Hugo stops to ask a serious question. Was Gwynplaine really free to react differently from the way he did? "Est-il possible à la feuille de refuser obéissance au vent? Est-il possible à la pierre de refuser obéissance à la gravitation? Questions matérielles, qui sont aussi des questions morales" (p. 381). Is Gwynplaine so conditioned biologically that he must seek out Josiane's sexuality, forgetting his divine Déa? Hugo puts the query in mythic terms that are quite revealing: "Lucifer passait tranquille. Il a aperçu la femme. Il est devenu Satan" (p. 311). This question must surely have haunted the poet ever since he first deceived his wife. Certainly, Henri Guillemin is convinced that this whole "problème charnel" is at the heart of *L'Homme qui rit*.[21] At any rate, Gwynplaine turns briefly away from the Truth. Hugo comments: "Que le dieu s'appelle Christ ou qu'il s'appelle Amour, il y a toujours une heure où il est oublié, même par le meilleur" (p. 145). Hopefully, the sinner's conscience will crow "comme le coq devant le jour" to bring him, like Peter, to his senses. But during this period of abandonment of responsibility, disaster can strike. This truism the hero discovers when he chooses to say "oui" to the evil Barkilphedro, who told him that he must decide either to be a lord and forget the past, or to be a clown and forget his rank. After summoning all the reasons that could be adduced to excuse his hero, the author concludes: "Toutefois, et sur ce point sa conscience le pressait, ce qui s'était offert, l'avait-il simplement subi? Non. Il l'avait accepté. . . . Gwynplaine pouvait dire non. Il avait dit oui" (p. 504).

Hugo reminds us that Gwynplaine's assent had more to it than the desire for wealth and social caste or for the body of Josiane. He had hoped, like his creator, to become a *porte-parole* for the masses of underprivileged, but this hope failed abysmally. He came to understand that "cette élévation à laquelle il avait cru, cette haute fortune, cette apparence, s'était effondrée sous lui" (p. 506). "Monte! avait signifié: Descends!" (p. 509). Why? Because he had, unlike the sage of the Biblical parable, sold the pearl of great price, "l'âme," for the inferior "chair." For Hugo, "ce n'est pas la chair qui est le réel, c'est l'âme" (p. 509). And flesh means not only woman but also society: "La société c'est le monde du corps; la nature, c'est le monde de l'âme" (p. 511), an odd conclusion to say the least.

Gwynplaine thus chooses Hell, thinking it will be Heaven, and this Hell

21. *Hugo et la sexualité* (Paris, 1954), p. 97.

has its own demonic imagery. We have already seen the vegetable and mineral worlds of the demonic when Gwynplaine was a youngster and encountered the gibbet and the cold stone houses. But aristocratic London is the true lair of evil, that stone city where the Green-Box will confront its adversary. Nearby there is a massive stone prison. The Southwark jail is a masterpiece of demonology: "La muraille haute était noire maçonnée à la saxonne, avec des crénaux, des scorpions et des carrés de grosses grilles. . . . Aucune fenêtre" (p. 332). And when "la pesante porte de chêne et de fer tourna sur ses gonds, une ouverture livide et froide s'offrit, pareille à une bouche d'antre. Une voûte hideuse se prolongeait dans l'ombre" (p. 332). Near the door there is "une échelle de potence" and another with a skull. This is the prison where Hardquanonne, the *comprachico* who can confirm the secret of the hero's birth, is tortured and dies. His body forms a cross as it lies in a deep pit, another version of the demonic religious motif in a cave that has been so frequent in Hugo's work.[22] The spider image reappears in the phrase: "l'araignée et la justice tendaient leurs toiles" (p. 333), but the dominant imagery of this scene is that of the octopus in its marine grotto: "Le mur suintait; il tombait de la voûte des gouttes d'eau. . . . L'espèce de pâleur diffuse qui tenait lieu de clarté devenait de plus en plus opaque" (p. 340). Here Gwynplaine "se sentait saisir par une sorte de main énorme et obscure" (p. 338). Here he feels himself "sous la pression de la hideuse force collective. De quelle façon se débattre avec cet anonyme horrible, la loi?" (p. 339). The octopus now represents society's law.

There are two other demonic stone dwellings besides the prison. The first is the palace where the hero has his encounter with Josiane and the other is the palatial legislative building of the Lords which is the lair of the Olympians, or society of evil gods. The stone edifices are decorated with monsters sculptured out of stone, and to reinforce this idea, Hugo provides the scene with other monsters, these not of stone but carved out of living flesh. Castration and defiguration were common, if we can believe Hugo's history: "Cette vivisection d'autrefois ne se bornait pas à confectionner pour la place publique des phénomènes pour les palais des bouffons . . . et pour les sultans et papes des eunuques" (pp. 25–26). An English king had had one man operated on so that he could crow like a

22. The prisoner is compared to Jesus "nu sur la croix" (p. 345).

rooster. In James II's toleration of the *comprachicos* the guilt is clear: "Le défiguré était fleurdelysé; on lui ôtait la marque de Dieu [his natural face], on lui mettait la marque du roi" (p. 29), a restatement of the idea of the man in the iron mask that is the theme of the unfinished *Les Jumeaux.*

Another elaboration of the demonic "mineral" world is that of money, used here with wider social implications than the gold coin in *Notre-Dame.* One day Gwynplaine picks up a farthing and contrasts its value, "représentant la misère du peuple," and its image "représentant, sous la figure d'Anne, la magnificence du trône." He permits himself a bitter comment and so later, when Gwynplaine is hauled off to the Southwark jail, Ursus assumes this is why and exclaims: "il a insulté les liards de sa majesté! un farthing, c'est la même chose que la reine! l'effigie sacrée, morbleu, l'effigie sacrée" (p. 287). All of this is heavy irony of course, for love and innocence, not the harsh metal of exploitation, are sacred.

The demonic gibbet, the representative of the vegetable world, is on occasion assimilated to the metallic one by Hugo. The demonic tree becomes the iron staff or mace of the wapentake, an official dressed in black who, in Hugo's fanciful history, seizes the victim in total silence. At each end of the staff the "bâton de fer [est] sculpté en couronne" (p. 324), and Hugo easily associates it with the royal scepter: "le sceptre . . . est le premier des bâtons" (p. 287). When the official appears in the idyllic Green-Box, "qu'on se figure Méduse passant sa tête entre deux branches du paradis," and the two servants of Ursus, named Phœbe and Venus, are turned to stone: "Deux pétrifications, c'étaient ces deux filles. Elles avaient des attitudes de stalactites" (p. 325). That night, when the wapentake appears at the head of the procession that is to bury Hardquanonne, "il avait au poing son bâton de fer" and the whole group is dehumanized by proximity: "A la suite du wapentake, défilèrent . . . avec la rigidité d'une série de poteaux qui marcheraient, des hommes silencieux" (p. 403).

The hero must next encounter the demonic animal world. Gwynplaine had been "le saint Georges combattant ce dragon . . . de la misère" (p. 258) for Déa, but poverty is not the real adversary, for it exists in nature as well as in the Hell of wicked cities. In London, Gwynplaine comes face to face with the Satanic Josiane, who like various other infamous noble-women of history is deemed a monster by Hugo: "Presque pas de femme dans les hauts rangs qui ne fût un cas tératologique" (p. 175). She has "l'aplomb mythologique" (p. 173) and claims that she regrets the death of Hercules because she would have liked to couple with him.[23] She is "un beau torse de femme [qui] en hydre se termine" (p. 174) and has the same "dilatation lumineuse" of the octopus and "sous l'eau, la transparence entrevue et trouble, un prolongement ondoyant, surnaturel, peut-être draconien et difforme" (p. 174). Nor is the religious imagery associated with the octopus lacking: "Quoi! la princesse descendait de son trône, l'idole de son autel. . . . Quoi! cette déité . . . cette irradiation . . . se penchait vers Gwynplaine" (p. 316). Just as Gilliatt saw the octopus on two occasions only, and the former was but a brief visual contact, so too does Gwynplaine have only two encounters with her, the first when she attends the play as a spectator, and then a later moment of desperate struggle. As the hero tries to find his way out of the palace to get back to Déa (having finally realized that he must go back to her), he wanders through a labyrinth of corridors in the palace, little dreaming that he is reenacting the eternal role of the fly in Claude Frollo's cell seeking the light. The hero enters a chamber where Josiane is asleep, and she is described as being behind a "toile d'argent, transparente." "Au centre de la toile, à l'endroit où est d'ordinaire l'araignée, Gwynplaine aperçut une chose formidable, une femme nue" (pp. 421–22).[24]

But soon the arachnoid imagery is replaced by that developed in *Les Travailleurs*. First, Gwynplaine hears running water in this room, coming from a fountain-bath of black marble. The place is called a grotto, and again the religious imagery intrudes violently with the erotic: the palace "tenait du cloître et du sérail," and "une galerie s'achevait en oratoire. Un confessional se greffait sur une alcôve" (p. 418). It is a "chapelle équivoque tout écaillée de nacres et d'émaux" (p. 419). Josiane on her bed is a "divinité" (p. 423) on its altar. When the hero sees her, he tries to flee but cannot, chained by the vision as Gilliatt had been held fast by the tentacles. He is even in danger of being drunk alive, at least in the language of imagery: "Gwynplaine subissait une sorte de résorption. Des

23. Gwynplaine is described as doing the labors of Hercules in the earlier pages (p. 125).
24. Actually, Hugo adds, she is not fully naked, but garbed in a transparent peignoir which makes her more attractive. There is an interesting parallel between Liberty and Lilith-Isis on the one hand and Déa and Josiane on the other. Both evil figures are veiled.

forces obscures le garottaient mystérieusement. Une gravitation l'enchaînait. Sa volonté, soutirée, s'en allait de lui" (p. 424). The temptress "ondulait, composant et décomposant des courbes charmantes. Toutes les souplesses de l'eau, la femme les a . . . elle était là, chair visible, et elle restait chimérique" (p. 425). Awaking, she leaps forward and seizes him. "Gwynplaine . . . recula, mais les ongles roses crispés sur son épaule le tenaient. Quelque chose d'inexorable s'ébauchait. Il était dans l'antre de la femme fauve, homme fauve lui-même" (p. 428). Hugo's imagery has at last come out into the open, but the possibilities of this scene, so superbly executed in *Les Travailleurs,* are spoiled when Josiane procedes to make an incredibly long speech which constitutes a vast, incoherent summary of Hugo's own thoughts on evil. She raves of chaos, Olympus, "fange," "vestale bacchante," and Eve, and if this were not enough, she adds remarks on the orgies of the Goddess cult of primitive religions. Then Josiane "le mordit d'un baiser" (p. 433), and we remember the octopus' attempt to bite Gilliatt. But in this struggle it is not the courage and blade of the hero that overcome the monster, it is a caprice of fate in the form of a royal message announcing that these two are to marry. Whereupon, now that he is no longer forbidden fruit, she loses interest in him at the very moment when he was ready to be overwhelmed by her. This outside intrusion blurs Hugo's position on the responsibility of the hero, for Gwynplaine did not by himself succeed in overcoming the temptation of the flesh or of matter.

From the animal world encountered in the boudoir, Gwynplaine moves to the more complex world of the aristocratic society of the times. Hugo had already made clear his attitude toward this privileged class from the earliest pages of the work, but he emphasizes its demonic qualities as he shows the nobility "at play." At the beginning of the eighteenth century, the pastimes of the wealthy idle lords in London were, according to Hugo, their activities in connection with various clubs. The republican clubs were gone, and in their place there were the She romps Clubs and the Club des Eclairs, dedicated to the public humiliation of women, the Hellfire Club which spent its time blaspheming, the Club des Coups de Tête, which killed men by butting them in the stomach, the Fun Club dedicated to vandalism, and the Mohock Club which had "ce but grandiose: nuire" (p. 182). The noblemen also enjoy sponsoring boxing contests of a most brutal kind, and Hugo has us witness the gory mutual destruction of two fighters while idle noblemen make their wagers. In short, noble amusement consisted in damaging the common people and insulting God, and the aristocracy is no better when "at work," as Gwynplaine finds out to his horror.

Just after Josiane repudiates him because of the Queen's wish that they should marry, Gwynplaine is led out of the palace by an official "au visage respectueux et sévère qui avait une baguette noire à la main" (p. 439). Again one finds the demonic symbol of authority, like the one held by the wapentake. In subsequent pages the phrase "l'huissier de la verge noire" is repeated constantly, as this official walks before Gwynplaine, leading him to the legislative assembly of the Peers. Here Hugo repeats an image used earlier: "Cette salle avait une voûte de châtaignier où ne pouvaient se mettre les toiles d'araignée; c'est bien assez qu'elles se mettent dans les lois" (p. 460). But as has often been observed, the central image of this scene is that of the Satyr on Olympus: "Qu'on s'imagine, sur la montagne réservée aux dieux, dans la fête d'une soirée sereine, toute la troupe des tout-puissants réunie, et la face de Prométhée . . . apparaissant tout à coup" (p. 481). It is "l'Olympe apercevant le Caucase," and the Titan is linked to the Satyr as Gwynplaine "sentait en lui un grandissement étrange" (p. 482).[25]

The hero's sense of outrage grows out of the legislative session in which he participates. The lords vote various bills, all of which serve to tax the downtrodden even more in order to augment their own privileges. Gwynplaine shocks them all by voting "non content"; then he rises to explain his vote. In order to be taken seriously, he manages to overcome his grinning mask and to recompose his features temporarily into normal form. The speech itself picks up some of the themes of the work: the gibbet that serves as a commentary on their "law" (p. 483), Déa's mother dead in the snow as judgment on their wealth, the theme of the prison ("le genre humain est au cachot," p. 485), and the whole demonic structure of their society is condensed into the image of the Tower of Babel, "construction manquée" (p. 484), a symbol of the false way to Heaven. By now, his emotion is so great that he can no longer control his features, and his grinning mask reappears. The reaction is immediate:

25. This point has been treated by various scholars. E.g., Pierre Albouy, *La Création mythologique chez Victor Hugo* (Paris, 1963), p. 247; J.-B. Barrère, *La Fantaisie de Victor Hugo*, II (Paris, 1960), 411, etc.

the nobles laugh Homerically (p. 490), mocking everything he says, ignoring his Truths. He explains to them that he has been initiated into Truth: "J'ai été jeté au gouffre. Dans quel but? pour que j'en visse le fond. Je suis un plongeur, et je rapporte la perle, la vérité" (p. 483). Later Hugo comments: "Il arrivait tout mouillé de l'eau du puits Vérité. Il avait la fétidité de l'abîme. Il répugnait à ces princes, parfumés de mensonges" (p. 508). There is a clear reprise of imagery of the sewers in *Les Misérables*. And when he cries out "je suis le peuple" (p. 489), his carved face looks in judgment at them all. "Tout ce que vous voyez, c'est moi. Vous avez des fêtes, c'est mon rire. Vous avez des joies publiques, c'est mon rire," etc. Like the Satyr, he becomes a cosmic figure and God is on his side: "Je me dresserai avec la poignée des haillons du peuple dans la main" (p. 486) and concludes: "Dieu hait ce que font les rois" (p. 489). Thus, in *L'Homme qui rit* myth and prophecy are combined: the hero on the quest for truth is also the one who brings judgment on an evil society and prophesies a better life for the future, whereas in *Les Misérables* the apocalyptic vision was left to the minor character Enjolras. This greater economy of structure is a rare example of concision in this prolix work and it is partly responsible for whatever power *L'Homme qui rit* succeeds in generating. But the power of the conclusion of this scene is only verbal. Unlike the Titan-Satyr, Gwynplaine cannot hope to overthrow the English peerage in the eighteenth century, for despite the liberties that Hugo took with historical accuracy, he could not tamper with fact beyond a certain point. Gwynplaine's appeal in the chambers is totally ineffective, and he is driven in defeat from Olympus. When immediately afterward he is challenged to a duel to the death by his half-brother (the theme of the *frères ennemis* again), he has had enough of the society of this world.

Having explored the mineral, vegetable, animal, and social forms of both the demonic and the paradisiac worlds of the "novel," we must ask what is the ultimate "divine" dimension of the evil world? While the King (or Queen) is likened to God and incarnates in one person the divine dimension of social evil, Josiane is a better incarnation of the demonic. She is the counterpart of Déa, the goddess of good who represents "l'âme," and because she is both rival for Gwynplaine's love and the symbol of the bonds of the flesh ("Josiane, c'était la chair"), she is a better choice than the Queen, who rarely makes an appearance in the text.

The Duchess is called a "déesse" (pp. 209, 300), an "Olympienne" (p. 302), whose glance reveals "des profondeurs d'un paradis" (p. 299), although that paradise is demonic. The antithetical struggle between soul and matter is in essence the same as that between Heaven and Hell. One can see in the light of this dualism that all the demonic, material forms that we have analyzed seem very heavy: prison, gibbets, even sex and society, whereas in the divine world, matter is transfigured and loses its weight. Instead of a prison which crushes body and soul, there is a temple-home that develops them. Instead of a gallows which destroys life, leaving a heavy corpse swinging, wrapped in chains, there is a divine ray of light from Heaven that saves, as shown in the play *Chaos vaincu*. Instead of earthy and debasing sex, exalting idealism; instead of an unfeeling and heavy-handed monarchy, a pure family and the larger promise of the rise of the common people. One can only associate this dualism with the Manichean tradition, even if elsewhere, as in *Dieu*, Hugo suggests that there are even nobler visions.

Gwynplaine had finally realized all these truths when he tried to translate them into social terms for the lords in his speech. Their incomprehension drove him from their midst, defeated, yet in some glory. Then the hero tried to return to the true paradise, the Green-Box, only to learn that once one has left Paradise it is not easy to return. The wagon had disappeared and even Tadcaster Inn, next to which it was parked, is closed and abandoned. Royal authority has had the entire fairgrounds closed up, and Ursus was ordered to leave the country. To expiate his crime of saying "oui," Gwynplaine goes to the Thames to commit suicide. But Hugo refuses the black endings of his youth. At the last moment, the hero is found by Homo the wolf, who leads him back to Déa. "On ne sait pas toutes les figures que peut prendre Dieu. Quelle est cette bête? la providence" (p. 516). Reunited with his beloved "épouse" and "étoile" (p. 527), he exclaims: "Je sors de l'enfer et je remonte au ciel" (p. 527).[26] But the idyll must be finished beyond the grave if spirit is really to disengage itself from matter. Déa is dying of a heart condition and expires in the hero's arms as they flee the country in a boat on the Thames. Like Gilliatt and like the *comprachicos* of the earlier portion, Gwynplaine cries out to God, "Grâce," but God is wiser than the suppli-

26. The parallel with Satan's flying towards the distant stars in *La Fin de Satan* is quite clear.

cant for He is preparing their eternal union. As Déa dies, she cries out: "Lumière!" and says: "Je vois" (p. 534). Gwynplaine then looks off into the air and as if he can see her soul, he too says: "Je viens." Now that he understands all, he consents to his fate: "Il cria: 'Oui!' " like Geestemunde and drops into the water and disappears. Once more the way down is the way to salvation. Even having sinned, he has been saved.

Léon Cellier is entirely correct in seeing *L'Homme qui rit* as a *roman initiatique* and the hero an *initié*.[27] It is the story of the fulfillment of a hero who, by descent to Hell and return, finally achieves wholeness. But the vision transcends the personal mythic quest to become a commentary on aristocratic society of the prerevolutionary period. By equating that society with the Hell into which the hero descends, Hugo has prepared the need for a revolution that will overthrow this wickedness and create a Heaven on earth. By uniting myth and prophecy, he has laid his groundwork for *Quatrevingt-treize*.

27. Cellier, pp. 214, 223.

221

THE FINAL VISION

QUATREVINGT-TREIZE

For YEARS, all of Victor Hugo's literary creation had been pointing to the French Revolution. As early as *Han d'Islande* he had portrayed oppressed miners rebelling against evil noblemen and unjust taxation. In *Bug-Jargal*, revolution is at the heart of the action, and *Cromwell, Hernani, Marie Tudor, Ruy Blas*, and *Les Burgraves* are all concerned with the problem of the masses of the nation and their political leaders. *Notre-Dame de Paris* foreshadows 1789 and *Les Misérables* is bathed in the afterglow of this famous historical event. *L'Homme qui rit* was written in part as a conscious effort to prepare for what Hugo considered to be the central event of history. In his later poetry Hugo articulated the meaning of the Revolution. In *La Légende des siècles* and *La Fin de Satan* he makes clear that this upheaval will create a New Adam and usher in an age that leads to the beatific vision of "Plein Ciel," where evil is apparently nonexistent and man is nearly divinized. One should not be surprised at this interest from "un enfant du siècle" whose father was a Napoleonic general, and Hugo himself wrote how central this moment was to his formation in one of his versions for a preface to *Quatrevingt-Treize*: "Dans mes longues heures de solitude, j'ai beaucoup étudié les temps dont nous sommes et les temps dont étaient nos pères. Ma pensée a pris une empreinte de la Révolution."[1]

What does surprise one, upon reflection, is the manner in which Hugo hesitated to come to grips with the subject. He turned around it, he pointed toward it, he anticipated or followed, he devoted volumes to Napoleon III and the Second Empire. In *La Fin de Satan* the section that would have dealt with 1789 is left unfinished, and in *La Légende* for the period of the Revolution, there is nearly a void where one might well have expected an outpouring of creativity. It can be argued that he was waiting

---

1. E.I.N., p. 353. Hugo used only one hyphen in his spelling of the title, and he capitalized the last word of it.

to treat this subject in his last great work of prose fiction, but it may also be that he was still uncertain how to reconcile his approval of 1789 with his horror of the Terror of 1793. At any rate, he had been thinking about such a work for many years. One note from his dossiers for the novel dates from about 1840, to judge from the handwriting (p. 355). This long-standing general interest crystalized by 1862 enough for him to write about it to Paul Meurice,[2] and in 1866, he composed a "plan d'une intrigue" (p. 452). But it was not until December, 1872, at the age of seventy when he was once again back on the island of Guernsey, that he began to write the novel.

Faced with the enormous scope of his task, Hugo was apparently very conscious of his age and declining strength. In the same preface from which we quoted above, he apologized for the inadequacy of his effort: "Mais le temps me manque. J'ai cru devoir, avant de partir, laisser un spécimen de ce travail inachevé. De là ces pages" (p. 353). In another version of a preface, he worried about the unity of his creation, which he saw as only "une série de récits . . . qui n'auront d'ailleurs d'autre cohésion entre eux que l'unité historique" (p. 353). The serene feeling of mastery is lacking, although Hugo did live to finish it and to give it some artistic coherence. Perhaps because of this very feeling of inadequacy, Hugo's effort for this work was considerable. The editor of the E.I.N. stresses, perhaps a little too much, the enormous research that went into its preparation, but there can be no doubt that Hugo read widely. He turned to Michelet for the events that took place in Paris and sought in one Duchemin-Descepeaux and in the memoirs of a royalist general, Joseph de Puisaye, material on the Vendée and Lantenac. For a work of this great importance, a great effort was needed. By the time he began to write, he had filled nineteen dossiers.[3] He wrote with reasonable rapidity and the work appeared in February, 1874.

In one respect particularly, *Quatrevingt-Treize* is unique in Hugo's work. There is a total absence of any love idyll (and therefore of the usual heroine of romance) or of any sexual struggle (and therefore of any demonic female). Henri Guillemin, speculating on this oddity, observed

2. *Correspondance*, II, letter of Oct. 18.
3. E.I.N., pp. 351–52. There were, of course, other sources, as diverse as Louis Blanc and Lamartine.

that we are dealing with "un livre austère," due in all likelihood to "les désordres de sa vie sexuelle à Paris,"[4] disorders which so appalled even Hugo that he banished himself from Paris to Guernsey and removed love and sex from his novel. This unprovable hypothesis is a shrewd one which we suspect is basically correct, but regardless of the reason, the absence of an important central love affair left the novel with a problem. In the past, Hugo structured his creation around the hero's quest for the ideal female figure. Now he would need a new center. In *Les Travailleurs de la mer* Hugo had spoken of the sanctity of the little girl and then, skipping over the phase of the nubile woman, had explained that she was resanctified by motherhood. In *Les Misérables* he was more at ease describing the young Cosette and her self-sacrificing mother, Fantine, than the young woman in love with Marius. For *Quatrevingt-Treize*, he combined the innocence of childhood and the plenitude of maternity by putting Michelle Fléchard and her three small children at the center of the action. By the way in which they are treated by others, Hugo would judge the opposing forces, for "celui qui n'a pas vécu encore n'a pas fait le mal, il est la justice, il est la vérité, il est la blancheur, et les immenses anges du ciel sont dans les petits enfants" (p. 311).

The opening chapter shows a battalion of soldiers of the Revolution sent from Paris searching cautiously through the dense Saudraie Forest in Brittany for royalist guerillas. They find signs of the enemy, but that is all:

> De temps en temps, on rencontrait des traces de campements, des places brûlées, des herbes foulées, des bâtons en croix, des branches sanglantes. Là on avait fait la soupe, là on avait dit la messe, là on avait pansé les blessés. Mais ceux qui avaient passé avaient disparu. Où étaient-ils? bien loin peut-être. Peut-être là tout près, cachés, l'espingole au poing. Le bois semblait désert. (p. 6)

The tautness of the style of this passage, which reflects the tension of the wary soldiers, communicates admirably a sense of the real which is so often weak in Hugo.[5] These fine pages which form the setting for the

4. Preface to *Quatrevingt-Treize* (Paris: Editions du Seuil, 1963), III, 471. See also Guillemin, *Hugo et la sexualité* (Paris, 1954), pp. 108–9. There were other reasons as well, the sickness of his son and his disillusionment with Parisian politics. See Elliott M. Grant, *The Career of Victor Hugo*, p. 298.

5. For a typical critical statement of this weakness in Hugo, see E. Auerbach, *Mimesis* (Princeton, 1953); original edition in German, 1946, p. 412.

initial action are carefully detailed without the verbiage that marred *L'Homme qui rit*. Further, the familiar imagery seems to have disappeared. The prose is limited to its denotative meaning. This "non-Hugolian" technique is not an invention of this late novel, but examples of it are rather infrequent in the earlier creations.

The soldiers soon come upon another aspect of reality: Michelle Fléchard and her three children, innocent victims of the fighting. At first the soldiers ask this simple woman all the wrong questions: "Quelles sont tes opinions politiques?" "Quelle est ta patrie?" "De quel parti es-tu?" But the woman for all her ignorance is wiser than they. She knows the fundamental reality of her existence: "Je suis avec mes enfants," she explains (p. 10). When asked, "D'où viens-tu?", she answers: "De là"; "Où vas-tu?"—"Je ne sais pas." Like Gwynplaine, she is alone in immensity. She has no *patrie* except her farm and no clear political allegiance, a condition which is the mark of those not educated enough to articulate political slogans. The sergeant understands the point finally and declares: "C'est une pauvre." When the battalion adopts the woman and her children in the name of the Republic, the act makes sense on the "real" plane of the soldiers' psychology. It also transcends reality and provides the novel's first example of symbolism: the Revolution takes the oppressed under its protection even when the poor are the enemy, as in this case, for her husband had died fighting in the service of the king.

The scene then shifts and moves out to sea, where the new royalist leader, the Marquis de Lantenac, is sailing from England to take charge of the insurrection. Despite the marine setting, which usually triggers Hugo's imagination into creating endless images, the clouds that were octopi, hydras, etc., lurking beneath a "voûte du ciel" are here just clouds, not monsters: "Le ciel avait comme un couvercle de nuages; mais les nuages ne touchaient plus la mer" (p. 38). Nor are the clouds an isolated case of this non-symbolic style. Even the dialogue between the two ship's officers combines exposition, humor, and psychology remarkably well. But in Hugo realism cannot remain just realism for long. Soon it must lead to a symbol, as in the case of Michelle Fléchard. The episode at sea is more than anecdote and more than Hugo's nostalgia for writing about the Channel: its function can only be to give the reader a chance to observe Lantenac in action.

Lantenac is not just another officer. A solitary figure who holds himself aloof from the others, he reminds one of Geestemunde, a real spiritual leader. He has an arresting presence:

> Un homme, en effet, venait de s'y embarquer, qui avait tout l'air d'entrer dans une aventure. C'était un haut vieillard, droit et robuste, à figure sévère. . . . un de ces hommes qui sont pleins d'années et pleins de force, qui ont des cheveux blancs sur le front et un éclair dans le regard. (p. 18)

As the ship makes its way through a thick fog (p. 21), there occurs the famous episode of the runaway cannon that careens wildly around the decks smashing everything in its path. This anthology piece can be viewed on more than one level: if Guillemin is correct in his surmise that Hugo's sexual aberrations are responsible for the suppression of a love story, a Freudian critic might well see their reappearance in the cannon, a disguised destructive phallus. Hugo, who constantly equated the flesh of the body with matter in general, calls the cannon "matter" and its escape from its bonds is "l'entrée en liberté de la matière." Elsewhere, it is a monster, a tiger, and it has a "volonté de démon" (p. 32). When, thanks to Lantenac and the sailor whose negligence had first caused the disaster, the weapon is finally mastered, its function in showing the royalist leader's psychology becomes clear. Lantenac has the sailor decorated for his bravery and then shot for his negligence, actions typical of an inflexible man of honor, of courage, and especially of logic. Throughout the early pages of the novel, Lantenac uses pure logic to justify all his acts. His reasoning is powerful and compelling, but it leaves little or no place for human charity.

After the hellish combat with the cannon and the execution of the sailor, the fog lifts as it did for the Durande in *Les Travailleurs:* "les brumes qui traînaient sur les vagues se déchirèrent, tout l'obscur bouleversement des flots s'étala à perte de vue dans un demi-jour crépusculaire" (p. 38). The battered ship finds itself surrounded by a revolutionary squadron that intends to blow it out of the water. The solemnity of the moment of death, the silence in which the action takes place before the gunfire begins, causes Hugo to revert to the language of myth. Referring to the squadron, he writes: "La catastrophe sortait du gouffre avec majesté. Elle ressemblait plutôt à une apparition qu'à une attaque. . . .

226

C'était on ne sait quel colossal silence. Avait-on affaire à quelque chose de réel? On eût dit un rêve passant sur la mer" (p. 40).

The description of the feverish preparation for battle aboard the *Claymore* abandons mythic language and shows the same absence of imagery as we found with the clouds. Hugo relies for his effects on that tense realism that was present in the search through the forest in the opening chapter. Again, the style reflects the anguish of the beleaguered combatants:

> Le capitaine donna ses ordres à voix basse. Le silence se fit dans le navire. On ne sonna point le branle-bas, mais on l'exécuta. La corvette était aussi hors de combat contre les hommes que contre les flots. On tira tout le parti possible de ce reste de navire de guerre. On accumula près des drosses, sur le passavant, tout ce qu'il y avait d'aussières et de grelins de rechange pour raffermir au besoin la mâture. . . . Chaque homme prit son poste. Tout cela sans dire une parole et comme dans la chambre d'un mourant. Ce fut rapide et lugubre. (p. 43)

But when the enemy opens fire, "la mer se couvrit de fumée et de feu" (p. 47). Smoke replaces fog in the blurring of reality at the moment of the passage from life to death, and the realism of smoke and fire in a naval battle serves Hugo's symbolism effectively.

Only Lantenac and a sailor escape the slaughter, fleeing in a small boat. It happens that the sailor is the brother of the man that Lantenac had had executed and he announces that he is going to kill his brother's assassin. Lantenac defends himself with crushing logic and with apocalyptic Catholic imagery. If the sailor kills him, "dans cette lutte des impies contre les prêtres, dans cette lutte des régicides contre le roi, dans cette lutte de Satan contre Dieu, tu es pour Satan" (p. 52). Lantenac sees the world as a struggle between two absolutes and in erecting this vision of a society of Evil opposed to a society of God, he recreates the basic structure of *L'Homme qui rit*. This attitude is more appropriate here than in Hugo's previous novel because historically and psychologically it was the way in which the Bretons interpreted reality. Thus, the sailor is already conditioned to believe the Marquis' words and throws himself at his leader's feet and begs forgiveness. Lantenac grants it because he needs the man's services.

227

Arriving safely on shore, Lantenac will soon be put to the test to see whether he is truly an emissary of God. His life is saved by the beggar Tellmarch who, like Michelle and her children, represents the poor. "Je suis un pauvre" (p. 72), he says. The beggar saves Lantenac from the soldiers on one condition: "que vous ne venez pas ici pour faire le mal." In all sincerity, Lantenac assures him that he has come "pour faire le bien" (p. 76), but deeds speak louder than words. He soon has thousands of Whites with him and they proceed to destroy a whole village that had befriended government troops. In the process, and at Lantenac's order, they shoot Michelle Fléchard and carry off her three children. To sin against a child was the sin of the *comprachicos;* here Lantenac shoots a mother and will have to expiate his crime. Yet, despite this devilish activity which later makes Tellmarch regret not having denounced him, Lantenac and the Bretons still see themselves on God's side fighting a holy war against Satanic revolution.

The demonic quality of the French Revolution is not only a warped belief of the royalists, however, it is also "reality" within the framework of the novel. Part II of *Quatrevingt-Treize* takes place in Paris, and despite his revolutionary sympathies, Hugo is so hostile to the excesses of its Jacobin phase that he portrays the Paris scene with demonic imagery. Thus the partisan beliefs of the Bretons coincide with the author's "objective" presentation. Paris, like London of *L'Homme qui rit,* is the wicked city where "on dansait sur les cloîtres en ruine, avec des lampions sur l'autel" (p. 94). Its special building representing the mineral world of the demonic is the Tour du Temple where Louis XVII is imprisoned. The evil tree of the vegetable world is the guillotine, whose metallic blade also assimilates it to the mineral world.[6] To die on it was "aller à la messe rouge," the image of a perverted or demonic cult. The gods of this Hades are the familiar figures Minos, Eaque, Rhadamanthe (p. 107) once again, but fortunately the mythological labels appear only in the chapter title. Their real names are Robespierre, Danton, and Marat and in the words of the latter: "Nous sommes les trois têtes de Cerbère." Behind these historical figures Hugo places the one man who is at the head of the demonic world. He is Cimourdain, an incarnation of inhuman justice. As fanatic in his devotion to the Revolution as Lantenac is to his cause, he is

6. Its sterility is emphasized: "La guillotine est une vierge; on se couche sur elle, on ne la féconde pas" (p. 118).

gifted with the same logical temperament and lacks equally a sense of charity. "Cimourdain était une conscience pure, mais sombre. Il avait en lui l'absolu. Il avait été prêtre, ce qui est grave. L'homme peut, comme le ciel, avoir une sérénité noire; il suffit que quelque chose fasse en lui la nuit. La prêtrise avait fait la nuit dans Cimourdain. Qui a été prêtre l'est" (p. 99). His continued chastity is dangerous: "rien de plus dangereux qu'un tel refoulement" (p. 99). Having lost his Christian faith, he replaces it with "la patrie" and "l'humanité." "Cette plénitude énorme," Hugo remarks with considerable wisdom, "au fond, c'est le vide." This man's instinct is usually to hate others, a sign of the demonic: "Défense lui était faite d'aimer, il s'était mis à haïr" (p. 99). He hates the past and even the present, looking forward to the future. He is "sublime," but "sublime dans un entourage de précipices. Les hautes montagnes ont cette virginité sinistre." He is a "vertu inaccessible et glaciale. Il était l'effrayant homme juste" (p. 103). The juxtaposition of "effrayant" and "juste" underlines the fact that Cimourdain cannot qualify as a pure demon. His rectitude and sense of justice are real virtues that Hugo does not deny. If he is "dans les ténèbres," nonetheless his truths shine forth from the darkness. So the demonic world of the Revolution is pure evil only in the eyes of Lantenac and the Vendée. In Hugo's eyes, its absolutist phase, though set in a demonic context, mixes good and evil in about equal proportions.

This moral mixture is less evident, but is visible, when Hugo looks at the Vendée from the point of view of the Revolution. There is no question that it, too, is demonic. It has its evil mineral world and symbol of feudalism, the Tourgue, where the final action takes place. Hugo emphasizes its torture chambers and compares its architecture to the social strata of earlier times: "L'étage supérieur était le cachot, l'étage inférieur le tombeau. Superposition ressemblante à la société d'alors" (p. 210). As the Tour du Temple contained the child-king Louis XVII, so will the Tourgue have as hostages the three children of Michelle Fléchard, symbols of the *peuple* and the new era. This castle is set in a forest, and although the search through the woods for guerrillas was presented realistically in the opening pages, by the time the reader comes to Part III ("En Vendée"), he begins to encounter the language of legend and myth. The forest is a "forêt de Brocéliande" (p. 155) which belongs to the "fées," for the superstitious Bretons believe as much in the gods of the ancient Druids as they do in orthodox Christianity, "croyant à la sainte Vierge et à la Dame blanche" (p. 156). They worship not only at Christian altars but at demonic ones: "la haute pierre mystérieuse debout," a religious form of what is expressed socially by the Tourgue. That this forest is an "antre" is made clear by Hugo's explanation that the guerrillas have actually created underground holes and tunnels from which to spring on the government troops. The Bretons are cats walking in the shadows[7] (p. 166), and "Le sous-sol de telle forêt était une sorte de madrépore percé et traversé en tous sens par une voirie inconnue de sapes, de cellules et de galeries" (p. 159). The word "madrépore" shows that Hugo had not entirely forgotten the marine imagery of the octopus' grotto or of the corridors in Josiane's palace. The forest even has a suggestion of the spider-web image. The grapevine system of communication in the area is expressed in these terms: it seemed as if the region "eût un même appareil nerveux, et qu'un point de ce sol ne pût tressaillir sans que tout s'ébranlât" (pp. 161–62), just as no part of a web can be disturbed without the vibrations' being felt at every point.

From the mineral world of the Tourgue and the Druid stones and the vegetable world of the evil forest, we move to the animal world, incarnate in L'Imânus, a brutish assistant to Lantenac, also called Gouge-le-Bruant, a name probably meaning "Face of Thunder" and suggestive of his forbidding appearance. His sobriquet "Imânus" comes from local Norman demonic superstitions about an evil being that Hugo traces back to the Latin *immanis*, or "monstrous." In this ferocious beast are concentrated the worst aspects of the Breton peasant. It is he who callously sets fire to the library in the Tourgue where the three children are captives in order to avenge "sur leurs petits, notre petit à nous, le roi qui est au Temple" (p. 288). With evil concentrated in this creature, Lantenac appears less wicked in his role of demonic man, just as Satan seemed more redeemable when Lilith-Isis incarnated (if that is the word) pure evil. Lantenac does raze hamlets and shoot prisoners, but his inherent nobility is more than a mark of cast. Just as the average Breton has a "grand cœur," there is some redeeming quality to Lantenac as well. "Un haut vieillard . . . à figure sévère . . . un éclair dans le regard," this man can only be of Hugo's elite, and his creator's desire of universal salvation

7. The shadows are both literal and figurative, for Hugo explains that it is ignorance that makes the Breton evil.

and national unity is so strong that he will save this noble Breton, despite his false belief in the monarchy, just as he would have liked to reconcile in his own family his Breton mother and Napoleonic father. Thus Hugo has balanced monarchy and Lantenac against the Jacobin phase of the Revolution and Cimourdain, and although each has a redeeming side, each is evil enough so that it cannot be a final solution.

Gauvain is the perfect synthesis of the two extremists and represents Hugo's own position, as is clear to even the most casual reader. This young man[8] is Lantenac's nephew, although he has turned republican and is now commanding general of the revolutionary armies in the field, and he is also the former beloved pupil of Cimourdain. All three had lived together before 1789 when Gauvain had grown up in the castle with his uncle and learned his democratic ideals under the tutelage of the marquis' priest, Cimourdain. Gauvain has many of the expected heroic traits. He is compared to Hercules (p. 180), he is handsome, and like a hero he is invulnerable, never having been wounded (pp. 180, 185). He is courageous and intelligent in battle, defeating a much larger force by an honorable military stratagem. After the battle, as Hugo's own father did in Spain, he gave a drink to a dying enemy soldier who tried to shoot him.[9]

But despite his heroic qualities, Gauvain is just as suspect to Cimourdain as he is a renegade in the eyes of Lantenac. Because the young man is known to exercise clemency on a large scale, the Three Heads of Cerberus have assigned Cimourdain to the army in order to watch over him. Reverting to that theme so prominent in *Cromwell, Hernani,* and *Notre-Dame de Paris,* the author carefully contrives the following situation: at Cimourdain's urging, Gauvain has agreed on pain of death to execute Lantenac if they can capture him. The three characters come together for their final encounter at the ancient castle, the Tourgue, where Lantenac is holed up with remnants of his force. There they are joined by Michelle Fléchard, who has recovered from her wounds and is now looking for her children. Her presence signifies that the others are about to be tested through her.

As she approaches the Tourgue, she enters one of those places of

8. His youth symbolizes the future as Lantenac's age does the past (p. 179).
9. "Après la bataille," *Légende des siècles, Le Temps présent,* no. 4, "Mon père, ce héros au sourire si doux." Gauvain, too, has a "doux sourire" (p. 336).

crisis so important in Hugo. The tower glows with "un rayonnement mystérieux" and seems, like the house at Plainmont, to "grandir lentement." The sense of reality is blurred as the Tourgue becomes "un énorme édifice qui semblait bâti avec des ténèbres plus noires que toutes les autres ténèbres qui l'entouraient." Confronted by this tower veiled in smoke, Michelle "avait le vertige" (p. 296) and no wonder, for as Hugo puts it: "La fumée est nuage, le nuage est rêve; elle ne savait plus ce qu'elle voyait. . . . Elle se sentait presque hors du réel." In her hallucination, seeing her three children surrounded by flames, she screams (p. 297). At this moment she passes from one state to another. She had been a simple human being; now she becomes mythic: "ce n'était plus Michelle Fléchard, c'était Gorgone. Les misérables sont formidables. La paysanne s'était transfigurée en euménide. Cette villageoise quelconque . . . venait de prendre brusquement les proportions épiques du désespoir." She even blasphemes: "Oh! s'ils devaient mourir comme cela, je tuerais Dieu" (p. 300).

It so happens that just at this moment the remnants of the defeated royalists have slipped out of the Tourgue by a secret tunnel. Lantenac, free to organize the rebellion once more, hears her cry and forsaking his cause, turns back into the tower. At the last moment Michelle cries out, as have so many Hugolian characters, "Grâce!" Because of her love for her children and because God is just, her prayer is heard and answered through Lantenac, the one man who knows the way back into the library. His return into the fire is an entrance into Hell, which Hugo explicitly labels "un enfer," comparing the flames to serpents and scarlet dragons, the swirling smoke to a "hydre noire." Its devil peers through the flames: "on eût dit que l'épouvantable Imânus tout entier était là changé en tourbillon d'étincelles" (p. 299). When the tall, austere marquis reappears with the children, he is revealed, as Hugo indicated in his chapter heading, as a savior—"In Daemone Deus." Michelle Fléchard is transported suddenly "de l'enfer dans le paradis." The soldiers who observe his cool courage are overawed by this "majesté de fantôme," and before this figure who has returned from Hell, there is "un recul d'horreur sacrée comme autour d'une vision." He is pale as death with his "regard de spectre."[10]

10. "C'était dans le sépulcre en effet que le marquis était descendu."

In Hugo's universe, anyone who goes through Hell is transfigured.[11] One of the republican soldiers who hears him cry out: "Vive le roi!" answers cogently: "Tu peux . . . dire des bêtises si tu veux, tu es le bon Dieu" (p. 305). By his action, "l'infernal Satan était redevenu le Lucifer céleste" (p. 317). Humanity had defeated the inhuman qualities in him, and "Lantenac s'était racheté de toutes ses barbaries par un acte de sacrifice" (p. 317). Hugo thus reminds all factions that above logic, above every "absolu révolutionnaire," there is "l'absolu humain." As for the mother and her children, having served their purpose of testing others, they disappear from the text and we hear no more about them.[12]

Upon his descent from the tower, Lantenac is immediately arrested and told that he will die at dawn on that other demonic device: the guillotine, the Revolution's counterpart to the feudal tower. Now it is Gauvain's turn to be tested. He had sworn to have Lantenac executed or to forfeit his own life. After great anguish and much inner debate, he concludes that the prisoner has indeed been transformed so that he is no longer Lantenac the criminal, and he should be spared. As Gauvain represents the human side of Revolution, he cannot permit himself to be outdone in humanity by the *ancien régime*. He arranges Lantenac's escape even though he knows that once free, the "hydre" of the Vendée (p. 316) may come to life again. Since what is important is not the military or political struggle but the salvation of the character, Lantenac disappears into the darkness and is not heard from again, leaving the reader totally ignorant of the future of the insurrection.

When Lantenac's escape is discovered the next morning, Gauvain is court-martialed and by the deciding vote of Cimourdain, condemned to death. Awaiting execution, he is visited by his former mentor, and the two have a long discussion concerning the future in the course of which the essential differences between them become clear. As Hugo had written earlier: "Ces deux hommes incarnaient, l'un la mort, l'autre la vie, l'un

11. He uses a ladder in the library to bring out the children. This image of an Axis Mundi is an inverted Jacob's ladder, which is an "échelle de sauvetage pour les autres" and for himself an "échelle de perdition" (p. 312). The theme of the ladder is repeated by the efforts of the Republicans to find a ladder to save the children. By a twist of fate, a demonic guillotine shows up in its place.

12. In *Han d'Islande*, there were three babies asleep in the demonic Tower of Vygla. The same situation has been recreated here, but with a vast difference in technique. What was only bric-a-brac of a Gothic novel in 1823 has become an episode that tests class values and human courage.

était le principe terrible, l'autre le principe pacifique, et ils s'aimaient" (p. 201). Here Hugo goes beyond the demonic apocalypses that dominated the London of *L'Homme qui rit* and the Paris of *Quatrevingt-Treize* to suggest a Revelation or perfect society that will grow out of the Revolution, one superior to the Green-Box of Ursus, Déa, and Gwynplaine in scope and superior to the vision of Cimourdain in humanity. Gauvain begins by criticizing the other's overly rationalistic view of man. According to him, his former teacher would turn society into an army barracks with his "république de l'absolu" (p. 337). Cimourdain proposes a progressive income tax, universal military service, and law based on strict social justice. Against this view Gauvain, and through him Hugo, argues for something more noble. He begins with the idea that behind the present state of the Revolution there is something which is as yet invisible, something sublime and beautiful. Behind an "échafaudage de barbarie" one can discern a holy temple, "un temple de civilisation," which will be the "république de l'idéal" (p. 337). Its order will not be equilibrium but harmony, not the meting out of justice under law but a soaring into the Heavens ("en plein azur"), as in "Plein Ciel." This Heavenly City of the future will overcome both the demonic cities of monarchical feudalism with their evil towers, and Jacobin absolutism with its guillotine. It will be a place of peace without poverty and without taxation. The expenses of the community are to be reduced to a minimum and the cost to be paid out of "la plus-value sociale" (p. 338). When Cimourdain asks him what on earth he means by that, Hugo-Gauvain explains that first one must eliminate the parasitic cost of priest, judge, and soldier. Then to create wealth, he urges that the fertility of the land be augmented by the fertilizer of human excrement, an idea that Hugo had lyrically propounded in *Les Misérables*. He also urges the use of water power, including harnessing the power of the ocean. Hugo's "science" even speaks of an underground network of veins through which circulate water, oil, and fire. If one will but exploit these riches, all will be well. In its ideal social structure, the child[13] will fit into a perfect family with the father who sires him, the mother who bears him, the teacher who instructs him, the community that makes a man of him, with the nation and humanity above all, and all of these steps being "des échelons de

13. Hugo's ultimate test of a society is the treatment it affords its children.

l'échelle qui monte à Dieu." Then "Dieu s'ouvre, on n'a plus qu'à entrer" (p. 340). The perfect society is based on the school, not the barracks as Cimourdain would wish, and will build monuments not to generals but to heroes and geniuses. There will be no more slaves, prisoners, or damned souls in Gauvain's dream of universal salvation. Echoing Hugo's Satyr, he reminds Cimourdain that man is made "non pour traîner des chaînes, mais pour ouvrir des ailes. Plus d'homme reptile" (p. 342). One sympathizes with Cimourdain, who begs the youthful enthusiast to come back to earth, reminding him of the necessity of limiting oneself to the possible (p. 340). But Gauvin is beyond human limitation. As the conversation draws to a close, one can see that "la clarté d'aurore qu'il avait dans la prunelle grandissait" (p. 342).

When on the following day he is led to the guillotine, "il ressemblait à une vision. Jamais il n'avait apparu plus beau" (p. 347), and Hugo compares him to an archangel. Although the guillotine onto which he climbs is evil, "ce lieu-là aussi est un sommet." In his apotheosis, "le soleil l'enveloppait, le mettait comme dans une gloire." He dies after crying: "Vive la République" (p. 348), in a scene curiously parallel to the one in *Han d'Islande* when Ordener is nearly executed. Both appear in a golden glow before the people who love them but are powerless to save them. As Gauvain's head falls, Cimourdain has to face *his* moment of truth. He had remained loyal to his principles by condemning to death the one man he had loved, but the satisfaction was empty. He expresses the failure of his ideal by blowing out his brains. Hugo comments: "et ces deux âmes, sœurs tragiques, s'envolèrent, l'ombre de l'une mêlée à la lumière de l'autre."

For the careful reader, the novel is more allegory than history. Thanks to the French Revolution, both monarchy and feudalism are overthrown, as they deserved to be, but those who will serve the poor in love will be the new elect, whatever their social class or political beliefs. Hugo looks forward to the time when Brittany will be converted to a more enlightened view of the world, when the Jacobins will have disappeared with Cimourdain, and an ideal national unity based on love can be forged. What are we to make of this vision? As for the ideas, there is little that can impress the modern reader. We agree that a school is better than a barracks and that man should harness the power of nature. But Hugo's naïveté in economics disqualifies him as a social planner, and his inability to convince us that evil can be eradicated marks his limitations as a theologian. The main value of the final ideas may in reality be literary rather than ideological. They harmonize in an aesthetic conclusion the opposing apocalyptic claims and resolve the dramatic tensions of the novel.

Because the social message, whatever its value, hangs on the central fact of the Revolution, the critic is obliged to comment on Hugo's manner of integrating the Parisian phase of the novel with the action in the field. Hugo decided not to choose 1789 and the capture of the Bastille, but to dramatize the Convention in such a way as to make it the culminating point to which both he and history had been pointing:

> Nous approchons de la grande cime.
> Voici la Convention.
> Le regard devient fixe en présence de ce sommet.
> Jamais rien de plus haut n'est apparu sur l'horizon des hommes.
> Il y a l'Himalaya et il y a la Convention.
> La Convention est peut-être le point culminant de l'histoire. (p. 129)

In the following pages, Hugo tries to provide some "mythic" language to support this impressive introduction, He invests the Convention with a religious aura ("à tout dogme, il faut un temple," p. 130) and on a smaller scale he describes the table of the presiding official at the sessions of the Convention, "contrebutée par quatre monstres ailés à un seul pied, qu'on eût dit sortis de l'Apocalypse pour assister à la révolution" (p. 133). Hugo also suggests that the participants are involved in an epic confrontation that transcends the humble reality of the place where it occurs:

> Qui voyait l'Assemblée ne songeait plus à la salle. Qui voyait le drame ne pensait plus au théâtre. Rien de plus difforme et de plus sublime. Un tas de héros, un troupeau de lâches. . . .
> Dénombrement titanique. (p. 135).

But the details of the description hardly support the epic tone that Hugo has tried to create. For example, Danton is shown humming "Cadet Roussel" to annoy Robespierre, and more generally, the arena seems full of petty men hurling petty insults: "Les imprécations se donnaient la réplique.—Conspirateur!—Assassin!—Scélérat!—Factieux!—Modéré —On se dénonçait. . . ." (p. 145). After such scenes as this Hugo is obliged to call this sea of men a "tas de fumées poussées dans tous les sens" (p. 146), an idea of chaos that leads him to create another image. The delegate G. of *Les Misérables* may have been presented as totally noble, but these politicians seem to be

> Esprits en proie au vent.
> Mais ce vent était un vent de prodige.
> Etre un membre de la Convention, c'était être une vague de
> l'Océan. (p. 146)

The imagery is clearly contradictory. If the Convention was a towering solid mountain, how could it also be a swirling sea? Furthermore, in an attempt to give a kaleidoscopic panorama of the daily life of the Parisians in 1793, Hugo gets lost in a welter of detail. He fails to create the epic forces that could forge the culminating point in history. When we also consider that the whole section on Paris and the Convention is only some 53 pages in length out of a total number of 348 pages, we feel that something is wrong. What Hugo believed was the most important event in all human history merited more detailed treatment.

Thus, *Quatrevingt-Treize* leaves one with a disappointing sense of incompleteness. The details of certain parts are often admirable, as Hugo starts with sharply defined reality, then introduces imagery that is historically and psychologically credible in terms of the opposing groups of combatants. As he had done before, he transforms imagery into myth, most successfully perhaps at the Tourgue.[14] But he was not content to stop here. By now literature was not enough for Hugo, prophetic ideology ranked higher. He had already given intimations of this hierarchy of values with Enjolras' speech at the barricade in *Les Misérables,* and in *L'Homme qui rit* had even structured the entire work so that it could contain both a mythical quest and an apocalyptic vision. In *Quatrevingt-Treize,* only Lantenac follows the mythic path; the hero Gauvain never descends into any hell. His role is really to preach to Lantenac and Cimourdain. By making exposition of prophetic ideas paramount, Hugo

14. For more detail on the artistic use of the Tourgue and the guillotine, see Pierre Georgel, "Vision et imagination plastique dans *Quatrevingt-Treize,*" *Lettres Romanes,* XIX (1965), 3–27.

announces the end of his effectiveness as a creator of fiction, just as a generation later *Les Trois Villes* and *Les Quatre Evangiles* would mark a similar change in Emile Zola. Further, as prophecy it cannot compel the respect of the modern reader, and in comparison with the gripping mythic visions that Hugo had unfolded, it represents a serious anticlimax. As if this were not enough, the Parisian center on which all the action in the field is based is woefully inadequate. Perhaps one might even make so bold as to surmise that the absence of the central woman, that spider at the center of the web, left a void in Hugo's work that not even the French Revolution could fill.

CONCLUSION

W<small>E EMBARKED</small> upon this study with a dual purpose. The first was to analyze the imagery and structure of the principal narrative works of Victor Hugo with the intention of showing their artistic nature and unity. For this part of our study no conclusion is necessary or possible. The various chapters are their own conclusion, and they show that each of the major works is a solidly built artistic creation, coherent in structure and imagery, even if marred in some instances by other defects.

The other goal was to examine how the author's literary devices and his general form evolved over a period of a lifetime, but despite the evolution, analysis of each work indicates that the imaginative center remained fairly constant throughout Hugo's career. In each plot there is some awesome cave inhabited by a fearsome creature; to this lair must come a hero who can only achieve atonement or success by confronting the monster, who is first portrayed as that—a monster, but then progressively as a spider, then as an octopus, and finally revealed as a woman. Otherwise, Hugo varied his techniques considerably. In the early period of *Han d'Islande* and *Bug-Jargal* he imitated traditional romances, parodying them in the former and taking them seriously in the latter. But the hero so necessary to romance was unable to dominate these works, and Hugo seemed more interested in exploring the villain who was in some way worthy of redemption. In *Notre-Dame de Paris*, Hugo subsumed the action under the power of fatality and, in an intricate historical romance, the forms explode in a rich burst of images, all based on sun, spider, web, and fly, whose "meaning" is to illustrate the omnipotence of fatality. The imagery is symbolic, therefore, but it stops short of any *mythopœia*. Hugo was still forming, as it were, the verbal tools that would make this latter step possible. Meanwhile, he experimented in the theater. From *Cromwell* to *Les Burgraves*, he wrestled with the problem of adapting fatality to the stage. At the same time he moved gradually in the direction of human freedom, trying to unite in various ways his growing awareness of man's freedom and responsibility with the images that he had developed.

It has long been recognized that *Les Burgraves* shows Hugo's first mature effort to move beyond imagery to myth. After having repudiated Classical mythology in the 1820's, he returned to it once more, recreating Hercules, the Titans, and Prometheus in various disguises. As the theater cannot really contain the epic because of its limitations of space and time, Hugo abandoned it for poetry and for prose fiction. *La Légende des siècles* shows the possibilities of epic poetry while the prose *Les Misérables* succeeds in placing Hugo's earlier imagery in a context of heroic quest that goes beyond traditional romance to form a new mythology set within the framework of contemporary French history. But Hugo's sense of true history, and more particularly, of human reality, is weaker than his desire to achieve the transcendent. The ability of Balzac to be subservient to humble objects, as in *Le Curé de Tours,* or that of Flaubert to place a truly unheroic hero at the center of his work, is beyond him. His "real" world may be studded with dates, places, and names, but it rarely gives the impression of being the world of every day. It is rather one of myth wherein heroes can wage their great struggles. As René Journet and Guy Robert put it, "Le but du romancier est de donner à ce mythe, par une sorte de peinture en trompe l'œil le relief du réel,"[1] but in Hugo we are always conscious of the illusion. Perhaps that is why *Les Travailleurs de la mer* is so successful. Set far from the world that we know, its monsters can freely become real. But despite his limitations at handling real life, Hugo had a strong sense of history and as *"mage"* he became insistent on going beyond literature to interpret the destiny of nations and of men. His final "novels" look forward to the creation of a perfect world and achieve their effects by transforming the familiar imagery into an apocalyptic vision.

The totality of Hugo's work has one central theme: a quest for the ideal. The images change their shape and their function but are in essence the same, possessing a unity that reveals, incidentally, that the idea of "two Hugos" separated by the death of Léopoldine in 1843 is an overstatement. Because of this constant presence of the quest for an ideal world, his creation may well stand in both its personal and social dimensions as one of the great expressions of the nineteenth century, which was preoccupied with this search. Thus he shares a common bond with such different spirits, for example, as Lamartine, Baudelaire, and, outside of

1. Introduction to *Le Manuscrit des Misérables* (Paris, 1963), p. 42.

literature, Karl Marx. While Lamartine's poetry tended to flee reality and soar upward to the Heavens, and while Marx saw the solution in a Communist paradise created after a journey through time, Hugo and Baudelaire both sensed that the road to the ideal, Baudelaire's "Anywhere out of this world," ran not directly upward but down into the Hell of private passions or social misery. Even if the two poetic giants of the century saw this truth in very different ways and with considerable difference in technique, one should not exaggerate their dissimilarities. Like Baudelaire, Hugo, by incorporating paths of descent into his work, conformed to the richest pattern of age-old myth, imparting to his creation a strength that, despite many weaknesses, has permitted it to stand the test of time and to speak eternally to the deepest stirrings of the human psyche.

BIBLIOGRAPHY

The following bibliography does not attempt, of course, to be an exhaustive compilation of books and articles pertinent to Hugo studies. I have included here only those editions of Victor Hugo's writing that have been of direct use, and as for the secondary source material, only those works that I have quoted or alluded to, as well as any that have contributed to this study.

I. *Editions of Victor Hugo's Works*

Le Conservateur Littéraire (1819–1821). Ed. Jules Marsan. Société des textes français modernes. 4 vols. Paris, 1922–1938.

Dieu (*L'Océan d'en haut*). Ed. critique par René Journet et Guy Robert. Paris, 1960.

Dieu (*Le Seuil du gouffre*). Ed. critique par René Journet et Guy Robert. Paris, 1961.

La Légende des siècles. Ed. Paul Berret. 6 vols. Paris, 1921–1927.

La Légende des siècles, La Fin de Satan, Dieu. Ed. Jacques Truchet. Bibliothèque de la Pléiade. Paris, 1950.

Le Manuscrit des Misérables. Ed. René Journet et Guy Robert. Paris, 1963.

Les Misérables. Ed. Maurice Allem. Bibliothèque de la Pléiade. Paris, 1951.

Les Misérables, variantes des Misères. Ed. M. F. Guyard. 2 vols. Paris, 1957.

Notre-Dame de Paris. Ed. M. F. Guyard. Classiques Garnier. Paris, 1959.

Œuvres complètes de Victor Hugo. Ed. Paul Meurice, Gustave Simon, Cécile Daubray. 45 vols. Edition de l'Imprimerie Nationale. Paris, 1904–1952.

Œuvres poétiques de Victor Hugo (*Avant l'exil, 1802–1851*). Ed. Pierre Albouy. Bibliothèque de la Pléiade. Paris, 1964.

Promontorium Somnii. Ed. René Journet et Guy Robert. Annales littéraires de l'Université de Besançon. Paris, 1961.

Victor Hugo, Romans. Ed. Henri Guillemin. 3 vols. Paris: Editions du Seuil, 1963.

Victor Hugo: Théâtre complet. Ed. J.-J. Thierry et Josette Mélèze. 2 vols. Bibliothèque de la Pléiade. Paris, 1963.

II. *Secondary Books and Articles*

Albouy, Pierre. *La Création mythologique chez Victor Hugo.* Paris, 1963.

Allevy, Marie-Antoinette. *La Mise-en-scène en France.* Genève, 1938.

Auden, William H. *The Enchafèd Flood.* New York, 1950.

Auerbach, Erich. *Mimesis: The Representation of Reality in Western Literature.* Princeton, 1953. Original edition in German, 1946.

Bach, Max. "Critique littéraire ou critique politique? Les derniers romans de Hugo vus par les contemporains," *French Review,* XXVIII (1954), 27–34.

——. "The Reception of Hugo's First Novels," *Symposium,* XVIII (1964), 142–55.

——. "Le Vieux Paris dans *Notre-Dame:* Sources et ressources de Victor Hugo," *PMLA,* LXXX (1965), 321–24.

Bachelard, Gaston. *L'Eau et les rêves.—Essai sur l'imagination de la matière.* Paris, 1942.

Barrère, Jean-Bertrand. *La Fantaisie de Victor Hugo.* 3 vols. Paris, 1949–1960.

——. *Victor Hugo, l'homme et l'œuvre.* Paris, 1952.

Baudouin, Charles. *Psychanalyse de Victor Hugo.* Genève, 1943.

Béguin, Albert. *L'âme romantique et le rêve.* Paris, 1946.

Bellessort, André. *Victor Hugo, sa vie son œuvre.* Paris, 1930.

Berret, Paul. *La Philosophie de Victor Hugo en 1854–1859 et deux mythes de la Légende des siècles.* Paris, 1910.

——. " 'Le Satyre' et le Panthéisme de Victor Hugo," *RHLF,* IX (1912), 376–81.

——. "Les Comprachicos et la mutilation de Gwynplaine dans L'Homme qui rit," RHLF, XXI (1914), 503–518.

Biré, Edmond. *Victor Hugo avant 1830.* Paris, 1883.

———. *Victor Hugo après 1830.* Paris, 1899.

———. *Victor Hugo après 1852, l'exil, les dernières années et la mort du poète.* Paris, 1894.

Blanchard, Marc. *Marie-Tudor: Essai sur les sources de la pièce avec des notes inédites de Victor Hugo.* Paris, 1935.

Brombert, Victor. "Victor Hugo, la prison et l'espace," *Revue des Sciences Humaines,* CXVII (jan.–mars, 1965), 59–79.

Brunetière, Ferdinand. *Victor Hugo.* Paris, 1902.

Butor, Michel. "Le Théâtre de Victor Hugo," *La Nouvelle Revue française,* XII (Dec., 1964), 1073–81; XIII (jan., 1965), 105–13.

———. "Victor Hugo, romancier," *Tel Quel* (Hiver, 1964), XVI, 60–77.

Campbell, Joseph. *The Hero with a Thousand Faces.* Meridian Books. New York, 1956.

Carlson, Marianna. *L'Art du romancier dans Les Travailleurs de la mer: les techniques visuelles de Hugo.* Archives des lettres modernes, IV, No. 38. Paris, 1961.

Cellier, Léon. " 'Chaos vaincu'—Victor Hugo et le roman initiatique," *Centenaire des Misérables* (1862–1962). *Hommage à Victor Hugo.* Strasbourg, 1962. Pp. 213–33.

Chateaubriand, François-René de. *Atala, René, Les Aventures du Dernier Abencérage.* Classiques Garnier. Paris, 1962.

Claudel, Paul. *Réflexions sur la poésie.* Paris, 1963.

Cormeau, Paul T. " 'Le Satyre' dans *La Légende des siècles* de Victor Hugo," *French Review,* XXXIX (1966), 849–61.

Ditchy, Jay K. *La Mer dans l'œuvre littéraire de Victor Hugo.* Paris, 1925.

Eliade, Mircea. *Images et symboles.* Paris, 1952.

Emery, Léon. *Vision et pensée chez Victor Hugo.* Lyon, n.d. [1939].

Escholier, Raymond. *Victor Hugo, cet inconnu.* Paris, 1951.

———. *La Vie glorieuse de Victor Hugo.* Paris, 1928.

Etienne, Servais. *Les Sources de "Bug-Jargal" avec en appendice quelques sources de Han d'Islande.* Bruxelles, 1923.

Europe: revue mensuelle, XL (février–mars, 1962). The entire issue is devoted to *Les Misérables.*

Frye, Northrop. *Anatomy of Criticism.* Princeton, N.J., 1957.

Gaudon, Jean. "Je ne sais quel jour de soupirail," in *Centenaire des Misérables. (1862–1962) Hommage à Victor Hugo.* Strasbourg, 1962.

———. *Victor Hugo, dramaturge.* Paris, 1955.

Georgel, Pierre. "Vision et imagination plastique dans *Quatrevingt-Treize*," *Lettres Romanes*, XIX (1965), 3–27.

Girard, René. "Monstres et demi-dieux dans l'œuvre de Hugo," *Symposium*, XIX (1965), 50–57.

Glachant, Paul et Victor. *Essai critique sur le théâtre de Victor Hugo.* 2 vols. Paris, 1902–1903.

Glauser, Alfred. *Victor Hugo et la poésie pure.* Genève. 1957.

Goncourt, Edmond and Jules de. *Journal; Mémoires de la vie littéraire.* Text intégral établi et annoté par Robert Ricatte. 22 tomes. Monaco, 1956.

Grant, Elliott M., *The Career of Victor Hugo.* Cambridge, Mass., 1945.

———. *Victor Hugo: A Select and Critical Bibliography.* Chapel Hill, N.C., 1967.

Graves, Robert. *The Greek Myths.* 2 vols. Baltimore, 1955.

Guiard, Amédée. *Virgile et Victor Hugo.* Paris, 1910.

Guillemin, Henri. *Hugo et la sexualité.* Paris, 1954.

Gusdorf, Georges. "Quel horizon on voit du haut de la barricade," *Centenaire des Misérables (1862–1962). Hommage à Victor Hugo.* Strasbourg, 1962. Pp. 175–96.

Guyon, Bernard. *La Vocation poétique de Victor Hugo. Essai sur la signification spirituelle des* "Odes et Ballades" *et des* "Orientales" *(1818–1828).* Gap, 1953.

Heugel, Jacques. *Essai sur la philosophie de Victor Hugo au point de vue gnostique.* Paris, 1930.

Hugo, Adèle. *Victor Hugo raconté par un témoin de sa vie.* 2 vols. Bruxelles, 1863.

Huguet, Edmond. *La Couleur, la lumière et l'ombre dans les métaphores de Victor Hugo.* Paris, 1905.

———. *Le Sens de la forme dans les métaphores de Victor Hugo.* Paris, 1904.

Hunt, Herbert J. *The Epic in Nineteenth Century France, a Study in Heroic and Humanitarian Poetry from* "Les Martyres" *to* "Les Siècles morts." Oxford, 1941.

―――. "Le Sens épique des Misérables," *Centenaire des Misérables* *(1862–1962)*. *Hommage à Victor Hugo*. Strasbourg, 1962. Pp. 127–38.

Journet, René and Robert, Guy. *Le Mythe du peuple dans les Misérables*. Paris, 1964.

―――. *Notes sur Les Contemplations*. Paris, 1958.

Lanson, Gustave. *Histoire de la littérature française*. 7è édition, Paris, 1902.

Larroutis, M. "J. de Maistre et V. Hugo: Le bourreau dans *Han d'Islande*," *Revue d'Histoire Littéraire*, LXII (1962), 573–75.

Leuillot, Bernard. "Présentation de Jean Valjean," *Centenaire des Misérables (1862–1962)*. *Hommage à Victor Hugo*. Strasbourg, 1962. Pp. 51–67.

Levaillant, Maurice. *La Crise mystique de Victor Hugo*. Paris, 1954.

Lote, Georges. *En Préface à Hernani—cent ans après*. Paris, 1930.

Mallion, Jean. *Victor Hugo et l'art architectural*. Paris, 1962.

Maurois, André. *Olympio, ou la vie de Victor Hugo*. Paris, 1954.

O'Connor, Sister Mary. *A Study of the Sources of "Han d'Islande" and Their Significance in the Literary Development of Victor Hugo*. Washington, D.C., 1942.

Péès, Simone. "L'Origine de la couleur scandinave dans le *Han d'Islande* de Victor Hugo," *Revue de littérature comparée*, IX (1929), 261–85.

Pendell, William D. *Victor Hugo's Acted Dramas and the Contemporary Press*. Baltimore, 1947.

Piroué, Georges. *Victor Hugo romancier: ou les dessous de l'inconnu*. Paris, 1964.

Pommier, Jean. "Premiers pas dans l'étude des 'Misérables,' " *Centenaire des Misérables (1862–1962)*. *Hommage à Victor Hugo*. Strasbourg, 1962. Pp. 29–37.

Py, Albert. *Les Mythes grecs dans la poésie de Victor Hugo*. Genève, 1963.

Renouvier, Charles. *Victor Hugo, le philosophe*. Paris, 1900.

―――. *Victor Hugo, le poète*. 3è édition, Paris, 1900.

Riffaterre, Michael. "La Vision hallucinatoire chez Victor Hugo," *Modern Language Notes*, LXXVIII (1963), 225–41.

Rigal, Eugène. " 'Le Glaive' de Victor Hugo et sa source," *Revue des Langues Romanes du midi* (Montpellier, 1901), pp. 464–73.

————. "Signification du 'Satyre' de Victor Hugo," *RHLF*, XIX (1912), 85–94.

Robertson, Mysie E. I. *L'Épithète dans les œuvres lyriques de Victor Hugo publiées avant l'exil.* Paris, 1926.

Roos, Jacques. *Les Idées philosophiques de Victor Hugo.—Ballanche et Victor Hugo.* Paris. 1958.

Rudwin, Maximilien. *Satan et le Satanisme dans l'œuvre de Victor Hugo.* Paris, 1926.

Russell, Olga W. *Etude historique et critique des Burgraves de Victor Hugo, avec variantes inédites et lettres inédites.* Paris, 1962.

Saint-Denis, Etienne de. "Victor Hugo et la mer anglo-normande," *Etudes classiques*, XXXI (juillet, 1963), 275–94.

Saint-Victor, Paul de. *Victor Hugo.* Paris, 1892.

Saurat, Denis. *Victor Hugo et les dieux du peuple.* Paris, 1948.

Savey-Casard, Paul. *Le Crime et la peine dans l'œuvre de Victor Hugo.* Paris, 1956.

Seebacher, Jacques. "La Mort de Jean Valjean," *Centenaire des Misérables (1862–1962). Hommage à Victor Hugo.* Strasbourg, 1962. Pp. 69–83.

Schroeder, Maurice Z. *Icarus: The Image of the Artist in French Romanticism.* Cambridge, Mass., 1961.

Simaïka, Raouf. *L'Inspiration épique dans les romans de Victor Hugo.* Genève, 1962.

Thomas, John H. *L'Angleterre dans l'œuvre de Victor Hugo.* Paris, 1933.

Tuzet, Hélène. "L'image du Soleil Noir," *Revue des Sciences Humaines*, LXXXVIII (oct.–déc., 1957), 497–502.

Venzac, Géraud. *Les Premiers maîtres de Victor Hugo.* Paris, 1955.

Vial, André. "Un beau mythe de *La Légende des siècles: Le Satyre*," *Revue des Sciences Humaines*, LXXXVII (juillett–sept., 1957), 299–317.

Viatte, Auguste. *Victor Hugo et les Illuminés de son temps.* Montréal, 1942.

Weber, Jean-Paul. *La Genèse de l'œuvre poétique.* Paris, 1960.

Zumthor, Paul. *Victor Hugo, poète de Satan.* Paris, 1946.

INDEX

This index includes (1) proper names, excluding those of scholars cited, for they are given credit in footnotes and bibliography, (2) all titles by Hugo and fictional characters in his works (listed after the works in which they appear), and (3) legendary or mythic figures.

* * *

The following are the abbreviations used for poetic *recueils:*